LABOR RELATIONS AND PUBLIC POLICY SERIES

No. 31

"WRONGFUL DISCHARGE" AND THE DEROGATION OF THE AT-WILL EMPLOYMENT DOCTRINE

by

ANDREW D. HILL

INDUSTRIAL RESEARCH UNIT
The Wharton School, Vance Hall
University of Pennsylvania
Philadelphia, Pennsylvania 19104-6358

631-B

Foreword

In 1968, the Industrial Research Unit inaugurated its Labor Relations and Public Policy Series as a means of examining issues and stimulating discussions in the complex and controversial areas of collective bargaining and the regulation of labor-management disputes. Thus far, thirty monographs have been published in this series. Eleven of these deal with various policies and procedures of the National Labor Relations Board. The other nineteen cover such significant issues as collective bargaining in the 1970s; welfare and strikes; opening the skilled construction trades to blacks; the Davis-Bacon Act; the labor-management situation in urban school systems; old age, handicapped, and Vietnam-era antidiscrimination legislation; the impact of the Occupational Safety and Health Act; the Landrum-Griffin Act; the effects of the AT&T-EEO consent decree; unions' rights to company information; employee relations and regulation; operating during strikes; union violence and the law; the impact of antitrust legislation on employee relations; prevailing wage legislation; comparable worth theory and practice; and the conflicts between labor and bankruptcy laws.

This study, *"Wrongful Discharge" and the Derogation of the At-Will Employment Doctrine*, is the thirty-first in the series and involves a thorough analysis of the judicial law making which has been altering the traditional and unique American theory of at-will employment which provides that either party may terminate an employment relationship at his or her discretion. To be sure, legislation such as the National Labor Relations Act, as amended; Title VII of the Civil Rights Act of 1964, as amended; and various other state and federal laws have provided significant exceptions to the at-will theory. What is new, however, is the judicial interference in the employment relationship. Citing such vague standards as "public policy exceptions" or declaring that an employee handbook is a contract, courts have assumed the right to pass judgment on the correctness of employee discharges or permanent layoffs and juries have awarded extremely lucrative damage awards. Yet specific legislation supporting judicial intervention on this broad scale does not exist.

Such judicial intervention varies considerably from state to state. Hence, following a careful development of the at-will theory, the book provides a detailed analysis of judicial action in four states—California, Michigan, Pennsylvania, and New York—which have pursued quite different approaches. This provides a backdrop for an analysis of the principles involved and an evaluation of the impact of judicial action. An appendix summarizes key developments in each state so that scholars and practitioners may check the legal situation throughout the country. Because the status of such case law is so volatile, supplements and new editions are planned for the future as appropriate.

The author, Andrew D. Hill, is a Phi Beta Kappa graduate of Brown University and received two graduate degrees from the University of Pennsylvania—J.D. from the Law School, and M.B.A. from the Wharton School. He also served with distinction as a research assistant in the Industrial Research Unit. In the last two years of his four-year program, Mr. Hill was awarded the Graduate Industrial Relations Fellowship endowed by the General Motors Corporation. He is a member of the Pennsylvania and District of Columbia Bars and an associate of the Washington, D.C. office of the Jones, Day, Reavis & Pogue national law firm.

Prior to going to press, the manuscript was read by five outstanding lawyers who specialize in employment law: Andrew M. Kramer, managing partner, Jones, Day, Reavis & Pogue, Washington, D.C.; Douglas S. McDowell, counsel to the Equal Employment Advisory Council, and partner, McGinnis and Williams, Washington, D.C.; Edward B. Miller, former chairman, National Labor Relations Board, and partner, Pope, Ballard, Shepard & Fowle, Chicago; Patricia Bergeson also of Pope, Ballard, Shepard & Fowle and Philip A. Miscimarra, Murphy, Smith & Polk, Chicago. All made valuable suggestions and all enthusiastically commended the author and urged publication. The Wharton Industrial Research Unit is very grateful to these distinguished legal practitioners for their contributions of time, effort, diligence, and wisdom.

The manuscript was edited by Kathryn Pearcy, Chief Editor of the Wharton Industrial Research Unit; she also constructed the case index. Mrs. Marthenia Perrin, the Unit's Business Manager, supervised the administrative aspects of the project.

The initial research was funded by the generous grant of the J. Howard Pew Freedom Trust in support of the Labor Relations and Public Policy Series. The interest in our work by Fred H. Billups, Jr., Vice President and Executive Director, the Pew Trusts;

Dr. John W. Gould, Vice-President; James McGann, Senior Program Associate; and Robert G. Dunlop, Member, Board of Directors, as well as the staff of the Glenmede Trust Company, which administers the Pew Foundations, is most heartening and much appreciated. Later research and publication were funded by gifts from William C. Griffith, a distinguished alumnus, and by the unrestricted membership fees of the Wharton Industrial Research Unit's Industry Research Advisory Group. Additional funding for the section dealing with Pennsylvania was provided by the William Penn Foundation and the Greater Philadelphia Chamber of Commerce.

As in all works published by the Wharton Industrial Research Unit, the author is solely responsible for the research and for all opinions expressed, none of which should be attributed to the grantors or to the University of Pennsylvania.

Herbert R. Northrup, Director
Industrial Research Unit
The Wharton School
University of Pennyslvania

Philadelphia
July 1987

Author's Preface

Managers at Port Huron Hospital thought that they were acting properly when they decided to discharge Karen Renny, a nurse at the hospital, for allegedly violating hospital procedure. Renny, however, felt the termination was unfair and challenged her discharge through the grievance procedure contained in the hospital's employee handbook. The hospital followed the procedure and at a final hearing before a six-member grievance board composed of employer and employee representatives, the board voted to uphold management's discharge decision.

But Renny was still unsatisfied and took her claim to a trial court, which determined that the decision of the grievance board was not final and binding. The trial court's decision was ultimately appealed to the Michigan Supreme Court where the entire bench affirmed the lower court's holding.[1] In resolving Renny's case, the state's supreme court held that an employer cannot insulate itself from a jury's review of a discharge decision by "unilaterally establishing a method of dispute resolution to which the employee must submit."[2] Even "[w]here an employee has expressly consented to submit a complaint to a joint employer-employee grievance board ... with the knowledge that the resulting decision is final and binding," the court explained, the decision shall be final only if a court determines that the procedures comport with "elementary fairness."[3]

The *Renny* case is illustrative of a growing trend among the courts across the United States to provide employees with some form of protection against various types of discharge by abrogating the traditional common law employment-at-will rule that the parties to an employment contract of indefinite duration are free to begin or end that relationship at any time and for any or no

---

[1] Renny v. Port Huron Hospital, 427 Mich. 415, 418, 398 N.W.2d 327, 329 (1986).
[2] *Id.*
[3] *Id.*

reason, absent an agreement to the contrary.[4] In the wake of this judicial activity there has developed a "disemployment industry" comprised of plaintiffs' lawyers advancing novel theories of wrongful discharge and "personnel administrators whose sole job function is to assure that each and every termination decision can be defended against later judicial attack."[5] The result of this trend has been an employment-at-will doctrine riddled with exceptions and exemptions depending on the jurisdiction and focus of each individual case. Moreover, "the developing body of judge-made law in this area is not performing the fundamental task of law: to provide for law-abiding citizens a clear and consistent scheme for guiding their conduct toward each other."[6]

The hospital's management in the *Renny* case, for example, probably felt that it was acting within the bounds of law when it decided to discharge Karen Renny. Indeed, by having a nonpartisan discharge review procedure in place and by following it

---

[4]An often-quoted opinion defining the traditional employment-at-will doctrine states that:

> [M]en must be left, without interference to buy and sell where they please, and to discharge or retain employees at will for good cause or for no cause, or even for bad cause without thereby being guilty of an unlawful act *per se*. It is a right which an employee may exercise in the same way, to the same extent, for the same cause or want of cause as the employer.

Payne v. Western & Atlantic R. R. Co., 81 Tenn. 507, 518-19 (1884), *rev'd on other grounds*, Hutton v. Watters, 132 Tenn. 527, 544, 179 S.W. 134, 138 (1915). The American Law Institute defines the doctrine of employment-at-will as follows:

> [U]nless otherwise agreed, mutual promises by principal and agent to employ and to serve create obligations to employ and to serve which are terminable upon notice by either party; if neither party terminates the employment, it may terminate by lapse of time or by supervening events.

Restatement (Second) of Agency, § 442 and comment (a) (1957). *See also* 9 S. Williston & W. Jaeger, *A Treatise on the Law of Contracts*, § 1017, at 129-30 and note 11 (3d ed. 1967 and Supp. 1986) which states that: "Where the contract is not for a fixed term, and is, therefore, terminable at will, though such notice as the nature of the contract made reasonable might be necessary, there seems no general principle analogous to that in the law of tenancies at will requiring notice of a certain length of time." *Id.*

[5]Cox v. Resilient Flooring Division of Congoleum Corp., 638 F. Supp. 726, 736 (C.D. Cal. 1986).

[6]*Id.* at 735. The need for clear guidelines also appears in decision-bargaining cases where the United States Supreme Court has stressed the need for certainty beforehand in fashioning guidelines to govern employer-employee relations: "An employer would have difficulty determining beforehand whether it was faced with a situation requiring bargaining or one that involved economic necessity sufficiently compelling to obviate the duty to bargain." NLRB v. First National Maintenance Corporation, 452 U.S. 666, 684 (1981).

consistently, most managers in the same position would conclude that the hospital's action was not "wrongful" in any way. Management's confusion over the current state of this area of employment law is evident. In fact, data from a recent survey reveal that approximately 60 percent of small business managers in Michigan are unaware of the shifting at-will framework.[7]

This study is designed to serve as an introduction to this complicated and rapidly changing area of the law. It must be noted that this study is not intended to be a dispositive treatise on the employment-at-will doctrine. This study does contain a fairly detailed and accurate exposition of the substantive law in several states and illuminates various public policy issues that do not vary from state to state and which should prove valuable even after the substantive law discussion becomes dated, as is inevitable in this rapidly changing area of law. It is also hoped that this study will acquaint its readers with the various legal theories and defenses that have been developed by the courts, and the preventive measures which some employers have adopted in response to the at-will problem. Because of the rapidly changing nature of at-will employment, the author strongly urges that before any action is taken or before any reader relies on any given statement within this study, he or she should attempt to verify the current status of the law.

Chapter I provides an historical overview of the employment-at-will doctrine and outlines the size and scope of the problem today. Chapters II and III examine the legal theories advanced to undercut the at-will rule and the defenses commonly used by employers when defending wrongful discharge lawsuits. Chapters IV through VII are a series of case studies discussing the development of at-will employment in California, Michigan, Pennsylvania, and New York respectively. Chapter VIII explores the possible economic and social consequences stemming from a modification of the at-will doctrine. Chapter IX discusses various preventive measures currently used by employers to protect themselves from liability in wrongful discharge lawsuits. Appendix A to this book provides

---

[7]*See* D. Sheffler, *Terminable At-Will Employment in Michigan: A Survey of Business Opinions and Current Employment Practices,* at v (Aug. 1985 and photo. reprint 1986) (Master of Business Adminstration thesis, Central Michigan University).

a brief summary of the state of the law in the remaining jurisdictions and Appendix B contains the text of proposed legislation which would require an employer to have "just cause" before discharging an employee.

Andrew D. Hill

Philadelphia, Pennsylvania
June, 1987

TABLE OF CONTENTS

TABLES AND FIGURES

CHAPTER I

Historical Development

The historical development of the employment-at-will doctrine is distinctly American in that it represents a clear departure from the English common law approach to service contracts of indefinite duration.[1] During the colonial period and the early years of the republic, American courts relied on the English rule that a hiring of indefinite duration was presumed to be yearly and required reasonable notice before it could be terminated by either party.[2] Beginning in the last quarter of the nineteenth century, however, American jurisprudence departed from its Anglo-Saxon origins and developed the employment-at-will doctrine, holding that employment for an indefinite term is "at will" and may be terminated at any time by either party to the agreement for any reason or no reason at all.[3] This ideological departure has left legal commentators puzzling for years over the reasons for the development of this uniquely American doctrine.[4]

---

[1]*See generally* Feinman, *The Development of the Employment-At-Will Rule*, 20 Am. J. Legal Hist. 118 (1976) [hereinafter cited as Feinman, *Development of At-Will*]; Jacoby, *The Duration of Indefinite Employment Contracts in the United States and England: An Historical Analysis*, 5 Comp. Lab. L. 85 (1982) [hereinafter cited as Jacoby, *Indefinite Employment Contracts*]; Summers, *Individual Protection Against Unjust Dismissal: Time for a Statute*, 62 Va. L. Rev. 481 (1976) [hereinafter cited as Summers, *Individual Protection Against Unjust Dismissal*].

[2]R. Morris, Government and Labor in Early America, at 219 (1965); Feinman, *Development of At-Will, supra* note 1, at 122. For a general statement of the English rule, see, 1 W. Blackstone, Commentaries on the Law of England, at 425-26 (Bell ed. 1771) [hereinafter cited as Blackstone, Commentaries] and discussion, at 6-7.

[3]*See* Payne v. Western & Atlantic R.R. Co., 81 Tenn. 507, 518-19 (1884), *rev'd on other grounds*, Hutton v. Watters, 132 Tenn. 527, 544, 179 S.W. 134, 138 (1915). *See also* Feinman, *Development of At-Will, supra* note 1, at 118-19; Comment, *Protecting At Will Employees Against Wrongful Discharge: The Duty to Terminate Only in Good Faith*, 93 Harv. L. Rev. 1816, 1824-28 (1980) [hereinafter cited as Comment, *Protecting At Will Employees*]; Note, *Implied Rights to Job Security*, 26 Stan. L. Rev. 335, 340-47 (1974) [hereinafter cited as Note, *Implied Rights*]; Annot., 62 A.L.R. 3d 271 (1975).

[4]The list of authors who have written on this topic is extensive, and a sampling includes: Feinman, *Development of At-Will, supra* note 1; Friedman, A History of American Law (1973), at 484-94 [hereinafter cited as Friedman, A History of American Law]; Jacoby, *Indefinite Employment Contracts, supra* note 1; Selznick, Law, Society and Industrial Justice (1969), at 122-37 (hereinafter cited as Selznick, Industrial Justice); Summers, *Individual Protection Against Unjust Dismissal, supra* note 1.

ENGLISH RULE

The approach developed by the English courts to deal with the problem posed by indefinite hirings focused on two basic questions: (1) "[w]hat is the *duration* of the relation presumed to be when none is specifically stated"; and (2) "[w]hat length of *notice* must be given before the relation can be terminated?"[5] Concern for the duration of employment appeared in English law as early as the mid-fourteenth century when King Edward III enacted the Statute of Labourers,[6] partially in response to the labor shortage resulting from the Black Death.[7] The Statute of Labourers prohibited a worker from departing from the service of an employer, or an employer from discharging from service any employee, "before the end of the term agreed upon without reasonable cause of license."[8] Even after the repeal of the Statute of Labourers in the mid-eighteenth century, English law mandated that an employer could not terminate his servant without reasonable notice, which varied depending on the custom in the particular trade.[9]

In 1771, the famous English legal commentator, William Blackstone, summarized the English approach in the following manner:

> If the hiring be general, without any particular time limited, the law construes it to be a hiring for a year; upon a principle of natural equity, that the servant shall serve and the master maintain him, throughout all the revolutions of the respective seasons, as well as when there is work to be done as when there is not.[10]

Indeed, Blackstone's rule was firmly rooted on principles of equity. That is, "injustice would result if ... masters could have the benefit of servants' labor during planting and harvest seasons but dis-

---

[5]Feinman, *Development of At-Will, supra* note 1, at 119 (emphasis added).

[6]*See* Feinman, *Development of At-Will, supra* note 1, at 120 note 8, *citing* 23 Edw. III, c.1 (1349); Statute of Labourers, 5 Eliz. I, c.4 (1562).

[7]SELZNICK, INDUSTRIAL JUSTICE, *supra* note 4, at 126.

[8]*Id.* (citation omitted). *See also* Feinman, *Development of At-Will, supra* note 1, at 120; Mauk, *A History and Analysis of the Employment-At-Will Doctrine,* 21 IDAHO L. REV. 202, 203 (1985) (hereinafter cited as Mauk, *A History and Analysis*), *citing,* BLACKSTONE, COMMENTARIES, *supra* note 2, at 425-26.

[9]As Professor Feinman notes:

> [w]hat constituted reasonable notice was a question of fact to be decided anew in each case, but certain conventions grew up. Domestic servants, who presumably no longer needed the benefit of the seasons, could be given a month's notice. Other types of employees could also be given a month's notice, three months was another common term, although some special cases required six or even twelve months' notice.

Feinman, *Development of At-Will, supra* note 1, at 121 (citations omitted).

[10]BLACKSTONE, COMMENTARIES, *supra* note 2, at 425.

charge them to avoid supporting them during the unproductive winter. . . ."[11] Similar inequity would result if servants who were supported during the unproductive winter season "could leave their masters' service when their labor was most needed."[12] The English rule as it was stated by Blackstone was not restricted, however, to agricultural and domestic workers; rather, "[t]he presumption that an indefinite hiring was a hiring for a year extended to all classes of servants."[13]

AMERICAN RULE

On the other side of the Atlantic, American courts often followed the English rule of yearly hirings when dealing with agricultural and domestic workers,[14] but when faced with other instances of indefinite hirings, American law, although purportedly relying on English precedent, reached results markedly different from its English sources. American law was marked by confusion and inconsistency on the indefinite hiring question.

Treatises and case law addressing this issue of employment law from the early to mid-nineteenth century show the general state of confusion which pervaded the American legal community during this period. For example, Tapping Reeve's 1846 treatise, *The Law of Baron and Femme, of Parent and Child, Guardian and Ward, Master and Servant, and Other Powers of the Court of Chancery*, stated the basic English presumption of yearly hirings, but noted quixotically that no such rule existed in Connecticut.[15] In New York, on the other hand, a state court of appeals in *Davis v. Gorton*[16] in 1857 found that the English rule was alive and well in the Empire State.

In 1852, Charles Manley Smith published the first volume devoted entirely to the subject of master-servant relations in the United States. On the subject of indefinite hirings, Smith stated that in the United States there was a presumption that "a general hiring was a

---

[11]Feinman, *Development of At-Will, supra* note 1, at 120.

[12]*Id.*

[13]*Id.* and note 10, *citing,* C. SMITH, MASTER AND SERVANT, at 41 (1852); Baxter v. Nurse, 134 Eng. Rep. 1171 (C.P. 1844); Beeston v. Collyer, 130 Eng. Rep. 786 (C.P. 1827).

[14]*See* authorities cited *supra* note 2.

[15]Feinman, *Development of At Will, supra* note 1, at 122-23 and note 36, *citing,* T. REEVE, THE LAW OF BARON AND FEMME, OF PARENT AND CHILD, GUARDIAN AND WARD, MASTER AND SERVANT, AND OTHER POWERS OF THE COURT OF CHANCERY, at 347 (1846).

[16]16 N.Y. 255 (1857).

yearly hiring for all servants."[17] This presumption, Smith continued,
was "rebuttable by custom or other evidence; and, in spite of a
yearly hiring, the relation was terminable on notice where that was
customary."[18] Clearly, American law lay somewhere between its
Anglo-Saxon origins and a new path which was, as of the mid-
nineteenth century, still not fully articulated.

Some scholars have suggested that the confusion present in American law at this time arose from the fact that master and servant law
was traditionally classified as a domestic relation,[19] and as such was
characterized by a personal and familial atmosphere. As the Industrial Revolution took hold in America, however, the employment relationship moved from the traditional domestic setting into a commercial context. The body of law surrounding employment relationships
did not fit this new commercialized pattern, with the result being
judicial uncertainty.

In the late nineteenth century, freedom of contract was one of the
most powerful forces in American jurisprudence. With advocates
such as Langdell and Holmes, the judiciary viewed freedom of contract as an integral part of the larger corpus of American liberties.[20]
Some commentators, in fact, suggest that the principle of freedom of
contract was the dominant force which pushed American law to
depart from the English rule and adopt the employment-at-will doctrine,[21] and that "[t]he essence of freedom of contract was the voluntary assumption of legal obligation. The law would provide a framework for the dealings of the parties, but they were free to design
their own relationships through contract and the law would then give
effect to their design."[22] To be sure, freedom of contract was per-
fectly complemented by the then dominant economic ideology of
laissez-faire in which individual action was sovereign.[23]

---

[17]Feinman, *Development of At-Will, supra* note 1, at 123 note 40, *citing* SMITH,
MASTER AND SERVANT, *supra* note 13, at 41.

[18]Feinman, *Development of At-Will, supra* note 1, at 123.

[19]*See, e.g.,* Comment, *Protecting At Will Employees, supra* note 3, at 1824-25;
Jacoby, *Indefinite Employment Contracts, supra* note 1; SELZNICK, INDUSTRIAL JUS-
TICE, *supra* note 4, at 122.

[20]*See generally* FRIEDMAN, A HISTORY OF AMERICAN LAW, *supra* note 4, at 464-68.

[21]*See, e.g.,* Jacoby, *The Duration of Indefinite Employment Contracts, supra* note 1,
at 92-94.

[22]Feinman, *Development of At-Will, supra* note 1, at 124 and note 56, *citing* J. W.
HURST, LAW AND THE CONDITIONS OF FREEDOM IN THE NINETEENTH CENTURY UNITED
STATES, at 14 (1956).

[23]*See, e.g.,* Brake, *Limiting the Right to Terminate at Will—Have the Courts Forgotten the Employer?,* 35 VAND. L. REV. 201, 208 (1982) [hereinafter cited as Brake,
Limiting the Right to Terminate]; Feinman, *Development of At-Will, supra* note 1, at
124-25. *See generally* M. HORWITZ, THE TRANSFORMATION OF AMERICAN LAW (1977).

Against this backdrop of individual freedom, Albany, New York lawyer Horace Wood published a treatise on master-servant relations which provided the legal community with a hard and fast rule to be applied to indefinite hirings, a rule which on the surface was in keeping with contemporary ideology. Wood's 1877 treatise articulated for the first time what would become the American doctrine of employment-at-will:

> With us the rule is inflexible that a general or indefinite hiring is *prima facie* a hiring at will, and if the servant seeks to make it out a yearly hiring, the burden is upon him to establish it by proof. A hiring at so much a day, week, month, or year, no time being specified, is an indefinite hiring, and no presumption attaches that it was for a day even, but only at the rate fixed for whatever time the party may serve.[24]

Although commentators have challenged the precedent on which Wood based his rule, his treatise formed the foundation of the American doctrine of employment-at-will from which all subsequent modifications and exceptions developed.[25]

For years legal scholars have offered different theories to explain why American common law parted with its English heritage by adopting the employment-at-will standard. Although the at-will doctrine appeared at a time when individual freedom was being trumpeted by American society, it would be theoretically inaccurate to state simply that the at-will rule was a natural outgrowth of the principle of freedom of contract.[26] As one authority points out, if contract law had been the basis for Wood's rule, "then the agreement established by the parties would have been enforced."[27] In other words, the intentions of the parties would have been the source of the law. "The duration of the hiring and the notice required would have been open questions in each case to be decided without presumptions of either yearly hirings or termination at will."[28] Under Wood's rule,

---

[24]H. G. WOOD, MASTER AND SERVANT, § 134, at 272-73 (2d ed. 1886).

[25]Wood cited the following four cases in support of his general statement of the employment-at-will doctrine: Wilder v. United States, 5 Ct. Cl. 462 (1869), *rev'd on other grounds*, 80 U.S. 254 (1872); Debriar v. Minturn, 1 Cal. 450 (1851); Tatterson v. Suffolk Mfg. Co., 106 Mass. 56 (1870); Franklin Mining Co. v. Harris, 24 Mich. 115 (1871).

Among those commentators who report that these four cases do *not* support Wood's Rule, *see, e.g.,* Summers, *Individual Protection Against Unjust Dismissal, supra* note 1, at 485; Note, *Implied Rights, supra* note 3, at 341 notes 53-54.

[26]*See* Feinman, *Development of At-Will, supra* note 1, at 125.

[27]*Id.*

[28]*Id.*

however, the nature of the transaction—the fact that it is an employment contract—was the critical determinant, whereas the intentions
of the parties were of only secondary importance.[29]

Another explanation offered for America's adoption of Wood's rule
is that it was "a response to changing social conditions and its presumption accurately reflected the public's perception of the usual
duration of employment contracts."[30] Despite the theory's general
attractiveness, it is difficult satisfactorily to determine the usual
duration of general hirings.[31]

Professor Jay Feinman posits a novel theory to explain this development in American employment law.[32] According to Feinman,
Wood's rule was "essentially an adjunct to the development of
advanced capitalism in America."[33] Noting first that the majority of
participants in the litigation that resulted in the change to the
employment-at-will doctrine were middle-level employees, Feinman
suggests that these suits were an attempt by a newly important
group in the economy to establish interests in their jobs by applying
traditional common law contract doctrine.[34] In Professor Feinman's
analysis, the courts rejected these plaintiffs' claims and opted
instead for the employment-at-will rule for reasons that "lie in the
class division fundamental to the capitalist system: the distinction
between owners and non-owners of capital."[35]

Whether or not Professor Feinman's interpretation is correct, it is
undeniable that the adoption of Wood's rule greatly facilitated the
termination of employment, a step which was critical to the advancement of the American economy at the end of the nineteenth century.
"High rates of unemployment and severe business cycles were fre-
quent manifestations of the turbulent fluctuations in the economy in
this period, and unemployment due to technological advances was
also common."[36] One way for businessmen to respond to these events
was by alternately hiring and discharging workers as conditions dic-
tated, a practice which was especially prevalent in labor-intensive
industries.[37]

---

[29]*Id.* at 130.
[30]*Id.*
[31]*Id.*
[32]*See* Feinman, *Development of At-Will, supra* note 1, at 131-35 for a detailed discussion of this proposition.
[33]*Id.* at 131.
[34]*Id.* at 132.
[35]*Id.*
[36]*Id., citing* R. Fels, American Business Cycles, 1865-1897 (1959).
[37]*Id.* at 134.

Whatever the reasons were for the American legal community's embrace of Wood's rule, the employment-at-will doctrine spread across the nation until it was generally adopted in every jurisdiction as a principle of common law. California, in fact, went so far as to codify the rule in its state code.[38] (This is particularly ironic in light of the fact that California courts have moved farther than all other courts in abrogating the at-will rule.)[39]

The doctrine of employment-at-will achieved constitutional status early in the twentieth century in *Adair v. United States.*[40] In *Adair* the United States Supreme Court struck down a section of federal law banning discrimination by railroads against their operating employees because of union membership. Seven years later the Court relied on *Adair* in *Coppage v. Kansas*[41] to hold that a Kansas statute prohibiting "yellow dog" contracts (in which employers demand as a condition of employment that their workers not become union members) was unconstitutional since it infringed on an employer's right to determine whom to hire, a violation of the due process clause of the fourteenth amendment.[42] These opinions have been seen as the "high water mark" of the Court's insistence on laissez faire principles in the labor area.[43]

It was not until the 1930s that the United States Supreme Court began to create significant exceptions to the employment-at-will doctrine.[44] In *NLRB v. Jones & Laughlin Steel Corp.,*[45] the Court upheld those provisions of the National Labor Relations Act (NLRA) forbidding employer coercion or discrimination against employees because of union activity. "[G]overnment's responsibility to ameliorate economic distress" following the Great Depression could justify, in the Court's reasoning, "the imposition of restrictions on an employer's autonomy."[46] The Court made it clear, however, that the provisions of the NLRA created only a limited, specific exception to the fundamental employment-at-will rule: "[t]he [National Labor

---

[38]*See* CAL. LAB. CODE § 2922 (West 1971 & Supp. 1987) which states, in relevant part, that: "An employment, having no specified term, may be terminated at the will of either party on notice to the other . . ." *id.*

[39]A discussion of the erosion of the employment-at-will doctrine in California may be found in chapter IV, at 55-75.

[40]208 U.S. 161 (1908).

[41]236 U.S. 1 (1915).

[42]*Id.* at 11-13. *See also* Brake, *Limiting the Right to Terminate, supra* note 23, at 208.

[43]*See* Comment, *Protecting At Will Employees, supra* note 3, at 1826.

[44]Brake, *Limiting the Right to Terminate, supra* note 23, at 208.

[45]301 U.S. 1 (1937).

[46]Brake, *Limiting the Right to Terminate, supra* note 23, at 208-09.

Relations] Board is not entitled to make its authority a pretext for interference with the right of discharge when that right is exercised for other reasons than antiunion intimidation and coercion."[47]

Other cases from the New Deal era added support to the Court's general view that employers were free to select and dismiss employees "as long as they did not violate a statutory provision designed to protect employees."[48] For instance, in *J. I. Case Co. v. NLRB,*[49] "where the defendant company had been charged with refusing to bargain collectively in violation of the NLRA, the Court held that '[t]he employer, except as restricted by the collective agreement itself and except that he must engage in no unfair labor practice or discrimination, is free to select those he will employ or discharge.'"[50]

The Court's general recognition of an employer's right to terminate at-will employees has prevailed in more recent opinions as well. In 1961, for instance, the Justices in *Cafeteria Workers Local 473 v. McElroy*[51] "distinguished the ability of the federal government to discharge employees from the 'complete freedom of action enjoyed by a private employer.'"[52] Likewise, many lower courts also applied the traditional employment-at-will rule up until the 1970s.[53]

In addition to judicial activity, it is important to note that even historically there have been a significant number of limited exceptions to the at-will rule. By law, public-sector employees are not subject to being discharged at will since their employment is governed by civil service provisions which generally allow dismissal only for "just cause."[54] Similarly, employees in the private sector whose employment is governed by collective bargaining agreements usu-

---

[47]*Id.* at 209, *quoting* NLRB v. Jones & Laughlin Steel Corp., 301 U.S. 1, 45 (1937).

[48]Brake, *Limiting the Right to Terminate, supra* note 23, at 209.

[49]321 U.S. 332 (1944).

[50]Brake, *Limiting the Right to Terminate, supra* note 23, at 209, *quoting* J. I. Case Co. v. NLRB, 321 U.S. 332, 335 (1944).

[51]367 U.S. 886 (1961).

[52]Brake, *Limiting the Right to Terminate, supra* note 23, at 210 *quoting* Cafeteria Workers Local 473 v. McElroy, 367 U.S. 886, 897 (1961).

[53]*See* Brake, *Limiting the Right to Terminate, supra* note 23, at 210 note 43, *citing* Buian v. J. L. Jacobs & Co., 428 F.2d 531 (7th Cir. 1970); Entis v. Atlantic Wire & Cable Corp., 335 F.2d 759 (2d Cir. 1964); Beeler v. Chicago, R.I. & P. Ry., 169 F.2d 557 (10th Cir. 1948), *cert. denied,* 335 U.S. 903 (1949); Brown v. Safeway Stores, Inc., 190 F. Supp. 295 (E.D.N.Y. 1960); Swaffield v. Universal Ecsco Corp., 271 Cal. App.2d 147, 76 Cal. Rptr. 680 (1969); Wilson v. Red Bluff Daily News, 237 Cal. App.2d 87, 46 Cal. Rptr. 591 (1965); Gressley v. Williams, 193 Cal. App.2d 636, 14 Cal. Rptr. 496 (1961); Russell & Axon v. Handshoe, 176 So.2d 909 (Fla. Dist. Ct. App. 1965); Carfizzi v. United Transp. Co., 20 App. Div.2d 707, 247 N.Y.S.2d 162 (1964); Winslow v. Roberts Numbering Mach. Co., 17 Misc.2d 18, 183 N.Y.S.2d 817 (Sup. Ct. 1959).

[54]Civil Service Reform Act of 1978, § 204(a), 5 U.S.C. § 7513(a)(1982). This guarantee covers virtually all civilian employees of the federal government who have completed either a probationary period or one year of current, continuous employment.

eral employment contract, it has been held that such a contract does not lack mutuality unless there is also a concomitant failure to supply consideration: "a unilateral contract does not lack mutuality unless there is also a failure of consideration."[30] Moreover, examination of the issue of consideration shows that the relative value of the consideration given is not relevant.[31] Therefore, "[u]nilateral contracts contemplate an offer which is accepted by performance rather than a promise of performance."[32] In this sense, the formalistic requirement of mutuality of obligation is satisfied in the unilateral contract typical of at-will employment relationships.

Under the umbrella of contract theory, courts have addressed three main lines of argument connected with exceptions to the employment-at-will rule.[33] One line argues that an implied contract may exist where an employee relies on oral assurances or representations contained in personnel policies or handbooks that appear to qualify or otherwise limit the employer's right to terminate the contract relationship. Closely related to the handbook issue, courts have had to consider the contractual significance of disclaimers which employers insert in handbooks or otherwise communicate to employees. Courts have had to grapple with the issue of promissory estoppel (also characterized as "detrimental reliance") where an employee has relied, to his detriment, on a promise or offer by an employer.

Personnel Policies. Several jurisdictions have held that promises, conditions, and benefits extended by employers to their employees in handbooks, personnel manuals, and application forms can be contractually binding in certain instances. More specifically, some courts have found that "oral and written statements of personnel policy which result in an employee's legitimate expectation of benefits are legally enforceable even though the employment relationship is of an indefinite term."[34]

Explicit "Just Cause" Provisions. The seminal case according handbook statements contractual significance is *Toussaint v. Blue Cross and Blue Shield of Michigan.*[35] In that case, plaintiff Charles Toussaint was discharged from Blue Cross after being employed by

---

[30]*Langdon*, 569 P.2d at 526-27 (cited in Mauk, *A History and Analysis, supra* note 9, at 213).

[31]*See* 1 A. CORBIN, CORBIN ON CONTRACTS, § 122 & note 51 (1950) *citing* Whitney v. Stearns, 16 Me. 394 (1839)("A cent or a peppercorn, in legal estimation, would constitute a valuable consideration.")

[32]*Langdon*, 569 P.2d at 527.

[33]*See* Mauk, *A History and Analysis, supra* note 9, at 214-25.

[34]*Id.* at 214. *See also* Toussaint v. Blue Cross and Blue Shield of Michigan, 408 Mich. 579, 292 N.W.2d 880 (1980).

[35]408 Mich. 579, 292 N.W.2d 880 (1980).

the company for five years in a middle management position. In cross-examination, when Toussaint was asked whether he had an employment contract, he responded that he felt certain sections of a supervisor's manual which he had been given upon accepting the job were evidence of a "contract."[36] In a 4-3 decision, the Michigan Supreme Court ruled in favor of Toussaint, holding that the company personnel manual that stated it was Blue Cross' policy to discharge employees "for just cause only" was sufficient to create an enforceable promise that Toussaint would not be terminated except for just cause.[37] Several jurisdictions have adopted the *Toussaint* rule according personnel manuals contractual weight.[38] The New Jersey Supreme Court in *Woolley v. Hoffman-La Roche, Inc.,*[39] for example, concluded that the pharmaceutical company was bound by its personnel policy manual provisions on termination to discharge its employees only for cause.

More recently, the Illinois Supreme Court in *Duldulao v. St. Mary of Nazareth Hospital Center,*[40] held that "an employee handbook or other policy statement creates enforceable contract rights if" (a) the handbook language contains "a promise clear enough that an employee would reasonably believe that an offer has been made"; (b) the handbook or policy statement is distributed "in such a manner that the employee is aware of its contents and reasonably believes it to be an offer"; and, (c) the employee "accept[s] the offer by commencing or continuing to work after learning of the policy statement."[41]

Moreover, in finding personnel handbooks to be "contracts," several courts have held that "fundamental rules of contract construction apply to policy statements authored by the employer."[42] Specifically, any ambiguities in the policy language, the courts conclude, should be construed against the party who wrote the contract and resolved in favor of the employees subject to the statements.[43] As

[36]*Id.* at 597 note 5, 292 N.W.2d at 884 note 5.

[37]*Id.* at 598, 292 N.W.2d at 899.

[38]*See, e.g.,* Weiner v. McGraw-Hill, Inc., 57 N.Y.2d 458, 443 N.E.2d 441 (1982)(statement in a company's personnel manual that the company would discharge an employee for just cause only enabled a discharged employee to sue employer for breach of contract); Rabago-Alvarez v. Dart Industries, Inc., 55 Cal. App. 3d 91, 127 Cal. Rptr. 222 (1976).

[39]99 N.J. 284, 297, 491 A.2d 1257, 1264 (1985).

[40]115 Ill.2d 482 (1987).

[41]*Id.* at 490.

[42]Mauk, *A History and Analysis, supra* note 9, at 219.

[43]*See id.* & note 82, *citing* Dangott v. A.S.G. Industries, Inc., 558 P.2d 379 (Okla. 1976); Dahl v. Brunswick Corp., 227 Md. 471, 356 A.2d 221 (1976); Hinkledey v. Cities Service Oil Co., 470 S.W.2d 494 (Mo. 1971).

one commentator warns, "employers can no longer offer attractive benefits and elaborate disciplinary procedures to employees, reaping the advantages of a more stable, productive and loyal workforce, and when challenged, pretend that the offerings were mere gratuities."[44]

Implicit "Just Cause" Provisions. Several courts, in extending the reasoning that contracts may arise from personnel handbooks, have found some contracts to mandate a just cause requirement for termination, even where no such protection appears in the company material. These implied contract cases usually "involve long-term employees and established industry practices of retaining more senior employees at times of reduction in the workforce."[45] Although such judicial action might be viewed by some as overreaching, one commentator offers an explanation for such decisions by examining the ramifications of disciplinary guidelines and programs of probationary employment frequently implemented by companies:

> The disciplinary guidelines impose an element of due process in the workplace, while the distinction between probationary and non-probationary employees clearly communicates the employer's intent to treat these distinct classes of employees differently in the event of discharge or discipline ...
>
> Take for example a situation where the employer has enumerated grounds for immediate termination ... The employer's policies may even establish levels of disciplinary action for offenses of differing gravities. Absent an unequivocal statement by the employer expressing a contrary intent, it is reasonable to assume that employees will rely upon such policies as defining the "causes" which will justify a spectrum of adverse personnel action. By its own proclamation then, the employer has both imposed a just cause condition upon the employment contract and through its chosen language and past application, given meaning to that condition.[46]

Such reasoning has heavily influenced several jurisdictions. In *Toussaint,* for instance, the Supreme Court of Michigan, in an opinion echoing much of the above logic, found that oral representations that the plaintiff "would be with the company 'as long as [he] did [his] job'"[47] created an implied contract which was enforceable against the employer. Such assurances, the court concluded, "may become

---

[44]Mauk, *A History and Analysis, supra* note 9, at 217.

[45]*Id.* at 224 note 101, *citing* Cleary v. American Airlines, Inc., 111 Cal. App. 3d 443, 168 Cal. Rptr. 722 (1980); Pugh v. See's Candies, Inc., 116 Cal. App. 3d 311, 171 Cal. Rptr. 917, *modified,* 117 Cal. App. 3d 520a (1981); Maloney v. E.I. DuPont de Nemours & Co., 352 F.2d 936 (D.C. Cir. 1965), *cert. denied,* 383 U.S. 948 (1966).

[46]Mauk, *A History and Analysis, supra* note 9, at 222-23.

[47]*Toussaint,* 408 Mich. at 597, 292 N.W.2d at 884.

part of the contract either by express agreement, *oral or written,* or as a result of an employee's legitimate expectations"[48] arising from policy statements in the handbook.

As alarming as such judicial reasoning may be to many employers, courts finding an implied just cause standard arising from personnel handbooks only represent the minority of jurisdictions. It appears that the rule among the majority of jurisdictions is still "that personnel policies are unilateral expressions of company policy and do not create an enforceable contract right to just cause dismissal."[49] Manuals or other corporate documents, according to the majority's rationale, are insufficient as actionable contracts of employment since these documents rarely contain all the necessary terms of employment, such as the duties of the position, the length of employment, and compensation.[50]

Disclaimers. Robert Williams and Thomas Bagby note that "the implied contract approach" to creating exceptions "to the strict application of the at-will rule ... is consistent in principle with the traditional notion that employment relationships are, at bottom, contracts between employers and workers."[51] "In other words," the authors state, "the exceptions are created within the framework of contract law principles, rather than outside that framework."[52] Therefore, "the legality of any given discharge still hinges essentially on what the court concludes the parties mutually intended."[53]

---

[48]*Id.* at 598, 292 N.W.2d at 885 (emphasis added).

[49]Green, *Prevention, supra* note 2, at 6, *citing* Heidick v. Kent General Hospital, Inc., 446 A.2d 1095 (Del. 1982)(court rejected argument that personnel booklet enumerating reasons for dismissal limited employer to such reasons); Beidler v. W.R. Grace, Inc., 461 F.Supp. 1013 (E.D. Pa. 1978), *aff'd,* 609 F.2d 500 (3d Cir. 1979)(court found no limitation on the employer's right to terminate an employee at will, despite the requirements of an exit interview, evaluations, notification to the employee of the result of the evaluations, and the availability of lesser penalties than dismissal); Johnson v. National Beef Packing Co., 220 Kan. 52, 551 P.2d 779 (1976)(court found no cause of action for breach of contract where manual did not describe all essential elements of the employment agreement).

[50]*See, e.g.,* Edwards v. Citibank, N.A., 100 Misc. 2d 59, 418 N.Y.S.2d 269 (Sup. Ct. 1979), *aff'd,* 74 A.D.2d 553, 425 N.Y.S.2d 327 (App. Div), *appeal dismissed,* 51 N.Y.2d 875, 414 N.E.2d 400, 433 N.Y.S.2d 1020 (1980); Chin v. American Tel. & Tel. Co., 96 Misc. 2d 1070, 410 N.Y.S.2d 737 (Sup. Ct. 1978), *aff'd,* 70 A.D.2d 791, 416 N.Y.S.2d 160 (App. Div.), *appeal denied,* 48 N.Y.2d 603, 421 N.Y.S.2d 1028 (1979).

[51]R. WILLIAMS & T. BAGBY, ALLIS-CHALMERS CORPORATION v. LUECK: THE IMPACT OF THE SUPREME COURT'S DECISION ON WRONGFUL DISCHARGE SUITS AND OTHER STATE COURT EMPLOYMENT LITIGATION (1986), at 17 [hereinafter cited as WILLIAMS & BAGBY, ALLIS-CHALMERS].

[52]*Id.*

[53]*Id.* at 17-18.

Largely in reaction to the courts that have adopted the implied contract analysis, many employers have inserted disclaimers or other explicit reservations of their rights to terminate an employee in company policy statements. In addition, many employers have instructed managers not to give employees or applicants broad assurances of continued employment. (The topic of handbook modification and other preventive measures are discussed in greater detail in chapters III and IX.) Where such language is clearly communicated to employees in authorized, published writings, most jurisdictions have held that such disclaimers serve to rebut a claim by a former employee that he relied upon the manual as a contract.[54] It must be noted, however, that an employer cannot completely insulate himself through use of disclaimers. "Despite the presence of disclaiming language ... [i]f contrary written or oral assurances are given to the employee ... such promises may constitute implied contracts."[55]

One of the first cases to address the effectiveness of handbook disclaimers was *Novosel v. Sears, Roebuck & Co.*[56] In *Novosel, a* federal district court, applying Michigan law, concluded that in light of clear language in the handbook stating that his employment was at-will and could be terminated at any time for any or no reason, the plaintiff could not have reasonably relied on such a manual as implying any contractually binding promise by Sears to discharge only for just cause.[57] Rather, the court reasoned, the disclaimer effectively precluded the plaintiff employee's legitimate expectation of a right to a "just cause" determination prior to termination.[58]

The Ninth Circuit Court of Appeals upheld the force of such disclaimers by granting summary judgment in favor of the employer on the basis of an employment-at-will disclaimer in the applications for

---

[54]*See, e.g.,* Reid v. Sears, Roebuck & Co., 122 L.R.R.M. 2153 (6th Cir. 1986); Bailey v. Perkins Restaurants, Inc. 1 IER Cases 1327 (N.D. Sup. Ct. 1986); Woolley v. Hoffman-LaRoche, Inc., 119 L.R.R.M. 2380, 2391 (N.J. 1985); Dell v. Montgomery Ward, 41 Daily Lab. Rep. at A-12-13 (March 4, 1987). *See also* Mauk, *A History and Analysis, supra* note 9, at 218. *See also* Novosel v. Sears, Roebuck & Co., 495 F.Supp. 344 (E.D. Mich. 1980)(court upheld employer's disclaimer reasoning that the discharged employee could not have reasonably relied on policy as a contract of job security); Kari v. General Motors Corp., 79 Mich. App. 93, 261 N.W.2d 222 (1977), *rev'd on other grounds,* 402 Mich. 926, 282 N.W.2d 925 (1978)(court held that employer's statement of "for information only" was a sufficient disclaimer) and discussion *infra,* at notes 55-57 and accompanying text.

[55]Mauk, *A History and Analysis, supra* note 9, at 219. *Accord* Schipani v. Ford, 102 Mich. App. 606, 302 N.W.2d 307 (1981).

[56]495 F. Supp. 344 (E.D. Mich. 1980).

[57]*Id.* at 346.

[58]*Id.*

employment. *Gianaculus v. Trans World Airlines, Inc.,*[59] forced the
court to resolve a conflict between the at-will disclaimers in the
applications and provisions of a policy manual which appeared to
limit TWA's right to discharge at-will employees. Each plaintiff in
Gianaculus had completed an employment application which stated
that "[i]f given employment, I hereby agree that such employment
may be terminated by the company at any time without advance
notice and without liability to me for wages or salary."[60] The Ninth
Circuit reasoned that since this application expressly stated the at-
will nature of the employment, it contradicted the suggestion that
certain provisions of TWA's "Management Policy and Procedure
Manual" limited the company's ability to discharge at will and,
thereby, precluded the application of an implied contract theory.[61]

Another issue that arises in this area is the modification of the
employment handbook *during* the term of employment. This problem is usually encountered in instances "where the employer unilaterally alters its policies, thereby depriving employees of previously
offered benefits and protections."[62] William Mauk observes that, in
deciding these cases, there are four basic questions which courts
focus on when a policy statement has been modified during the
course of employment: "was the modification with mutual consent
. . . ; was there new consideration for the modification . . . ; did the
modification involve 'vested' or 'accrued' benefits . . . ; [and,] will
the modification operate both prospectively and retrospectively?"[63]

Ledl v. Quik Pik Stores, Inc.,[64] illustrates the application of this
four-question approach. In that case, the court upheld the insertion
of the disclaiming language after an employee was hired. The
employee in *Ledl* had been told when she accepted employment that
she would continue to be employed so long as her performance was
satisfactory.[65] Seven and one-half years later, she signed an employment agreement expressly containing the at-will language describing the nature of the employment.[66] The court, considering the four
basic questions outlined above, rejected the plaintiff's argument
that the employment agreement was an adhesion contract and not

---

[59]761 F.2d 1391 (9th Cir. 1985).
[60]*Id.* at 1393.
[61]*Id.* at 1394.
[62]Mauk, *A History and Analysis, supra* note 9, at 219.
[63]*Id.*
[64]133 Mich. App. 583, 349 N.W.2d 529 (App. 1984).
[65]*Id.* at 586, 349 N.W.2d at 531.
[66]*Id.* at 586-87, 349 N.W.2d at 531.

supported by new consideration, and upheld the dismissal of the wrongful discharge claims on the basis of the at-will language in the agreement.[67]

Promissory Estoppel. Another branch of common law contract theory which courts in some jurisdictions have applied is the principle of promissory estoppel. Promissory estoppel provides an equitable basis for recovery in wrongful discharge actions. The *Restatement (Second) of Contracts* defines the principle as: "[a] promise which the promisor should reasonably expect to induce action or forbearance on the part of the promisee or a third person . . . is binding if injustice can be avoided only by enforcement of the promise."[68] Application of the principle of promissory estoppel can transform "a non-binding agreement . . . into a binding one where one party has relied to his detriment on the representation of the other party."[69]

The theory of promissory estoppel is often applied in a discharge situation "where an employee has resigned one position in reliance upon alternative employment and the offer of employment is either subsequently withdrawn or the employee is terminated shortly after the move."[70] In general, only a few jurisdictions have accepted the promissory estoppel argument as applicable to wrongful discharge cases.[71]

Tort Theories[72]

Tort theory gives rise to various exceptions to the employment-at-will doctrine by imposing duties on the employer from the outside, as a matter of law. The tort exceptions are "based not on the express or implied agreement of the parties," as in contract theory, "but on

---

[67]*Id.* at 587-88, 349 N.W.2d at 531-32.

[68]RESTATEMENT (SECOND) OF CONTRACTS § 90(i) (1981).

[69]Green, *Prevention, supra* note 2, at 6.

[70]Mauk, *A History and Analysis, supra* note 9, at 224, *citing* Grouse v. Group Health Plan, Inc., 306 N.W.2d 114 (Minn. 1981)(plaintiff entitled to opportunity to perform duties to employer's satisfaction where employee had resigned former job in reliance on offer of new employment that was revoked prior to commencement); McMath v. Ford Motor Co., 77 Mich. App. 721, 259 N.W.2d 140 (1977). *See also* McIntosh v. Murphy, 469 P.2d 177 (Ha. 1970). *Contra* Justice v. Stanley Aviation Corp., 530 P.2d 984 (Colo. Ct. App. 1974); Weiner v. McGraw-Hill, 57 N.Y.S.2d 458, 443 N.E.2d 441 (1982).

[71]*See* Green, *Prevention, supra* note 2, at 6.

[72]The law of torts concerns the redress of civil, as opposed to criminal, wrongs. Tort law serves to satisfy citizens' demands for retribution against wrongdoers, imposing punishment on such wrongdoers, deterring future acts, and providing compensation to those injured by the acts of others. Tort theories are conventionally applied in cases involving accidents (*i.e.,* negligence) and physical attack (*i.e.,* assault and battery) and not in the context of employment relationships.

some external state policy that is deemed to supersede the parties' agreement."[73] Williams and Bagby note that "the public policy exceptions can be reconciled with the traditional contractual view of employment, for the law generally recognizes that a contract provision which is illegal or contrary to public policy cannot be enforced."[74] Thus, the authors conclude, when courts prohibit discharges on public policy grounds, they are "simply refusing to enforce the at-will employment contract to the extent that it authorizes discharge on a ground that the state deems improper."[75]

Courts have applied tort theory to the employment relationship in a variety of contexts. There have been a large number of "individual rights" and "privacy" cases that are closely related to typical employment-at-will claims. These claims include allegations of libel, slander, tortious interference with a contractual relationship,[76] defamation, intentional infliction of emotional distress,[77] negligence (such as negligent hiring or performance appraisals) and invasion of privacy. Although several individual rights issues are discusssed in various portions of the text, a detailed exploration of these theories exceeds the scope of this study. The two tort theories which have emerged as having the most viability in the wrongful discharge arena are breach of public policy and breach of the implied covenant of good faith and fair dealing.

Public Policy Torts. A number of jurisdictions recognize an exception to the employment-at-will rule based on considerations of public policy. Under this theory, an employee may recover tort damages for a discharge which contravenes public policy. It is important to note that generally the public policy exception is not intended to encompass statutes that supply administrative machinery for

---

[73]WILLIAMS & BAGBY, ALLIS-CHALMERS, *supra* note 51, at 19.

[74]*Id.*

[75]*Id.*

[76]As Green notes, a few courts have recognized a cause of action for "intentional interference with contractual relations or wrongful inducement of breach of contract in cases involving employment-at-will relationships." Green, *Prevention, supra* note 2, at 12, *citing* Cleary v. American Airlines, 111 Cal. App. 3d 443, 456-57, 168 Cal. Rptr. 722, 730 (2d Dist. 1980); Yaindl v. Ingersoll-Rand Corp., 281 Pa. Super. 560, 422 A.2d 611, 625 (1980).

[77]Most courts require employer's conduct to be extreme and outrageous in order to recognize a tort action for intentional infliction of emotional distress. *See* Green, *Prevention, supra* note 2, at 11-12, *citing* Agarwal v. Johnson, 25 Cal. 3d 932, 160 Cal. Rptr. 141 (1979)(racial epithet and termination by employer); Alcorn v. Anbro Engineering, Inc., 2 Cal. 3d 493, 86 Cal. Rptr. 88 (1970)(racial epithets); Agis v. Howard Johnson Co., 371 Mass. 140, 355 N.E.2d 315 (1976)(waitresses fired in alphabetical order until thief discovered). *But see* Rawson v. Sears, Roebuck & Co., 119 L.R.R.M. 2670 (D. Colo. 1982)(claim dismissed where employee with 33 years of service alleged that employer maliciously fired plaintiff and would not let him resign with dignity).

relief.[78] Rather, the public policy cause of action refers to claims seeking to remedy an employer action that offends some public policy and for which there is no other relief is available other than a private cause of action against the employer.

Such policy may be found "in the form of a legislative enactment or may arise from the rulemaking authority of an administrative agency."[79] Other possible sources of public policy include industry standards, codes of conduct, or ethical codes[80] inherent to the particular trade or industry.[81] Indeed, the myriad sources of public policy contribute to the ambiguity surrounding this area of employment law. At times "the public policies and the prohibitions against their violation are clearly expressed," but "[i]n other instances they are implied as necessary and consistent with a body of law providing rights and protections in the employment context generally."[82]

Statutory sources provide the clearest expression of public policy. As discussed above, there are at least fifteen statutes and their attendant rules on the federal level and whistleblower protection acts in some states which directly and specifically proscribe application of the at-will doctrine.[83] Expressions of public policy arising from common law, on the other hand, are not as clear as those rooted in a statutory context. As one of the earliest cases adopting the public policy argument, *Petermann v. Int'l Brotherhood of Teamsters* noted, "[t]he term 'public policy' is inherently not subject to precise definition."[84] Despite this difficulty, that court observed that:

---

[78]*See* Amicus Brief of the Equal Employment Advisory Council, Mein v. Masonite Corporation, No. 60422 (Ill. S. Ct. 1985) at 20 note 9: "the courts ... have recognized that the tort of wrongful discharge is available only when 'the aggrieved employees have been without any method to gain redress.'" *See* Tarr v. Riberglass, Inc., 115 L.R.R.M. 3688, 3690 (D. Kan. 1984). They have held that "the public policy exception not only requires 'a clear mandate of public policy,' but also a situation where the employee is without remedy." Wehr v. Burroughs, 438 F. Supp. 1052, 1055 (E.D. Pa. 1977). *See also* Bruffett v. Warner Communications, Inc., 692 F.2d 910, 919 (3d Cir. 1982); Wolk v. Saks Fifth Avenue, 115 L.R.R.M. 3064, 3065 (3d Cir. 1984); McCluney v. Jos. Schlitz Brewing Co., 489 F. Supp. 24, 26 (E.D. Wis. 1980); Checkey v. BTR Realty, Inc., 575 F. Supp. 715, 717 (D. Md. 1983). These decisions all refused to extend the public policy tort to cover public policies already protected in the state's anti-discrimination statutes."

[79]Mauk, *A History and Analysis, supra* note 9, at 229.

[80]*See, e.g.,* Pierce v. Ortho Pharmaceutical Corp., 84 N.J. 58, 72, 417 A.2d 505, 512 (1974)(ethical standards may provide source of public policy).

[81]*See* Mauk, *A History and Analysis, supra* note 9, at 229.

[82]*Id.*

[83]*See* federal and state statutes cited *supra* notes 9-14 and accompanying text.

[84]174 Cal. App. 2d 184, 188, 344 P.2d 25, 27 (1959).

> By "public policy" is intended that principle of law which holds that
> no citizen can lawfully do that which has a tendency to be injurious to
> the public or against the public good ... Public Policy [rests on] the
> principles under which freedom of contract or private dealing is
> restricted by law for the good of the community. Another statement
> sometimes referred to as a definition, is that whatever contravenes
> good morals or any established interests of society is against public
> policy.[85]

According to the *Petermann* court's definition, public policy could
arguably reach whatever actions the court desired.

Subsequent decisions, however, have not been as broad as *Petermann* in their development of a common law concept of public policy.[86] Some jurisdictions, for example, have required that the public
policy involved be "clear" or "substantial."[87] Other jurisdictions,
such as New York, completely abjure the concept of a judicially
defined public policy, holding that any public policy "must be legisla-
tively expressed in a statute which not only declares the policy but
explicitly protects or encourages the activity in which the employee
is engaged" in order to provide the basis for an independent cause of
action.[88] Courts have applied the public policy tort theory to reach a
wide variety of activities within the employment relationship. For
the purposes of the discussion in this study, the public policy exception will be divided into the following four categories: (1) refusal to
commit unlawful acts; (2) performance of public obligations; (3) exercise of statutory rights or privileges; and, (4) reports of an employer's unlawful conduct.[89]

Refusal to Commit Unlawful Acts. The seminal case in this area
of public policy is the *Petermann* case mentioned earlier in this chapter. In that case, the plaintiff had been discharged by his employer
for refusing to perjure himself before a legislative committee inves-
tigating the union. Although there was no statute at that time
explicitly protecting an employee who refused to commit perjury,
the *Petermann* court found the employer's decision to terminate
Petermann reprehensible, noting that the employer could have been
cited for contempt if it had sought to compel the employee to perjure

---

[85]*Id.* (citations ommitted).

[86]*See* Mauk, *A History and Analysis, supra* note 9, at 231.

[87]*Id.* & note 129, *citing* Larsen v. Motor Supply Co., 117 Ariz. 507, 573 P.2d 907
(1977); Lempe v. Presbyterian Medical Ctr., 41 Colo. App. 465, 590 P.2d 513 (1978);
Ward v. Frito-Lay, Inc., 95 Wis. 2d 372, 290 N.W.2d 536 (1980); Jones v. Keogh, 137
Vt. 562, 409 A.2d 581 (1979); Geary v. U.S. Steel Corporation, 456 Pa. 171, 319 A.2d
174 (1974).

[88]Mauk, *A History and Analysis, supra* note 9, at 231. *See, e.g.,* Murphy v. American Home Products Corp., 58 N.Y.2d 293, 461 N.Y.S.2d 232, 448 N.E.2d 86 (1983).

[89]*See* Mauk, *A History and Analysis, supra* note 9, at 232-45.

himself in a court case.[90] In California, the basic principles of *Peter-mann* have been consistently followed in cases recognizing the public policy exception where refusal to commit unlawful acts forms the basis of discharge.[91]

Courts in many other jurisdictions have followed the *Petermann* reasoning to construct a public policy exception for employees discharged for refusing to commit unlawful acts. Other grounds where courts have recognized a cause of action include: refusal to illegally manipulate pollution sampling results;[92] refusal to engage in illegal price-fixing;[93] refusal by a married woman to engage in sexual relations with her supervisor;[94] refusal to accede to preferential hiring demands made by a union;[95] refusal to participate in a conspiracy to violate the Clayton Act;[96] and, refusal to hide evidence of a bank's non-compliance with the federal consumer credit laws.[97]

As Mauk and Green have noted, the New Jersey courts, through a series of decisions, have been very active in extending the public policy tort to reach cases where the employee was discharged for refusing to commit unethical acts.[98] Typically, these cases involve actions in the medical profession where ethical considerations are frequently documented. In the leading case, *O'Sullivan v. Mallon,*[99] a New Jersey court held that a cause of action may lie where an X-ray technician was dismissed "for refusing to perform the catheterization of a patient, a procedure, which under state law was authorized to be performed only by a licensed physician or nurse."[100]

---

[90]*See Petermann,* 174 Cal. App. 2d at 189, 344 P.2d at 27.

[91]*See, e.g.,* Crossen v. Foremost-McKesson, Inc., 537 F. Supp. 1076 (N.D. Cal. 1982); Tameny v. Atlantic Richfield Co., 27 Cal. 3d 167, 610 P.2d 1330, 164 Cal. Rptr. 839 (1980)(discharge for refusal to fix prices in violation of Clayton Antitrust Act held actionable). *See* detailed discussion of employment-at-will in California in chapter IV, *infra,* at 55-75.

[92]*See* Trombetta v. Detroit, Toledo & Ironton R.R., 81 Mich. App. 489, 265 N.W.2d 385 (1978).

[93]*See* Mauk, *A History and Analysis, supra* note 9, at 233 note 142, *citing* Tameny v. Atlantic Richfield Co., 27 Cal. 3d 167, 610 P.2d 1330, 164 Cal. Rptr. 839 (1980). *See also* Sheets v. Teddy's Frosted Foods, Inc., 179 Conn. 471, 427 A.2d 385 (1980).

[94]*See* Mauk, *A History and Analysis, supra* note 9, at 233 note 144 *citing* Monge v. Beebe Rubber Co., 114 N.H. 130, 316 A.2d 549 (1974).

[95]*See* Mauk, *A History and Analysis, supra* note 9, at 233 note 144, *citing* Sherman v. St. Barnabas Hospital, 535 F.Supp. 569 (E.D. N.Y. 1982).

[96]*See* Mauk, *A History and Analysis, supra* note 9, at 233 note 145, *citing* Ostrofe v. H. S. Crocker Co., 740 F.2d 739 (1982), *cert. denied,* 469 U.S. 1200 (1985).

[97]*See* Mauk, *A History and Analysis, supra* note 9, at 233 note 146, *citing* Harless v. First Nat'l Bank in Fairmont, 162 W. Va. 116, 246 S.E.2d 270 (1978).

[98]*See* Green, *Prevention, supra* note 2, at 7-8; Mauk, *A History and Analysis, supra* note 9, at 234-36.

[99]160 N.J. Super. 416, 390 A.2d 149 (1978).

[100]Mauk, *A History and Analysis, supra* note 9, at 233.

From a more recent case, however, it appears that ethical considerations will support an independent cause of action only in limited
circumstances. In *Warthen v. Tom's River Community Memorial
Hospital,*[101] for instance, "a nurse was discharged for refusing to
dialyze a terminally ill patient and relied upon a code of ethics for
nurses in support of her wrongful discharge claim."[102] In *Warthen,*
the "plaintiff had originally told her supervisor that she had 'moral,
medical and philosophical objections' to performing the procedure."[103] A New Jersey appellate court, however, upheld the grant of
summary judgment in favor of the employer, holding that "all
patients have a fundamental right to expect that medical treatment
will not be terminated against their will" and this right "clearly
outweighs any policy favoring the right of a nurse to refuse to participate in a treatment which he or she personally believes threatens
human dignity."[104] "The code of ethics relied upon by the plaintiff
referred to procedures for nurses to follow when personally opposed
to the delivery of care in a particular case."[105]

Performance of Important Public Obligations. Closely related to
public policy exceptions recognized because of an employee's refusal
to commit an unlawful act are those cases in which the courts have
recognized an independent cause of action for the discharge of an
employee for performing an important public obligation. Illustrative
of this line of cases is *Nee's v. Hocks.*[106] In that case, the Oregon
Supreme Court affirmed a lower court jury damage verdict for an
employee who had been discharged for indicating her availability for
jury duty against her employer's wishes. "Despite the absence of
express statutory prohibition, the court found that a strong public
policy encouraging jury service was implicit in the Oregon constitution, statutes, and decisional law."[107]

The "important public obligation" line of reasoning outlined in
Nee's has found favor in other jurisdictions where courts have recognized a cause of action based on a breach of public policy for the

---

[101]118 L.R.R.M. 3179 (N.J. Super. Ct. App. Div. 1985).
[102]Green, *Prevention, supra* note 2, at 8.
[103]*Id., quoting Warthen,* 118 L.R.R.M. at 3180.
[104]*Warthen,* 118 L.R.R.M. at 3182.
[105]Green, *Prevention, supra* note 2, at 8.
[106]272 Or. 210, 536 P.2d 512 (1975).
[107]Mauk, *A History and Analysis, supra* note 9, at 235. *Accord* Reuther v. Fowler &
Williams, Inc., 255 Pa. Super. 28, 386 A.2d 119 (1978).

discharge of an employee for supplying information of illegal conduct by a fellow employee[108] and the termination of an employee for refusing to conceal illegal corporate practices.[109]

Exercise of Statutory Rights or Privileges: Retaliatory Discharge. In this area of tort-based exceptions,"[t]he basis of the employee's claim is that the employer, by its retaliatory conduct, seeks to compel indirectly that which it may not directly affect."[110] As Mauk notes, '[t]he employer acts to defeat or inhibit the employee's exercise of statutory rights, thereby subverting the purposes of the statute but not directly violating the law itself."[111]

The earliest and most common type of case applying this kind of public policy involves an employee discharged for filing a worker's compensation claim. In *Frampton v. Central Indiana Gas Co.,*[112] which is typical of most of these worker's compensation cases, the Indiana Supreme Court held that an employee who was discharged for filing a worker's compensation claim provided for by state law could maintain an action for wrongful discharge. The public policy underlying the worker's compensation statute, the *Frampton* court reasoned, required the recognition of a cause of action based on a dismissal in retaliation for filing a claim.[113]

A number of jurisdictions have extended the retaliatory discharge branch of public policy tort theory to recognize causes of action in areas other than the filing of a worker's compensation claim. Among those areas, courts have found actionable an employer's discharge of its employee "in order to prevent a pension fund from vesting, for refusing to take a polygraph test where statutorily prohibited ... and for retaining counsel to negotiate a wage claim and to assist in the presentation of testimony against an employer in a minimum wage proceeding."[114]

---

[108]Mauk, *A History and Analysis, supra* note 9, at 235, *citing* Palmateer v. Int'l Harvester Co., 85 Ill. App. 3d 50, 406 N.E.2d 595 (1980), *rev'd,* 85 Ill. 2d 124, 421 N.E.2d 876 (1981).

[109]Mauk, *A History and Analysis, supra* note 9, at 235, *citing* Adler v. American Standard Corp., 291 Md. 31, 432 A.2d 464 (1981).

[110]Mauk, *A History and Analysis, supra* note 9, at 236.

[111]*Id.*

[112]260 Ind. 249, 297 N.E.2d 425 (1973).

[113]*Id.* at 253, 297 N.E.2d at 428. *See also* Kelsay v. Motorola, Inc., 74 Ill.2d 172, 384 N.E.2d 353 (1978); Sventko v. Kroger Co., 69 Mich. App. 644, 245 N.W.2d 151 (1976).

[114]Mauk, *A History and Analysis, supra* note 9, at 238 notes 181-84, *citing* Hovey v. Lutheran Medical Ctr., 516 F. Supp. 554 (E.D.N.Y. 1981); Savodnik v. Korvettes, Inc., 488 F. Supp. 822 (E.D.N.Y. 1980); Perks v. Firestone Tire & Rubber Co., 611 F.2d 1363 (3d Cir. 1979); Montalvo v. Zamora, 7 Cal. App. 3d 69, 86 Cal. Rptr. 401 (1970).

Recently the United States Court of Appeals for the Third Circuit recognized a potentially broad public policy exception based on the exercise of a legal right. In *Novosel v. Nationwide Insurance Co.*,[115] the plaintiff was discharged when he refused to aid his employer's lobbying effort for the elimination of no-fault insurance. Judge Adams, delivering the opinion of the court, held that a cause of action for wrongful discharge is stated when the termination is alleged to have contravened a public policy that "strikes at the heart of the citizen's social rights, duties and responsibilities."[116] Specifically, the court found that public policy includes the rights to freedom of speech protected by the First Amendment to the United States Constitution.[117]

The suspicion among many in the legal community that *Novosel* might represent a judicial overstep by the Third Circuit has been supported by subsequent federal cases which retreat from *Novosel's* expansive holding. In *Wolk v. Saks Fifth Avenue, Inc.*,[118] for instance, Judge Adams stepped back significantly from his stance in *Novosel,* stressing instead the gradual emergence of change in the common law and stating that:

> *Novosel* must be understood against the backdrop of the limited role of a federal court sitting in diversity jurisdiction. While a federal court must be sensitive to the doctrinal trends of the jurisdiction whose law it applies, *it is beyond the authority of a federal court in such circumstances to create entirely new causes of action.*[119]

In addition to *Wolk,* other limits have been placed on the extension of public policy protection in this area. Notably, in *Bruffett v. Warner Communications, Inc.*,[120] the Third Circuit Court of Appeals reasoned that where a statute contains an adminstrative machinery for addressing alleged violations of the statute, including alleged retaliation, such as Title VII, that administrative machinery cannot be sidestepped by a plaintiff who files a state law public policy wrongful discharge claim.[121] In *Rozier v. St. Mary's Hospital,*[122] an Illinois appellate court rejected extending a retaliatory discharge tort action "to a hospital employee discharged allegedly for reporting to

---

[115]721 F.2d 894 (3d Cir. 1983).

[116]*Id.* at 899.

[117]*Id.* at 897.

[118]728 F.2d 221 (3d Cir. 1984) discussed *infra* chapter IV, at 108-109.

[119]728 F.2d at 223 (citations omitted and emphasis added).

[120]692 F.2d 910 (3d Cir. 1982).

[121]*See also* Bonham v. Dresser Industries, Inc., 569 F.2d 187 (3d Cir. 1977), *cert. denied,* 439 U.S. 821 (1978).

[122]88 Ill. App. 3d 994, 411 N.E.2d 50 (1980).

the news media incidents of patient abuse."[123] As the court in that case noted, "if such a cause of action generally could be maintained, employers, particularly those in small businesses, would be thrust into an economic dilemma by every employment decision."[124]

Report of Employer's Unlawful Conduct: Whistleblowing. A few jurisdictions have recognized a cause of action for employees discharged for reporting to superiors or government authorities that other employees or the employer itself are violating the law, even where no statute requires such reporting or prohibits such retaliatory discharge, and where the employee himself was not required to engage in any wrongdoing. At present, nineteen states have enacted statutes protecting "whistleblowers," covering both private- and public-sector employees.[125] In all other jurisdictions the "whistleblower" exception relies predominantly "upon a judicial perception of public policy."[126]

The leading case involving the whistleblower's exception is *Sheets v. Teddy's Frosted Foods, Inc.*[127] In *Sheets,* the Connecticut Supreme Court recognized an action for wrongful discharge where a quality control director was discharged allegedly for his efforts to ensure that the employer's products complied with state labeling and licensing requirements. In contrast, however, the Pennsylvania Supreme Court in *Geary v. United States Steel Corp.*[128] refused to recognize a cause of action for an employee who was discharged allegedly for reporting to his supervisors his fears about one of the company's industrial tubing products. The *Geary* court dismissed the plaintiff's claims, holding that Geary had bypassed the employer's chain of command and created a nuisance.[129] Although the court acknowledged the possibility of employer abuse "where an employee must exercise independent, expert judgment in matters of product safety,"[130] the justices noted that Geary did not hold himself out as that sort of employee.

---

[123]Mauk, *A History and Analysis, supra* note 9, at 238.

[124]88 Ill. App. 3d at 999, 411 N.E.2d at 54.

[125]*See, e.g.,* MICH. COMP. LAWS ANN. §§ 15.361-369 (West 1981).

[126]Mauk, *A History and Analysis, supra* note 9, at 240.

[127]179 Conn. 471, 427 A.2d 385 (1980). *See also* Harless v. First National Bank in Fairmont, 162 W. Va. 116, 246 S.E.2d 270 (1978)(cause of action recognized where office manager of bank's consumer credit department was discharged allegedly in retaliation for bringing to his supervisor's attention bank's non-compliance with consumer credit laws).

[128]456 Pa. 171, 319 A.2d 174 (1974).

[129]*Id.* at 180, 319 A.2d at 179-80.

[130]*Id.* at 181, 319 A.2d at 178.

Implied Covenant of Good Faith and Fair Dealing

In a small but growing minority of jurisdictions across the nation, courts have found an implied covenant of good faith and fair dealing to exist in the employment relationship, thereby limiting the employer's right to discharge an employee at will. "The covenant encompasses an obligation to refrain from interfering with the one party's right to receive the benefits of the contract."[131] In wrongful discharge suits, courts usually will imply a covenant of good faith and fair dealing to prevent automatic losses or forfeitures of rights earned, or almost earned by an employee.

Although this theory has received much attention by courts in wrongful discharge litigation, the judiciary is split over whether an employee's allegation of bad faith on the part of the employer lies in contract or in tort.[132] For purposes of this discussion, the implied covenant will be viewed as giving rise to a duty imposed by law, rather than one arising out of contract, thereby sounding in tort.[133] Obviously this is the "worst case" scenario employers fear most since a tort action may lead to the plaintiff's recovery of compensatory and punitive damages.

The first case recognizing a bad faith cause of action in the employment setting was *Monge v. Beebe Rubber Co.*[134] In that case the plaintiff was a married female employee who refused to date her foreman. The court found the employer's behavior egregious and in bad faith, and recognized the plaintiff's cause of action under the good faith reasoning: "a termination by the employer of a contract of employment at will which is motivated by bad faith or malice . . . is not [in] the best interest of the economic system or the public good and constitutes a breach of the employment contract."[135] In a later case, however, the *Monge* court's ruling was restricted.[136] Today under New Hampshire law, a court will apply a two-part test before recognizing a wrongful discharge tort action based on this theory,

---

[131]Mauk, *A History and Analysis, supra* note 9, at 245.

[132]*Compare* Fortune v. National Cash Register Co., 373 Mass. 96, 364 N.E.2d 1251 (1977) *with* Rees v. Bank Bldg. & Equip. Corp., 332 F.2d 548, 550 (7th Cir.), *cert. denied,* 379 U.S. 932 (1964).

[133]*See* Mauk, *A History and Analysis, supra* note 9, at 246.

[134]114 N.H. 130, 316 A.2d 549 (1974).

[135]*Id.* at 133, 316 A.2d at 551.

[136]*See, e.g.,* Howard v. Dorr Woolen Co., 120 N.H. 295, 414 A.2d 1273 (1980)(restricts *Monge* holding to situations where an employee is discharged because he "performed an act encouraged by public policy or refused to do that which public policy would condemn." *Id.* at 297, 414 A.2d at 1274).

requiring that: (1) the employer's action be motivated by bad faith, malice or retaliation; and, (2) the discharge be in violation of public policy.[137]

Fortune v. National Cash Register Co.[138] was one of the first cases to specifically apply the affirmative duty of good faith and fair dealing to the employment setting. In that case, the Massachusetts Supreme Judicial Court applied the good faith covenant to affirm a jury verdict against an employer who had allegedly discharged its salesman of forty years in order to deprive him of a large commission. Although the *Fortune* court recognized that a duty did exist in this particular case, it refused to conclude that *all* employment contracts contain such an implied covenant.[139] Soon after *Fortune*, however, the California Supreme Court handed down *Tameny v. Atlantic Richfield*[140] which, although decided on public policy grounds, implied that the court would recognize an implied covenant in all employment relationships. With the subsequent cases of *Cleary v. American Airlines*[141] and *Pugh v. See's Candies, Inc.*,[142] California expressly adopted the stance that an implied covenant of good faith and fair dealing is present in all employment contracts.

In *Cleary*, the California Appellate Court's recognition of the plaintiff's breach of the implied covenant claim rested on two important factors. As the court pointed out:

> Two factors are of paramount importance in reaching our result that the plaintiff has pleaded a viable cause of action. One is the longevity of service by plaintiff—18 years of apparently satisfactory performance. Termination of employment without legal cause after such a period of time offends the implied-in-law covenant of good faith and fair dealing contained in all contracts. As a result of this covenant, a duty arose on the part of the employer, American Airlines, to do nothing which would deprive the plaintiff, the employee, of the benefits of the employment bargain—benefits described in the complaint as having accrued during plaintiff's 18 years of employment.
>
> The second factor of considerable significance is the expressed policy of the employer (probably in response to the demands of employees who were union members), set forth in Regulation 135-4. This policy involves the adoption of specific procedures for adjudicating employee disputes such as this one. While the contents of the regulation are not before us, its existence compels the conclusion that the employer

---

[137]*See* Mauk, *A History and Analysis, supra* note 9, at 247, *citing* Cloutier v. Great Atlantic & Pacific Tea Co., 121 N.H. 915, 921, 436 A.2d 1140, 1143 (1981).

[138]373 Mass. 96, 364 N.E.2d 1251 (1977).

[139]*Id.* at 104, 364 N.E.2d at 1257.

[140]27 Cal. 3d 167, 610 P.2d 1330, 164 Cal. Rptr. 839 (1980).

[141]111 Cal. App. 3d 443, 168 Cal. Rptr. 722 (1980).

[142]116 Cal. App. 3d 311, 171 Cal. Rptr. 917 (1981).

had recognized its responsibility to engage in good faith and fair dealing rather than in arbitrary conduct with respect to *all* of its employees.[143]

Similarly, in *Pugh,* the appellate court permitted the plaintiff's action in light of the "totality of the parties' relationship," which the court found to include the personnel policies of the employer, the employee's longevity of service, actions or communications by the employer reflecting assurances of continued employment, and the practices of the particular industry in question.[144]

Not all jurisdictions, however, have accepted the implied covenant exception to the at-will rule. Some courts, in fact, have expressly declined to imply a covenant of good faith and fair dealing in the at-will employment relationship.[145] Notably, the New York Court of Appeals, the state's highest court, rejected the good faith and fair dealing exception in *Murphy v. American Home Products, Inc.,*[146] where the court stated that:

> [T]he implied obligation is in furtherance of other terms of the agreement of the parties. No obligation can be implied, however, which would be inconsistent with other terms of the contractual relationship. Thus, in the case now before us, plaintiff's employment was at will, a relationship in which the law accords the employer the unfettered right to terminate the employment at any time. In the context of such employment it would be incongruous to say that the employer impliedly agreed to a provision which would be destructive of his right to termination.[147]

Judicial reasoning adopting the implied covenant exception has been the source of great criticism in the legal community. As Williams and Bagby note, such reasoning "reflects the lengths to which those courts have had to reach to try to fit their holdings within the framework of contract law principles generally recognized as governing employment relationships."[148] In their view, such reasoning approaches employment "more as a property right than as a contractual relationship."[149] That is, "[t]he job is treated as a personal entitlement of which the possessor (the employee) cannot be deprived

---

[143]111 Cal. App. 3d at 455-56, 168 Cal. Rptr. at 729.

[144]116 Cal. App. 3d at 327, 329, 171 Cal. Rptr. 933, 935.

[145]*See* WILLIAMS & BAGBY, ALLIS-CHALMERS, *supra* note 51, at 22 & note 81, *citing* Walker v. Modern Realty of Missouri, Inc., 675 F.2d 1002 (8th Cir. 1982); Muller v. Stromberg Carlson Corp., 427 So.2d 266 (Fla. App. 1983); Martin v. Federal Life Ins. Co., 109 Ill. App. 3d 596, 440 N.E.2d 998 (1982).

[146]58 N.Y.2d 293, 448 N.E.2d 86 (1983).

[147]*Id.* at 304-05, 448 N.E.2d at 91.

[148]WILLIAMS & BAGBY, ALLIS-CHALMERS, *supra* note 51, at 22.

[149]*Id.*

without a reason which the courts recognize as sufficient."[150] In short, "the decisions reflecting this approach seem to view the employee's job rights as growing stronger with continued time in possession of the job, much as property rights are acquired or strengthened by possession over a prolonged period of time."[151]

CONCLUSION

The abrogation of the employment-at-will doctrine has occurred at both the legislative and judicial levels. Statutory provisions have given limited protection to certain employees based upon certain characteristics or collective activities who would otherwise be classified as at-will employees. The courts have applied principles of both contract and tort law to create an array of exceptions to the traditional common law rule of terminations. In fashioning these exceptions, however, the courts have also had to confront the defensive legal theories used by employers faced with wrongful discharge claims, which will be examined in the following chapter.

---

[150]*Id.*
[151]*Id.*

CHAPTER III

Legal Defenses

Having examined the various legal theories supporting wrongful discharge claims, it is necessary to review briefly the procedural defenses which an employer might use when confronted with a wrongful discharge lawsuit. The discussion which follows highlights the most commonly employed defenses and is not intended to be an exhaustive survey of all available arguments. To be sure, the defenses available to any employer faced with a wrongful discharge claim vary according to the particular facts of the situation.

The most prevalent defenses fall into two broad doctrinal categories: the statute of frauds and the preemption doctrine.[1] The statute of frauds defense is a contract-based rule which provides that any contract not capable of performance within one year must be in writing in order to be binding upon another party. The preemption doctrine arises from the notion that the legislature, by enacting certain statutes, provides the appropriate rights and remedies available to a party in a particular situation; therefore, any private cause of action stemming from an incident addressed by the statute must be preempted in order to avoid undermining the legislative purpose.[2] As one might expect, the preemption doctrine spans a wide variety of employment situations, including instances in which employees are covered by collective bargaining agreements, state workers' compensation statutes, and various kinds of anti-discrimination legislation.

STATUTE OF FRAUDS

Attempts by discharged employees to assert breach of contract claims against a former employer are often barred by the statute of frauds which requires contracts not capable of performance within one year to be in writing. It is usually the case that "an employee

---

[1]For a detailed discussion of the various issues surrounding the preemption doctrine, see C. MORRIS, THE DEVELOPING LABOR LAW, chapter 31 (1983).

[2]*See* W. HOLLOWAY & M. LEECH, EMPLOYMENT TERMINATION RIGHTS AND REMEDIES at 137 (1985) [hereinafter cited as HOLLOWAY & LEECH, EMPLOYMENT TERMINATION].

hired for an indefinite period typically has no written contract."[3]
Discharged employees bringing an action for wrongful discharge,
therefore, attempt to show the existence of an oral contract for permanent employment. Such claims arising from oral contracts, however, frequently run afoul of a state's statute of frauds. These statutes, whose origins date back to English legislation in the
seventeenth century, provide in relevant part that:

> no action shall be brought upon any agreement that is not to be per-
> formed within the space of one year from the making thereof, unless
> the promise or agreement upon which such action shall be brought, or
> some memorandum or note thereof, shall be in writing . . . [4]

The purpose of these statutes, as Professor Corbin suggests, is to
avoid leaving to memory the terms of a contractual relationship that
is longer than one year.[5]

Most states have enacted their own statute of frauds[6] legislation

---

[3]Note, *Weiner v. McGraw-Hill, Inc.: Is Employment in New York Still at Will?*, 3
PACE L. REV. 245, 254 (1983) [hereinafter cited as Note, *New York At Will?*].

[4]Statute of Frauds, 29 Car. 2, ch. 3 (1677) (cited in HOLLOWAY & LEECH, EMPLOY-
MENT TERMINATION, *supra* note 2, at 55).

[5]2 A. CORBIN, CORBIN ON CONTRACTS § 444, at 534 (1950). Professor Corbin provides
further explanation of the rationale behind the statute of frauds as follows:

> Where actions on contracts are long delayed, injustice is likely to be done
> because of bad memory and because witnesses have died or moved away, so
> that mistakes will be made and perjury is more likely to be successful. And in
> the case of a contract whose performance is to cover a long period of time,
> actions are likely to be long delayed. These may be supposed to have been the
> reasons that underlay . . . this provision.

Id. (cited in *Note, New York At Will?, supra* note 3, at 255 note 74).

[6]HOLLOWAY & LEECH, EMPLOYMENT TERMINATION, *supra* note 2, at 55 note 39, *citing*
the following state statutes: ALA. CODE § 8-9-2 (1975); ALASKA STAT. § 09.25.010
(1973); ARIZ. REV. STAT. ANN. § 44-101 (1967); ARK. STAT. ANN. § 38-101 (1962); CAL.
CIV. CODE § 1624 (West 1973); COLO. REV. STAT. § 38-10-112 (1982); CONN. GEN. STAT.
§ 52-550 (1973); DEL. CODE ANN. tit. 6, § 2714 (1974); D.C. CODE ANN. § 28-3502
(1981); FLA. STAT. § 725.01 (1969); GA. CODE § 13-5-30 (1982) (except for contracts
with an overseer); HAWAII REV. STAT. § 656-1 (1976); IDAHO CODE § 9-505 (1979); ILL.
REV. STAT. ch. 59, § 1 (1972); IND. CODE § 32-2-1-1 (1979); IOWA CODE § 622.32 (1950);
KAN. STAT. ANN. § 33-106 (1981); KY. REV. STAT. § 371.010 (1981); ME. REV. STAT.
ANN. tit. 33, § 51 (1964); MD. ANN. CODE art. 39 C, § 1 (1957); MASS. GEN. LAWS ANN.
ch. 259, § 1 (West 1959); MICH. COMP. LAWS § 566.132 (1967); MINN. STAT. § 513.01
(1945); MISS. CODE ANN. § 15-3-1 (1972); MO. REV. STAT. § 432.010 (1952); MONT. CODE
ANN. § 13-606 (1979); NEB. REV. STAT. § 36-202 (1978); NEV. REV. STAT. § 111.220
(1979); N.H. REV. STAT. ANN. § 506.2 (1968); N.J. REV. STAT. § 25-1-5 (1940); NEW
MEXICO, by case law, *Childers v. Talbott*, 4 N.M. 168, 16 ¶ 275 (1888); N.Y. GEN.
OBLIG. LAW § 5-701 (McKinney 1977); N.D. CENT. CODE § 9-06-04 (1975); OHIO REV.

similar in wording to the one quoted above.[7] Notable exceptions are Pennsylvania, North Carolina, and Louisiana which do not have any statute of frauds legislation.[8] Generally, courts on both the state and federal levels have interpreted the statute's bar narrowly, applying it "only to cases that inescapably fall within the language of the statute."[9] In the case of at-will hirings either party to the contract, by definition, may terminate the relationship at any time; thus, many courts have reasoned that the contractual relationship is capable of performance within the one-year limit and not barred by the statute of frauds.[10] Under such legal construction, termination is viewed by the courts as performance of the contract, rather than its destruction.[11] In other words, termination does not defeat the contract, it simply advances the period of fulfillment.[12]

Problems of interpretation do arise, however, when the option to terminate the contract is unilateral. Simply stated, a unilateral contract is one in which there is "a promise in return for an act,"[13] such as where an employer promises some form of job security to a worker in return for the employee's work. "[I]t is sometimes argued that the [employer's] promise is unenforceable if made more than a year before performance of the promise is due."[14] As Holloway and Leech explain, "an employer may orally promise a stock option or dismissal only for good cause *after* one year of employment."[15] In such a

---

CODE ANN. § 1335.05 (Page 1979); OKLA. STAT. tit. 15, § 136 (1983); ORE. REV. STAT. § 41.580 (1981); R.I. GEN. LAWS § 9-1-4 (1956); S.C. CODE ANN. § 32-3-10 (1976); S.D. COMP. LAWS ANN. § 58-8-2 (1978); TENN. CODE ANN. § 23-201 (1980); TEX. BUS. & COMM. CODE ANN. § 26.01 (Vernon 1968); UTAH CODE ANN. § 25-5-4 (1953); VT. STAT. ANN. tit. 12, § 181 (1973); V.I. CODE ANN. tit. 28, § 244 (1976); VA. CODE § 11-2 (1950); WASH. REV. CODE § 19.36.010 (1974); W. VA. CODE § 55-1-1 (1981); WIS. STAT. § 241.02 (1981-82); WYO. STAT. § 16-1-101 (1977).

[7]New York's statute of frauds, for example, provides in pertinent part that:
   a. Every agreement, promise or undertaking is void, unless it or some note or memorandum thereof be in writing, and subscribed by the party to be charged therewith, or by his lawful agent, if such agreement, promise or undertaking:
   1. By its terms is not to be performed within one year from the making thereof or the performance of which is not to be completed before the end of a lifetime.
N.Y. GEN. OBLIG. LAW Section 5-701 (a) (1) (McKinney 1978 & Supp. 1987).
[8]*See* HOLLOWAY & LEECH, EMPLOYMENT TERMINATION, *supra* note 2, at 55.
[9]*Id.* at 56.
[10]*See* Note, *New York At Will?, supra* note 3, at 256 & note 80, *citing* Blake v. Voight, 134 N.Y. 69, 31 N.E. 256 (1892) (an employment contract which has as one of its terms a bilateral option to terminate within one year, is capable of performance within a year, and, thus, not within the statute of frauds).
[11]*Blake,* 134 N.Y. at 72, 31 N.E. at 259.
[12]*Id.* at 73, 31 N.E. at 257.
[13]HOLLOWAY & LEECH, EMPLOYMENT TERMINATION, *supra* note 2, at 56.
[14]*Id.*
[15]*Id.* (emphasis added).

situation, the employer's promise is not due, and the contract is not enforceable, until the act of one year's employment is fully performed. Another problem of interpretation arises in the context of a bilateral contract—an exchange of promises where one promise is within the statute of frauds, but the other is not. In this instance, most courts have avoided the harsh result of the statute of frauds bar and have held that the contract is not governed by the statute.[16]

The general rule of application, as Professor Williston notes, is that

> A promise which is not likely to be performed within a year, and which in fact is not performed within a year, is not within the Statute if at the time the contract is made there is a possibility in law and in fact that full peformance such as the parties intended may be completed before the expiration of a year.[17]

Therefore, arrangements such as "employment for life" or "permanent employment" entertain the possibility of performance within one year in the event of the employee's death and have therefore been adjudged to be beyond the scope of the statute of frauds (*i.e.*, on this basis, oral contracts "for life" might be upheld and enforced).[18] Of course, "some cases give less weight to a mere possibility that a contract may unexpectedly end."[19] It is crucial to note here the exactitude with which courts will interpret the language of an oral arrangement. For instance, in at least one case a court has held that employment "until retirement" is separate and distinct from a promise of "permanent" or "lifetime" employment and is subject to the statute of frauds' bar.[20]

Once it is determined that an agreement is within the statute of frauds, the inquiry focuses on "whether there is a writing sufficient to comply with the statute."[21] Generally, letters containing language which fixes the term of employment have been held sufficient to sat-

---

[16]*Id.* at 57 & note 44, *citing* Marek v. Knab Co., 10 Wis. 2d 390, 103 N.W.2d 31 (1960); Miller v. Riata Cadillac Co., 517 S.W.2d 773 (Tex. 1974).

[17]3 WILLISTON, WILLISTON ON CONTRACTS § 495, at 576-78 (3d ed. 1960).

[18]HOLLOWAY & LEECH, EMPLOYMENT TERMINATION, *supra* note 2, at 57 note 48, *citing* Fireboard Products v. Townsend, 202 F.2d 180 (9th Cir. 1953); Kitsos v. Mobile Gas Serv. Corp., 404 So.2d 40 (Ala. 1981); Sax v. Detroit, Grand Haven & Milwaukee Ry., 125 Mich. 252, 84 N.W. 314 (1900).

[19]HOLLOWAY & LEECH, EMPLOYMENT TERMINATION, *supra* note 2, at 57-58, *discussing* Sinclair v. Sullivan Chevrolet Co., 31 Ill.2d 507, 202 N.E.2d 516 (1964); *accord* Gilliland v. Allstate Ins. Co., 69 Ill. App. 3d 630, 388 N.E.2d 68 (1979).

[20]HOLLOWAY & LEECH, EMPLOYMENT TERMINATION, *supra* note 2, at 57 note 49, *citing* McKinney v. Nat'l Dairy Council, 491 F.Supp. 1108 (D. Mass. 1980) (applying New York law).

[21]HOLLOWAY & LEECH, EMPLOYMENT TERMINATION, *supra* note 2, at 59.

isfy the statute's writing requirement.[22] Under the "Massachusetts Rule" which some courts apply, the fixing of an annual salary, such as "Jones will be paid $X per year," implies "an annual employment and standing alone is sufficient to support a finding that there was a hiring for that period."[23] Furthermore, at least one court has held that it is not required that the writing be signed in order to be found sufficient for statute of frauds purposes.[24]

Some authors have pointed out that in cases "[w]here it appears that the statute of frauds requires the contract to be in writing and there is none sufficient to satisfy the statute, the employee ... argues that his detrimental reliance upon the employer's promise estops the employer from raising the statute as a defense."[25] This use of an equitable estoppel argument to defeat the statute of frauds defense has been modified in some jurisdictions. For instance, in Illinois, the conduct of the promissor must amount to concealment or misrepresentation of a material fact before the equitable estoppel argument can take effect.[26]

The statute of frauds is sometimes asserted by employers where there is an oral modification to a written contract. In this situation, an employer may argue that a salary increase in excess of that provided for in the written contract amounts to a new oral contract between the parties.[27] As such, the argument goes, the contract is unenforceable because of the statute of frauds' mandate that the contract be in writing. Despite the argument's legal creativity, courts have uniformly held that this situation merely is an oral amendment to a written contract and not an entirely new contract between the parties: "Therefore, the written agreement as orally amended complies with the statute of frauds."[28] In a similar vein, written contracts which are subject to automatic renewal without a new writing have been held to not require a new writing for each renewal term.[29]

---

[22]*Id.* at 59 note 61, *citing* Standing v. Morosco, 43 Cal. App. 748, 184 P. 954 (1925).

[23]HOLLOWAY & LEECH, EMPLOYMENT TERMINATION, *supra* note 2, at 59 note 62, *citing* Southwell v. Parker Plow Co., 234 Mich. 292, 207 N.W. 872 (1926).

[24]HOLLOWAY & LEECH, EMPLOYMENT TERMINATION, *supra* note 2, at 60 note 64, *citing* Graver v. Valve & Primer Corp., 47 Ill. App. 3d 152, 361 N.E.2d 863 (1977).

[25]HOLLOWAY & LEECH, EMPLOYMENT TERMINATION, *supra* note 2, at 60.

[26]*Id.*, *citing* Sinclair v. Sullivan Chevrolet Co., 31 Ill. 2d 507, 202 N.E.2d 516 (1964).

[27]*See* HOLLOWAY & LEECH, EMPLOYMENT TERMINATION, *supra* note 2, at 61.

[28]*Id.* & note 72, *citing* Evatt v. Campbell, 234 S.C. 1, 106 S.E.2d 447 (1959); Molotowsky v. Grauer, 113 N.Y.S. 679 (App. Div. 1908).

[29]*See* HOLLOWAY & LEECH, EMPLOYMENT TERMINATION, *supra* note 2, at 61 note 73, *citing* McIntyre v. Smith-Bridgman & Co., 301 Mich. 629, 4 N.W.2d 36 (1942); Conrad v. Ellison-Harvey Co., 120 Va. 458, 91 S.E. 763 (1917).

In summary, commentators agree that the statute of frauds defense provides limited force for employers involved in wrongful discharge litigation. The primary weakness of this defense is "that most jurisdictions construe the statute so that it rarely, if ever, operates on any employment contract."[30] In the District of Columbia, however, the statute of frauds defense has been recognized in several cases.[31] Even in those few jurisdictions that apply the statute of frauds, it is relatively easy to circumvent the statute by introducing evidence to prove that all contractual obligations encompassed within the employment relationship could be discharged within the one-year limit.[32]

PREEMPTION DOCTRINE

Another important employer defense to wrongful discharge claims rests in the doctrine of preemption. Preemption may occur at the federal level where, as Williams and Bagby note, "the exercise of state power clashes with the implementation of some aspect of federal labor relations policy to such an extent that it is deemed necessary to displace or modify the state law, regulation, or judicial decision in order to prevent the federal policy from being undermined."[33] Legal support for the doctrine of federal preemption lies in the supremacy clause of the United States Constitution which provides, in relevant part, that:

> This Constitution and the Laws of the United States which shall be made in Pursuance thereof ... shall be the supreme Law of the Land; and the Judges in every State shall be bound thereby, any Thing in the Constitution or Laws of any State to the Contrary notwithstanding.[34]

Preemption may also occur at the state level. Here, the preemption defense provides that a statutory scheme intended by the legislators to provide regulation of a specific aspect of the employment relationship may bar, or preempt, an otherwise viable cause of action.[35] "The idea," as Holloway and Leech explain, "is that the legislature, hav-

---

[30]HOLLOWAY & LEECH, EMPLOYMENT TERMINATION, *supra* note 2, at 62.

[31]*See, e.g.*, Hodge v. Evans Financial Corp., 778 F.2d 794 (D.C. Cir. 1985); Prouty v. National R.R. Passenger Corp., 572 F. Supp. 200, 203 (D. D.C. 1983).

[32]*See* HOLLOWAY & LEECH, EMPLOYMENT TERMINATION, *supra* note 2, at 62.

[33]R. WILLIAMS & T. BAGBY, ALLIS-CHALMERS CORPORATION V. LUECK: THE IMPACT OF THE SUPREME COURT'S DECISION ON WRONGFUL DISCHARGE SUITS AND OTHER STATE COURT EMPLOYMENT LITIGATION, at 9 (1986) [hereinafter cited as WILLIAMS & BAGBY, ALLIS-CHALMERS].

[34]U.S. CONST. art. VI.

[35]*See* HOLLOWAY & LEECH, EMPLOYMENT TERMINATION, *supra* note 2, at 137.

ing spelled out the appropriate rights and remedies, intended that they be all that are available."[36] Therefore, the authors continue, "permitting other actions in this situation would undermine the legislative purpose."[37]

At both the federal and state levels, the preemption doctrine operates potentially to limit the potential expansion of discharge remedies available to a plaintiff within that jurisdiction. The discussion below addresses the five topical areas of litigation in which the preemption doctrine has received significant judicial attention.

Employees Covered By Collective Bargaining Agreements

The National Labor Relations Act[38] (NLRA) expressly provides for the enforcement in court of collective bargaining agreements and permits employee suits for discharge in violation of the agreement.[39] It has long been settled that enforcement of the rights embodied in a collective bargaining agreement is controlled by federal law, not state law.[40] That is, Section 185 of the NLRA [Section 301 of the Labor Management Relations Act (LMRA)] preempts state contract law in this area. Until recently, courts had consistently held that where a grievance procedure was available under a collective bargaining agreement, the employee was limited to redress under that process and could not pursue a direct court action for wrongful discharge or any other employment-related tort or contract claim based on state law.[41]

Despite the relatively clear case law indicating preemption of state common law claims by those employees covered by a collective bargaining agreement, courts on both the state and federal levels have recently displayed a willingness to allow such employees to proceed

---

[36]*Id.*

[37]*Id.*

[38]29 U.S.C. § 157 *et seq.* (1982).

[39]29 U.S.C. § 185a (1982).

[40]*See* Textile Workers Union of America v. Lincoln Mills of Alabama, 353 U.S. 448 (1957) (cited in HOLLOWAY & LEECH, EMPLOYMENT TERMINATION, *supra* note 2, at 150 note 103).

[41]*See* WILLIAMS & BAGBY, ALLIS-CHALMERS, *supra* note 33, at 23 note 86, *citing* Olguin v. Inspirational Consolidated Copper Co., 740 F.2d 1468 (9th Cir. 1984); Moore v. General Motors Corp., 739 F.2d 311 (8th Cir. 1984); Beers v. Southern Pacific Trans. Co., 703 F.2d 425 (9th Cir. 1983); Jackson v. Consolidated Rail Corp., 717 F.2d 1045 (7th Cir. 1983); Viestenz v. Fleming Companies, Inc., 681 F.2d 699 (10th Cir.), *cert. denied,* 103 S. Ct. 303 (1982); Magnuson v. Burlington Northern, Inc., 576 F.2d 1367 (9th Cir. 1978), *cert. denied,* 439 U.S. 930 (1978); Broniman v. Great Atl. & Pac. Tea Co., 353 F.2d 559 (6th Cir. 1965), *cert. denied,* 384 U.S. 907 (1966); Cokely v. P.G. & E., 35 Empl. Prac. Dec. (CCH) ¶ 135, 295 (N.D. Cal. 1984); Mims v. Capitol Printing Ink Co., 428 F. Supp. 12 (D.D.C. 1976).

with tort- and contract-based wrongful discharge claims. The most significant decision in this area of employment law is *Garibaldi v. Lucky Food Stores, Inc.*[42] In that case, the Ninth Circuit Court of Appeals held that an employee's "state damage action was not barred by an adverse finding by an arbitrator that the plaintiff was discharged for cause."[43] The *Garibaldi* case involved a truck driver, covered by a collective bargaining agreement, who alleged that he was discharged for notifying health officials that the milk he was delivering was spoiled.[44] Upon his termination, Garibaldi filed a grievance pursuant to the terms of the collective bargaining agreement.[45] Eventually the claim went to arbitration where it was determined that he had been discharged for cause.[46] After this, Garibaldi filed an action for damages in California state court, claiming that his discharge was in violation of state public policy, was a breach of the implied covenant of good faith and fair dealing, and constituted an intentional infliction of emotional distress.[47]

The Ninth Circuit relied on an earlier United States Supreme Court decision, *Alexander v. Gardner-Denver Co.*,[48] to reach the conclusion that Garibaldi was not barred from seeking a court remedy, although he had chosen to arbitrate and had lost. As the *Garibaldi* court reasoned, "the state law may protect interests separate from those protected by the NLRA, provided those interests do not interfere with the collective bargaining process."[49] In the instant case, the court felt that the protection of state public policy would not interfere with the collective bargaining process, in particular:

> A claim grounded in state law for wrongful termination for public policy reasons poses no significant threat to the collective bargaining process; it does not alter the economic relationship between the employer and the employee. The remedy is in *tort*, distinct from any contractual remedy an employee might have under the collective bargaining contract. It furthers the state's interest in protecting the general public—an interest which transcends the employment relationship.[50]

---

[42]726 F.2d 1367 (9th Cir. 1984), *cert. denied*, 105 S. Ct. 2319 (1985).

[43]WILLIAMS & BAGBY, ALLIS-CHALMERS, *supra* note 33, at 24.

[44]*Garibaldi*, 726 F.2d at 1368.

[45]*Id.*

[46]*Id.*

[47]*Id.*

[48]415 U.S. 36 (1974) (employee may pursue a remedy in federal court under Title VII of the Civil Rights Act of 1964 although his grievance had been previously submitted to arbitration).

[49]*Garibaldi*, 726 F.2d at 1375-76 (footnotes omitted).

[50]*Id.* at 1375 (emphasis in original) (footnotes omitted).

It is important to note that the public policy at issue in *Garibaldi* was expressed in a California statute which specifically prohibited the delivery of adulterated milk.[51]

Two California decisions subsequent to *Garibaldi* have limited the scope of that decision. In *Buscemi v. McDonnell Douglas Corp.*,[52] the Ninth Circuit held that an employee's remedies were limited to the grievance and arbitration procedures provided by the collective bargaining agreement and rejected his state damage action since the alleged conduct by the employer did not violate either public policy or a statute. Then, in *Olguin v. Inspiration Consolidated Copper Co.*,[53] the same court rejected an employee's wrongful discharge claim, reasoning that even if the claim was based on state tort law, it was preempted since the collective bargaining agreement in question provided equal or greater protection of job security than state tort law provided for nonunionized employees.

In addition to the *Garibaldi* line of cases, *Midgett v. Sackett-Chicago, Inc.*[54] illustrates another significant decision permitting a state wrongful discharge cause of action to an employee covered by a collective bargaining agreement. The plaintiffs in *Sackett* were union members covered by a collective bargaining agreement which provided a grievance and arbitration procedure for dispute resolution. Plaintiffs, who alleged they had been discharged in retaliation for filing a worker's compensation claim, completely bypassed the contract grievance process and filed a suit directly in state court.[55]

The Illinois Supreme Court recognized the plaintiffs' tort action, stating that "in order to provide a complete remedy it is necessary that the victim of a retaliatory discharge be given an action in tort, independent of any contract remedy the employee may have based on the collective-bargaining agreement."[56] The Court relied heavily on an earlier workers' compensation claim case, *Kelsay v. Motorola, Inc.*,[57] noting that the essential factor present in that case was a judicial recognition of the importance of permitting the allowance of punitive damages against an offending employer. According to the *Sackett* Court's rationale:

---

[51]*Id.* at 1371.

[52]736 F.2d 1348, 1350 (9th Cir. 1984).

[53]*See* 740 F.2d 1468, 1474 (9th Cir. 1984).

[54]105 Ill. 2d 143, 473 N.E.2d 1280 (1984), *cert. denied,* 106 S. Ct. 278 (1985). The Illinois Supreme Court reaffirmed its earlier *Midgett* holding in Gonzalez v. Prestress Engineering Corp., 115 Ill. 2d 1, 503 N.E.2d 308 (Ill. 1986) *pet. for cert. filed* March 14, 1987.

[55]*Midgett,* 105 Ill. 2d at 145-46, 473 N.E.2d at 1281.

[56]*Id.* at 149, 473 N.E.2d at 1283.

[57]74 Ill. 2d 172, 384 N.E.2d 353 (1978).

> [T]here is no reason to afford a tort remedy to at-will employees but to
> limit union members to contractual remedies under their collective
> bargaining agreements . . . . If there is no possibility that an employer
> can be liable in punitive damages, not only has the employee been
> afforded an incomplete remedy, but there is no available sanction
> against a violator of an important public policy of this State. It would
> be unreasonable to immunize from punitive damages an employer who
> unjustly discharges a union employee, while allowing the imposition
> of punitive damages against an employer who unfairly terminates a
> nonunion employee. The public policy against retaliatory discharge
> applies with equal force in both situations.[58]

Not surprisingly, many commentators have criticized decisions
such as *Garibaldi* and *Sackett.*[59] The courts appear in these decisions to be departing from "the traditional legal view of employment
as an essentially contractual relationship."[60] What is most alarming,
these critics note, is that this departure takes place in a setting
where "the parties' mutual understanding of the terms that should
govern the relationship . . . is a written document which presumably
has been carefully negotiated and which contains its own agreed-
upon procedure for resolving questions about its meaning."[61] A 1987
ruling by the U.S. Court of Appeals for the Seventh District emphasized the necessity of exhausting the remedies in a collective bargaining agreement rather than allowing the state courts "through
the guise of worker's compensation laws, to circumvent the arbitration and grievance procedures envisioned by Congress as exclusive."
Allowing jurisdiction to state courts would shift "the burden of
resolving labor disputes to the courts, rather than . . . arbitration,
thus frustrating the policy underlying federal labor laws."[62]

---

[58]*Midgett*, 105 Ill. 2d at 150, 473 N.E.2d at 1283-84.

[59]*See, e.g.,* WILLIAMS & BAGBY, ALLIS-CHALMERS, *supra* note 33, at 29. For other
cases providing a state cause of action for discharged employees covered by a collective bargaining agreement, see *id.* at 28 note 105, *citing* Peabody Galion v. Dollar,
666 F.2d 1309 (10th Cir. 1981); Harper v. General Dynamics Corp., 117 L.R.R.M.
3197 (S.D. Cal. 1984); Messenger v. Volkswagen of America, 585 F. Supp. 565 (D. W.
Va. 1984); Spainhouer v. Western Electric Co., 615 S.W.2d 190 (Tex. 1981); Vaughn v.
Pacific Northwest Bell Tel. Co., 289 Or. 73, 611 P.2d 281 (1980).

[60]WILLIAMS & BAGBY, ALLIS-CHALMERS, *supra* note 33, at 29.

[61]*Id.*

[62]Lingle v. Norge Division of Magic Chef, Inc.; Martin v. Carling National Brew-
eries, Nos. 85-2971 & 86-1763 (Ill. App. 1987).

Employees Covered By Anti-Age Discrimination Legislation

The Age Discrimination in Employment Act of 1967[63] (ADEA) has a compulsory statutory requirement which protects employees and applicants for employment from age discrimination if they are age 40 or older. The Act does not preempt or supercede state or local laws prohibiting age discrimination. Therefore, in a wrongful discharge claim, inquiry must be made to the appropriate state age discrimination statute.

It has generally been held that a "common law tort claim for wrongful discharge based on a plaintiff's age is preempted by state age discrimination statutes."[64] *Mahoney v. Crocker Bank*[65] is illustrative of this line of cases. In that case, a federal district court held that a former bank official's claim for relief "for wrongful discharge on account of age is preempted by the remedies available ... under the California Fair Employment and Housing Act."[66] In reaching this conclusion, the court relied on two factors.[67] First, the right to be protected against age discrimination "did not exist at common law" prior to the enactment of the California statute; and, second, the state legislature "had provided a comprehensive remedial scheme for age discrimination."[68] As the *Mahoney* Court stated, "[w]here a right not existing at common law is created by statute, and a statutory remedy for its violation is provided, the statutory remedy is exclusive and no other remedy may be pursued."[69]

Indeed, subsequent decisions in many jurisdictions have established that a state age discrimination statute provides the *exclusive* remedy for a wrongful discharge action based on age discrimination.[70] It must be noted, however, that in at least one jurisdiction,

---

[63]29 U.S.C. § 621 *et seq.* (1982).

[64]*See* R. Green, *An Ounce of Prevention: Avoiding Litigation By Lawfully Terminating Employees,* at 23 (unpublished paper presented at a meeting of the American Financial Services Association May 13-14, 1986) [hereinafter cited as Green, *Prevention*].

[65]571 F. Supp. 287 (N.D. Cal. 1983).

[66]*Id.* at 294.

[67]*See* Green, *Prevention, supra* note 63, at 23.

[68]*Id.*

[69]*Mahoney,* 571 F. Supp. at 293 (citations omitted).

[70]*See, e.g.,* Hudson v. Moore Business Forms, Inc., 609 F. Supp. 467, 474 (N.D. Cal. 1985); Wilson v. Vlasic Foods, Inc., 116 L.R.R.M. 2419, 2421 (C.D. Cal. 1984); Greene v. Union Mutual Life Ins., 623 F. Supp. 295, 299 (D. Me. 1984); Dykstra v. Crestwood Bank, 119 L.R.R.M. 2058 (Ill. App. Ct. 1983); Strauss v. A.L. Randall Co., 144 Cal. App. 3d 514, 194 Cal. Rptr. 520 (2d Dist. 1983).

Nevada, a court has held that the state age discrimination law does not preempt the bringing of a common law wrongful discharge claim.[71]

Employees Covered By the Employee Retirement Income Security Act

Where an employee has alleged that he was discharged for the purpose of depriving him of benefits arising from an employee benefit plan governed by the Employee Retirement Income Security Act of 1974[72] (ERISA) courts have uniformly held that common law claims for wrongful discharge are preempted.[73] Indeed, "[e]ven where plaintiff fails to mention ERISA in the complaint, courts will recharacterize the complaint as asserting a claim under ERISA and hold the common law cause of action preempted."[74] The clarity of the preemption doctrine in this area of employment law arises from the Act's "express congressional declaration that it supercedes all state (but not federal) law that relates to employee benefit plans, unless the state law regulates insurance, banking, or securities."[75]

In case law, the United States Supreme Court in *Alessi v. Raybestos-Manhattan, Inc.*[76] held that the ERISA preemption provision must be broadly construed. In that case, the Court held that ERISA preempted a New Jersey statute prohibiting a pension plan from offsetting worker's compensation benefits.[77] Prior to the *Alessi*

---

[71]*See* Green, *Prevention, supra* note 63, at 23, *citing* Savage v. Holiday Inn Corp., 118 L.R.R.M. 3301 (D. Nev. 1985).

[72]29 U.S.C. § 1001 *et seq.* (1982).

[73]*See, e.g.*, Metropolitan Life v. Taylor, 55 L.W. 4468 (U.S. 1987); Pilot Life v. Dedeaux, 55 L.W. 4471 (U.S. 1987); Shaw v. Delta Airlines, 103 S. Ct. 2890, 32 FEP Cases 121 (1983); Nolan v. Otis Elevator, 102 N.J. 30, 505 A.2d 580 (1986) (ERISA preempts state suit challenging retirement plan). *See also* Green, *Prevention, supra* note 63, at 25, *citing* Johnson v. Transworld Airlines, Inc., 149 Cal. App. 3d 518, 196 Cal. Rptr. 896 (1983); Provience v. Valley Clerks Trust Fund, 209 Cal. Rptr. 276 (3d Dist. 1984) (plaintiff's tort claims of fraud, bad faith denial of benefits, and intentional infliction of emotional distress held to be preempted by ERISA); Ziskind v. Retail Clerks Int'l Assoc., 3 Empl. Ben. Cas. 1012 (E.D. Cal. 1982) (common law claims of breach of contract, negligent misrepresentation, negligent infliction of emotional distress held to be preempted by ERISA). *See also* Witkowski v. St. Anne's Hospital, 113 Ill. App. 3d 745, 447 N.E.2d 1016 (1983). *But see* Kelly v. Int'l Bus. Mach., 573 F. Supp. 366 (E.D. Pa. 1983) (claim for intentional infliction of emotional distress not preempted by ERISA).

[74]Green, *Prevention, supra* note 63, at 25.

[75]HOLLOWAY & LEECH, EMPLOYMENT TERMINATION, *supra* note 2, at 146, *citing* 29 U.S.C. § 1144 (1975).

[76]451 U.S. 504 (1981).

[77]*Id.* at 526.

ally are protected from unjust dismissal by "just cause" provisions in their union contracts.[55] According to estimates made by the U.S. Bureau of Labor Statistics, 96 percent of all collective bargaining agreements in the United States contain some form of job security provisions; 80 percent allow dismissal only for "just cause"; and grievance and arbitration procedures are included in 99 percent of all collective bargaining agreements.[56]

Because of these historical exceptions, workers in the private sector who are not protected against unjust dismissal by either collective bargaining agreements or statutory provisions form the bulk of employees potentially classified by the courts as working under contracts terminable at will. Professor Theodore St. Antoine of the University of Michigan Law School estimates that at present between 70 and 75 million workers are unprotected by any "just cause" requirements or statutory provisions.[57] Based on figures released by the Federal Mediation and Conciliation Service, one scholar calculates that between 6,500 and 7,500 employees under contracts terminable at will are discharged each year for reasons that most arbitrators would find unjustifiable.[58]

More often now than ever before, these discharged at-will employees are taking their claims to court. Figure I-1 illustrates that the number of employment-at-will cases reported annually at the appellate level has surged over the last few years. The momentum for this flood of litigation has come from the decisions of state and federal courts applying state law, which, within the last fifteen years, have begun eroding the traditional employment-at-will doctrine. As of June, 1987, forty-two states recognize an exception to the common law doctrine either based upon the employer's alleged violation of public policy or breach of an implied contract and permit employees to sue their former employers for wrongful discharge. Only Alabama, Iowa, Louisiana, Mississippi, North Dakota, Rhode Island, and Utah do not. (See Appendix A).

---

[55]Comment, *Job Security for the At-Will Employee: Contractual Right of Discharge for Cause*, 57 Chi-Kent L. Rev. 697, 707 (1981). A 1979 survey revealed that 79 percent of collective bargaining agreements prohibit discharge without cause. *Id.*, at 707 note 57. However, less than one-third of the workforce is covered by collective bargaining agreements. Comment, *Protecting At-Will Employees, supra* note 3, at 1816 note 2. *See generally* Peck, *Unjust Discharge From Employment: A Necessary Change in the Law*, 40 Ohio St. L. J. 1, 8-10 (1974) [hereinafter cited as Peck, *Unjust Discharge From Employment*].

[56]U.S. Bureau of Labor Statistics, Directory of National Unions and Employee Associations (1979), at 59, 74.

[57]Bureau of National Affairs (BNA), *The Employment-At-Will Issue: A BNA Special Report*, Daily Lab. Rep., No.225 (November 19, 1982), at 7.

[58]Peck, *Unjust Discharge From Employment, supra* note 55, at 8-9.

Figure I-1
*Number of Reported Employment-at-Will Cases
at the Appellate Level*

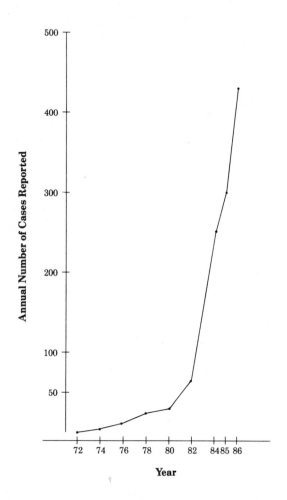

Sources: Data provided by the research special projects division of the Bureau of National Affairs, Inc., Washington, D.C. and the American Bar Association, Committee on Employee Rights and Responsibilities, Judicial Subcommittee (1986).

In many ways the graph understates the size of the wrongful discharge litigation explosion, since it only shows the cases reported at the appellate level. Approximately 75 percent of wrongful discharge claims filed never get to trial, and of those that do, a still smaller number proceed to the appellate level.

Judicial erosion of the common law employment-at-will rule, which will be discussed in the following sections, rests primarily on application of either "contract" or "tort" theories to circumvent application of the at-will rule. State jurisdictions have employed these two legal doctrines in various ways and to differing degrees to permit exceptions to the employment-at-will doctrine. Exceptions to the at-will rule are recognized in a number of jurisdictions. Of course, some state courts have gone farther than others in their recognition of either tort- or contract-based exceptions to the employment-at-will doctrine. For the purpose of gaining an overall view of the courts' activities in this area of employment law, the state jurisdictions may be divided into the following four basic categories, according to the number and breadth of exceptions recognized: significant modification, moderate modification, limited modification, and insignificant modification. States representative of each of these four groups include, respectively, California, Michigan, Pennsylvania, and New York. The development and current status of employment-at-will in each of these representative states will be discussed in detail in chapters IV through VII. In addition, a brief survey noting the current status of the at-will doctrine and the cases on which any exceptions have been recognized for the remaining state jurisdictions is included in Appendix A.

On the international level, the United States is the only major industrial nation in the world which adheres to the employment-at-will doctrine.[59] Although a complete discussion of other countries' treatment of employment termination is beyond the scope of this study, it should be noted that Canada,[60] France,[61] Germany,[62] Great

---

[59]Matthews, *A Common Law Action for the Abusively Discharged Employee*, 26 HASTINGS L. J. 1435, 1447 note 54 (1975); Summers, *Individual Protection Against Unjust Dismissal, supra* note 1, at 508.

[60]CANADA LABOUR CODE § 61.5.

[61]*See* W. MCPHERSON & F. MEYERS, THE FRENCH LABOR COURTS: JUDGMENT BY PEERS ch. 3 (1966); BLANC-JOUVAN, THE SETTLEMENT OF LABOR DISPUTES IN FRANCE IN LABOR COURTS AND GRIEVANCE SETTLEMENTS IN WESTERN EUROPE 16-36 (B. Aaron ed. 1971)(cited in Summers, *Individual Protection Against Unjust Dismissal, supra* note 1, at 510 note 137).

[62]*See* Law of August 10, 1951, An Act to Provide Protection Against Unwarranted Dismissals, [1951] BGBI I 499, translated in 1951, I.L.O. LEGISLATIVE SERIES 1951 Ger. F. R. 4 (cited in Summers, *Individual Protection Against Unjust Dismissal, supra* note 1, at 511 note 141).

Britain,[63] Italy,[64] Japan, and Sweden,[65] have enacted legislation
which requires that employers have "good cause" before terminating an employment relationship.[66]

[63]*See* Industrial Relations Act 1971 §§ 22-33, 41 HAL. STAT. 2062 (1971)(cited in
Summers, *Individual Protection Against Unjust Dismissal, supra* note 1, at 513 note
155).
 [64]Workers' Charter, STATUTO DE LAVORATORI, Law 300 of May 30, 1970.
 [65]*See* LAGEN OM ANSTALLNINGSSKYDD, SVENSK FORFATTNINGSSAMLING 1974:12
[translated as Act Concerning Employment Security in Sweden, Document No. 1525
(1974)] (cited in Summers, *Individual Protection Against Unjust Dismissal, supra*
note 1, at 517 note 180),
 [66]For a detailed discussion of the "good" or "just cause" legislation present in foreign jurisdictions, see Summers, *Individual Protection Against Unjust Dismissal,*
supra note 1, at 508-19. *See also id.* at 508 note 130, *citing* II ACTS OF FIFTH INTERNA-
TIONAL CONGRESS OF LABOUR LAW AND SOCIAL SECURITY 1963, REGULATION OF DIS-
PUTES CONCERNING EMPLOYER'S EXERCISE OF DISCIPLINARY POWERS; I.L.O., DIS-
MISSAL PROCEDURES IN NINE COUNTRIES (1959); I.L.O. INTERNATIONAL LABOR
CONFERENCE, 46th Sess., Report VII (1), (2) on *Termination of Employment* (1961-62);
Dismissal Procedures: A Comparative Study, 81 INT'L LAB. REV. 403 (1960).

CHAPTER II

Legal Doctrines

In an attempt to provide employees with some form of protection against certain types of discharge, a clear trend has developed in various legislatures,[1] the scholarly press,[2] and particularly the

---

[1]South Dakota, for instance, has abrogated the employment-at-will doctrine by statute which provides, in relevant part, that "the length of time which an employer and employee adopt for the estimation of wages is relevant to a determination of the term of employment." S. D. C. L. ANN. § 60-1-3 (1978 & Supp. 1987). In addition, Puerto Rico has passed a statute requiring just cause for termination even where the period of employment is not specified. See P. R. LAWS ANN. tit. 29, § 185a-b (1985 & Supp. 1986). Colorado, Connecticut, New Jersey, Wisconsin and Pennsylvania have considered but have not passed just cause legislation. See, e.g., Pa. H.B. 1020, 169th Pa. Gen. Assem. (1985 Sess.).

[2]Much has been written on the topic of employment-at-will. For a recent bibliography on at-will literature, see Employment-At-Will: Bibliography, J & E. Cook, eds. (1985).

Among the many commentators, see, e.g., C. BAKALAY, JR. & J. FEERICK, DEVELOPING RIGHTS OF EMPLOYEES IN THE WORKPLACE (1981); C. BAKALAY, JR. & J. GROSSMAN, MODERN LAW OF EMPLOYMENT CONTRACTS: FORMATION, OPERATION AND REMEDIES FOR BREACH (1983); J. BARBASH, J. FEERICK & J. KAUFF, UNJUST DISMISSAL AND AT WILL EMPLOYMENT (1982); R. BERENBEIM, NONUNION COMPLAINT SYSTEMS (1980); R. COULSON, THE TERMINATION HANDBOOK (1981); THE EMPLOYMENT AT WILL ISSUE, M. DICHTER & A. GROSS, eds. (1981); F. FOULKES, PERSONNEL POLICIES IN LARGE NON-UNION COMPANIES (1980); A. WESTIN, WHISTLEBLOWING, LOYALTY AND DISSENT (1980).

For law review articles, see, e.g., Bakalay, Erosion of the Employment-at-Will Doctrine, 7 J. CONTEMP. L. 63 (1982); Bellace, Individual Rights in the Workplace, 16 U. MICH. J. L. REF. 199 (1983); Berger, Defining Public Policy Torts in At-Will Dismissals, 34 STAN. L. REV. 153 (1981); Blades, Employment-At-Will vs. Individual Freedom: On Limiting the Abusive Exercise of Employer Power, 67 COLUM. L. REV. 1404 (1967) [hereinafter cited as Blades, Employment-At-Will vs. Individual Freedom]; Brake, Limiting the Right to Terminate at Will—Have the Courts Forgotten the Employer?, 35 VAND. L. REV. 201 (1982); Catler, The Case Against Proposals to Eliminate the Employment-At-Will Rule, 5 I. REL. L. J. 471 (1983); Comment, Protecting At Will Employees Against Wrongful Discharge: The Duty to Terminate Only in Good Faith, 93 HARV. L. REV. 1816 (1980); Comment, Protecting Employees at Will Against Wrongful Discharge: The Public Policy Exception, 96 HARV. L. REV. 1931 (1983); Estreicher, At-Will-Employment and the Problem of Unjust Dismissal: The Appropriate Judicial Response, 54 N. Y. ST. B. J. 146 (1982); Feinman, Development of the Employment-At-Will Rule, 20 AM. J. LEG. HIST. 118 (1976); Green, An Ounce of Prevention: Avoiding Litigation by Lawfully Terminating Employees (unpublished manuscript presented at meeting of the American Financial Services Association, May 13-14, 1986) [hereinafter cited as Green, Prevention]; Harrison, The "New" Terminable-at-Will Employment Contract: An Interest and Cost Incidence Analysis, 64 IOWA L. REV. 327 (1984); Hoffman, Written Contracts for Employment-At-Will

courts[3] which has resulted in the doctrine of employment-at-will being riddled with exceptions and exemptions depending on the jurisdiction and the focus of each individual case. A recent survey, in fact, notes that more than two-thirds of American jurisdictions have abandoned an absolute employment-at-will rule.[4] This chapter is designed to provide an overview of these general exceptions and the legal doctrines which support them, so that the later discussion regarding the status of the employment-at-will doctrine in each representative jurisdiction can be viewed in context. Exceptions to the at-will rule fall into two broad categories: those created by legislative act; and those created judicially, largely by the state courts. Judicially created exceptions to the rule are rooted in basic principles of contract and tort law.

LEGISLATIVELY CREATED EXCEPTIONS

Throughout the years, federal and state legislatures have created exceptions to the employment-at-will doctrine that protect workers who would otherwise be classified as at-will employees based upon certain common characteristics or collective activities. For example, the National Labor Relations Act (NLRA) of 1935 prohibits discharges in retaliation for union organizing activity[5] and layoff or terminations resulting from certain closings, relocations, or other actions that have not been accompanied by "decision-" or "effects-bargaining".[6] Additionally, Title VII of the Civil Rights Act of 1964[7]

Employees—Measures to Prevent and Defend Wrongful Discharge Lawsuits (unpublished manuscript presented at the 1983 Mid-Winter Meeting of the ABA Committee on the Development of the Law of Individual Rights and Responsibilities in the Workplace); Lewis, *Employment Protection: A Preliminary Assessment of the Law of Unfair Dismissal,* 12 I. REL. L. J. 19 (1981); May, *The Covenant of Good Faith and Fair Dealing: A Common Ground for the Torts of Wrongful Discharge from Employment,* 21 SANTA CLARA L. REV. 1111 (1981); Summers, *Individual Protection Against Unjust Dismissal: Time for a Statute,* 62 VA. L. REV. 481 (1976) [hereinafter cited as Summers, *Individual Protection Against Unjust Dismissal*].

[3]Several services exist which report only employment-at-will cases, *see, e.g.,* EMPLOYMENT-AT-WILL: A 1986 STATE-BY-STATE SURVEY, D. CATHCART & M. DICHTER, eds. (National Employment Law Institute 1987); K. McCULLOCH, TERMINATION OF EMPLOYMENT (1986) [hereinafter cited as McCULLOCH, TERMINATION]. *See also The Employment-At-Will Issue: A BNA Special Report,* DAILY LAB. REP. No. 225 (November 19, 1982) [hereinafter cited as *BNA Special Report*]; *Modern Status of the Rule that Employer May Discharge for Any Reason,* Annot., 12 A.L.R.4th 544 (1982).

[4]Bureau of National Affairs, *Employment-At-Will Information Package* (1986); *See also* Perritt, *Employee Dismissal Law and Practice,* § 1.11 (Supp. 1985).

[5]29 U.S.C. §§ 157, 158(a)(3) (1982).

[6]*See* NLRB v. First National Maintenance Corporation, 452 U.S. 666 (1981).

[7]42 U.S.C. § 2000e-2(a)(1) (1982).

and the Federal Age Discrimination in Employment Act[8] (among other federal employment discrimination statutes[9]) forbid employee terminations which discriminate on the basis of race, color, religion, sex, national origin, age, handicap, or other "protected" characteristics. There are also several specific provisions against retaliatory dismissals based on any individual's invocation of rights guaranteed under these statutes.[10]

---

[8]29 U.S.C. § 623(a)(1) (1982).

[9]*See* Mauk, *A History and Analysis of the Employment-At-Will Doctrine*, 21 Idaho L. Rev. 201, 226 note 109 (1985) [hereinafter cited as *Mauk, A History and Analysis*], listing the following statutes enacted at the federal level: National Labor Relations Act §§ 8(a)(1),(3),(4) (1935), 29 U.S.C. §§ 158(a)(1),(3),(4) (1982)(prohibits discharge for union activity, protected concerted activity, or filing charges or giving testimony under the Act); Fair Labor Standards Act §§ 15, 16 (1938), 29 U.S.C. §§ 215(a)(3), 216(b) (1982)(prohibits discharge for exercising rights guaranteed by minimum wage and overtime provisions of the Act); Occupational Safety and Health Act of 1970 § 11, 29 U.S.C. § 660(c) (1982)(prohibits discharge of employees in reprisal for exercising rights under the Act); Civil Rights Act of 1964, Title VII, § 703, 42 U.S.C. §§ 2000(e)-2, 2000(e)-3(a) (1982)(prohibits discharge based on race, color, religion, sex or national origin and reprisal for exercising Title VII rights); Age Discrimination in Employment Act of 1967, §§ 4, 12, 14, 29 U.S.C. §§ 623, 631, 633(a) (1982)(prohibits age-based discharge by private employers and federal government of persons between ages of 40 and 70 and reprisals for exercising statutory rights); Rehabilitation Act of 1973, §§ 503, 504, 29 U.S.C. §§ 793, 794 (1982)(prohibits federal contractors or any program or activity receiving federal assistance from discriminating against handicapped persons); Employment Retirement Income Security Act of 1974, §§ 510, 511, 29 U.S.C. §§ 1140, 1141 (1982)(prohibits discharge of employees in order to prevent them from attaining vested pension rights); Vietnam Era Veterans Readjustment Assistance Act, § 404(a) (1974), 38 U.S.C. §§ 2021(b)(1), 2024(c) (1982)(provides protection, for a limited period, against discharge without just cause of returning service people); Energy Reorganization Act of 1974, § 210, 42 U.S.C. § 5851 (1982)(prohibits discharge of employees who assist, participate, or testify, in any proceeding to carry out the purposes of the Act or the Atomic Energy Act of 1954); Clean Air Act, § 322 (1955), 42 U.S.C. § 7622 (1982)(prohibits discharge of employees who commenced, caused to commence, or testified at proceedings against employer for violation of the Act); Federal Water Pollution Control Act, § 507 (1948), 33 U.S.C. § 1367 (1982)(prohibits discharge of employees who institute or testify at a proceeding against employer for violation of the Act); Railroad Safety Act, § 212 (1980), 45 U.S.C. § 441(a), (b)(1) (1982)(prohibits railroad company from discharge of employees who filed complaints, instituted, or caused to be instituted, any proceeding under or related to enforcement of federal railroad safety laws, or testified, or who refuse to work under conditions they reasonably believe to be dangerous); Consumer Credit Protection Act, § 304 (1968), 15 U.S.C. § 1674(a) (1982)(prohibits discharge of employees because of garnishment of wages for any one indebtedness); Civil Service Reform Act of 1978, § 204(a), 5 U.S.C., § 7513(a) (1982)(permits removal of federal civil service employees "only for such cause as will promote the efficiency of the service"); Judiciary and Judicial Procedure Act, § 6(a)(1), 28 U.S.C. § 1875 (1982)(prohibits discharge of employees for service on grand or petit jury).

[10]Specific protections against retaliatory discharges include: Consumer Credit Protection Act, § 304(a), 15 U.S.C. § 1674(a)(1982); Fair Labor Standards Act, § 15(a)(3), 29 U.S.C. § 215(a)(3)(1982); Age Discrimination in Employment Act of 1967, § 4(a), 29 U.S.C. § 623(a)(1982); Occupational Safety and Health Act, § II(c), 29 U.S.C. § 660(c)(1982); Vietnam Era Veterans Readjustment Act, 38 U.S.C., § 2021(1982).

State legislatures have created additional protection for various at-will employees.[11] Several states, for instance, have statutes prohibiting discharges based upon political activity or affiliation.[12] Other states, such as Michigan, have enacted "Whistleblower Protection Acts" designed to prohibit the discharge of employees who report a violation of the law.[13] Another common provision found in state laws is a general prohibition against retaliatory discharge for filing a workers' compensation claim.[14]

At present there is legislation pending in many states to forbid dismissal without cause for all employees. Such legislation is patterned after existing arbitration procedures found in collective bargaining agreements. The proposed laws are intended to extend statutory protection from unfair dismissal to nonunion employees or to "give discharged employees recourse to an impartial panel for remedial actions."[15]

JUDICIALLY CREATED EXCEPTIONS

The second general area of exceptions to the traditional employment-at-will doctrine has been created through various judicial interpretations of common law tort and contract theories, largely at the state level. In applying these legal theories, however, the courts and commentators have often been ambiguous in distinguishing whether an action lies in contract or in tort. "Commentators and courts frequently use the terms 'wrongful discharge,' 'abusive discharge,' and 'discharge against public policies' interchangeably and often to describe the same legal theory."[16] This ambiguity is aggravated by "a tendency to combine tort and contract theories and the inclination to plead causes of action in general rather than specific terms."[17]

---

[11]*See* Mauk, *A History and Analysis, supra* note 9, at 227 note 110, *citing,* N.Y. Exec. Law §§ 296(1)(a), (e) (McKinney 1980)(civil rights); CAL. LAB. CODE, §§ 1420(a), (e) (West 1971 & Supp. 1975)(civil rights); CAL. LAB. CODE § 6310 (West Supp. 1980)(health and safety); N.Y. Lab. Law § 736 (McKinney Supp. 1981)(polygraphs); CAL. LAB. CODE § 432.2 (West 1971)(political activity); N.Y. JUD. LAW § 532 (McKinney 1968)(jury duty); CAL. LAB. CODE § 230 (West 1971)(jury duty).

[12]*See, e.g.,* MASS. GEN. LAWS ANN. ch. 56 § 33 (1978); CAL. LAB. CODE § 1102 (West 1971).

[13]*See, e.g.,* MICH. COMP. LAWS ANN. §§ 15.361-15.369 (West 1981 & Supp. 1987).

[14]*See, e.g.,* ILL. REV. STAT. ch. 48 § 138.4(h)(Supp. 1982); MO. ANN. STAT. § 287.780 (Vernon Supp. 1982); TEX. REV. CIV. STAT. ANN. art. 8307(c) (Vernon Supp. 1982).

[15]*BNA Special Report, supra* note 3, at 11. *See also* Note, *"Just Cause" Termination Rights for At-Will Employees,* 1982 DET. C. L. REV. 591, 615.

[16]Mauk, *A History and Analysis, supra* note 9, at 207.

[17]*Id.*

Distinguishing between tort and contract theories is important for several reasons. Determination as to whether a wrongful discharge action rests on a tort theory or a contract theory, or both, "orients the parties to the elements of proof" necessary to the suit's success and "permits anticipation of potential defenses."[18] More importantly, classification as either a tort or contract claim greatly affects the availability of particular remedies.

Contract and tort remedies differ in both their scope and purpose. Contract remedies, as one court recently summarized, are awarded:

> to fully recompense the non-breaching party for its losses sustained because of the breach, not to punish the breaching party... In the context of a contract for personal services, this rule entitles the wrongfully discharged employee or agent to recover the contract price diminished by the expenses saved and by the amount he received or could have earned from other suitable employment available because of his discharge.[19]

In contrast, tort remedies provide a much larger and frequently more lucrative array of potential damages, including general damages for pain and suffering, and, where appropriate, punitive damages.

It is also important to note the theoretical disparity which exists between tort and contract doctrines. "The distinction to be made," one observer notes, "focuses on the duty which has allegedly been breached and asks whether that duty arises from a promise set forth in the contract or is one imposed by law."[20] The Kansas Supreme Court similarly observed that "[a] breach of contract may be said to be a material failure of performance of a duty arising under or imposed by *agreement;*" a tort, on the other hand, is "a violation of a duty imposed by *law,* a wrong independent of contract."[21]

Contract Theory

One of the essential requirements of a binding contract is mutuality of obligation. This requirement "is best understood as the requirement of a *quid pro quo* for the creation of legally enforceable obligations."[22] As Professor Corbin explains, "mutuality of obligation ... express[es] the idea that each party is under a legal duty to

---

[18]*Id.* at 208.

[19]*Id., quoting,* Anderson v. Gailey, 100 Idaho 796, 801, 606 P.2d 90, 95 (1980).

[20]Mauk, *A History and Analysis, supra* note 9, at 209.

[21]*Id., quoting,* Malone v. University of Kansas Medical Center, 220 Kan. 371, 374, 552 P.2d 885, 888 (1976)(emphasis added).

[22]Langdon v. Saga Corp., 569 P.2d 524, 527 (Okla. App. 1977)(cited in Mauk, *A History and Analysis, supra* note 9, at 211).

the other; each has made a promise, and each is an obligor."[23] As some legal scholars are quick to point out, however, the concept of mutuality of obligation is a principle of bilateral contract law, that is, a principle arising out of an exchange of promises,[24] such as "I promise to paint your garage, if you promise to pay me $100." Employment contracts, particularly at-will ones, are generally unilateral. The difference, they argue, lies in the fact that "a unilateral contract is characterized by an offer which extends a promise followed by performance," rather than a simple exchange of promises.[25] Unilateral contracts by their very nature do not entail an exchange of promises. They are generally characterized as an exchange of performance by one party for a promise by another, such as, "if you paint my garage, I will pay you $100."

Not surprisingly, a defense frequently used by employers faced with wrongful discharge actions based on contract theory is to claim that the contract is invalid and non-binding on the grounds that there is no mutuality of obligation. (This and other possible employer defenses are discussed in more detail in chapter III). Although this defense was successful at one time in some jurisdictions,[26] most state and federal courts now generally follow the view that "the requirement for mutuality of obligation [is] ... simply the requirement that there be consideration."[27] Consideration is a legal requirement that in order for there to be a binding contract there must be either "detriment to the promisee or benefit to the promisor."[28] In other words, "[c]onsideration is a promise which is bargained for and culminates in an agreement."[29] Applied to the context of the unilat-

---

[23]1A A. CORBIN, CORBIN ON CONTRACTS, § 152 (1963)(cited in *Langdon,* 569 P.2d at 527).

[24]*See* Mauk, *A History and Analysis, supra* note 9, at 211.

[25]*Id.* at 212. Professor Corbin explains the difference between a unilateral and bilateral contract as follows:

> The differences between a unilateral and a bilateral contract ... lie both in the operative acts of the parties and also in the legal relations created thereby...
> In the case of a unilateral contract, there is only one promisor; and the legal result is that he is the only party who is under an enforceable legal duty. The other party to this contract is the one to whom the promise is made, and he is the only one in whom the contract creates an enforceable legal right. In a bilateral contract both parties are promisors and both parties are promisees; and the legal effect of such a contract is that there are mutual rights and mutual duties.

1 A. CORBIN, CORBIN ON CONTRACTS § 21, at 52 (1950)(citations omitted).

[26]*See, e.g.,* Simmons v. Westinghouse Electric Corp., 311 So. 2d 28, 31 (La. App. 1975); Pitcher v. United Oil and Gas Syndicate, 174 La. 66, 139 So. 2d 760 (1972).

[27]*Langdon,* 569 P.2d at 526-27 (cited in Mauk, *A History and Analysis, supra* note 9, at 213).

[28]1 S. WILLISTON, WILLISTON ON CONTRACTS § 103 (3d ed. 1967).

[29]*Id.* & note 7 (citations omitted).

decision, a majority of the circuit courts had accepted an expansive view of the ERISA preemption based on the broad language of the statute and the clear legislative history favoring preemption.[78]

One of the leading cases addressing the specific issue of ERISA's preemption of common law wrongful discharge claims is *Gordon v. Matthew Bender & Co.*[79] In that case, a federal district court in Illinois held "that a state law claim that an employer acted in bad faith in discharging an employee ten months before he fulfilled the eight-year vesting requirement of a pension plan was preempted" by ERISA.[80] Many other courts at both the state and federal levels have followed the *Gordon* decision, using ERISA to preempt state wrongful discharge claims.[81]

Employees Covered By Sex or Religious Discrimination Statutes

As one authority notes, "[i]f the reason for a tort or contract claim is premised upon some form of age, sexual, racial, or religious bias ... then limitation of the common law remedy may result from state human rights/fair employment practices acts or Title VII [of the Civil Rights Act of 1964 (Title VII)]."[82] The Third Circuit Court of Appeals, for instance, in *Wolk v. Saks Fifth Avenue*,[83] held that a plaintiff's ability to bring a common law wrongful discharge action as a result of sexual harassment was curtailed by the availability of full relief under the Pennsylvania Human Relations Act and Title VII and by various administrative requirements and jurisdictional prerequisites of these statutes. Thus, these two statutes operated to preempt the plaintiff's public policy tort action under state law.

It must be noted, however, that not all jurisdictions agree on this area of the preemption doctrine. For example, in Oregon it has been held that a state statute prohibiting sex discrimination does not bar an independent wrongful discharge claim based on sexual harassment.[84]

---

[78]*See, e.g.,* Bucyrus-Erie Co. v. Dept. of Industry and Labor, 599 F.2d 205 (7th Cir. 1979), *cert. denied,* 444 U.S. 1031 (1980).

[79]562 F. Supp. 1286 (N.D. Ill. 1983).

[80]HOLLOWAY & LEECH, EMPLOYMENT TERMINATION, *supra* note 2, at 147.

[81]*See, e.g.,* Authier v. Ginsberg, 757 F.2d 796, 801 (6th Cir. 1984) and cases cited *supra* note 72.

[82]HOLLOWAY & LEECH, EMPLOYMENT TERMINATION, *supra* note 2, at 150 & note 102, *citing* Shaffer v. Nat'l Can Corp., 565 F. Supp. 909 (E.D. Pa. 1983); Strauss v. A.L. Randall Co., 144 Cal. App. 3d 514, 194 Cal. Rptr. 520 (1983).

[83]728 F.2d 221, 222-24 (3d Cir. 1984).

[84]*See* Green, *Prevention, supra* note 63, at 23, *citing* Holien v. Sears, Roebuck & Co., 117 L.R.R.M. 2853 (Ore. 1984).

Employees Covered By Workers' Compensation Statutes

It is frequently the case that an employee filing a wrongful discharge claim will seek punitive damages by alleging an intentional tort for the infliction of emotional distress arising from the discharge. These claims, however, clash with many state workers' compensation statutes. Crucial to the workers' compensation scheme is the "employee's statutory surrender of the right to sue the employer for industrial injury."[85] Thus, "state statutes creating the right to compensation contain strict 'exclusivity' provisions that bar court suits for any bodily injury arising out of, and in the course of, employment."[86] A claim for the intentional infliction of emotional distress[87] presents special problems in light of these exclusivity provisions, since such a claim is often accompanied by some sort of physical injury.[88] In California, where the law of wrongful discharge has received great attention by the judiciary, the California Supreme Court has held that the state's worker's compensation statute provides the exclusive remedy for claims of intentional infliction of emotional distress.[89] In other instances, however, the specific nature of the employer's actions have led courts to conclude that the exclusivity provisions do not bar common law actions against the employer.

For example, in *Maggio v. St. Francis Medical Center, Inc.*,[90] the plaintiff brought an action based on his discharge for reporting his supervisor's alleged illegal activities to senior managers in the hospital's administration. In *Maggio,* the defendant and certain of its officers intentionally engaged in a pattern of outrageous, harassing conduct directed at the employee which caused him to have two nervous breakdowns.[91] "The court found that the exclusivity statute did not apply" in the instant case "because the action by its nature met the intentional tort exception."[92] That exception, as developed by case law, "requires an intentional tort plus specific intent to

---

[85]Holloway & Leech, Employment Termination, *supra* note 2, at 147.

[86]*Id.*

[87]In order to maintain a cause of action for intentional infliction of emotional distress, there must be extreme and outrageous behavior intended to cause severe emotional distress or indicate reckless indifference to that risk. *See* Restatement (Second) of Torts § 46.

[88]*See* Holloway & Leech, Employment Termination, *supra* note 2, at 149.

[89]*See* Cole v. Fair Oaks Fire Protection District, 1 IER Cases 1644 (Ca. S. Ct. Jan. 2, 1987). *See also* Green, *Prevention, supra* note 63, at 25, *citing* Hollywood Refrigeration Sales Co. v. Superior Ct., 210 Cal. Rptr. 619 (2d Dist. 1985); Gates v. Transvideo Corp., 93 Cal. App. 3d 196, 155 Cal. Rptr. 486 (2d Dist. 1979).

[90]391 So.2d 948 (La. App. 1980).

[91]*Id.* at 949.

[92]Holloway & Leech, Employment Termination, *supra* note 2, at 149.

inflict injury" and has been held to be "necessary to prevent the exclusivity provision from becoming a license to attack employees."[93] In short, then, the exclusivity provision of a state's workers' compensation statute has been held not to preempt common law wrongful discharge actions where the physical injury was intentional.[94]

CONCLUSION

The employer faced with a wrongful discharge claim has procedural defenses available through either application of the statute of frauds or some strain of the preemption doctrine. Of course, depending on the particular facts of the case, other legal defenses may also be available. As discussed, the statute of frauds defense will most likely provide little protection, since most jurisdictions rarely apply the statute to employment contracts and, even where the courts do, it is relatively easy for a plaintiff to sidestep the statute's narrow bar. The preemption doctrine, which may apply to a myriad of employment situations, can provide protection to employers by limiting the expansion of discharge remedies available to a plaintiff through state common law.

Having established the framework of legal doctrines which surround the at-will employment controversy, both those which have been used by the judiciary to create the wrongful discharge cause of action and those which employers may utilize when confronted with these claims, this study will next examine how these theories have been developed in a number of specific jurisdictions. As mentioned in chapter I, the series of state case studies which follows in chapters IV through VII should provide the reader with an overview of the great disparity which characterizes the judiciary's development of the at-will issue, ranging from states which have almost completely abrogated the traditional employment-at-will doctrine, to those jurisdictions which have left the rule basically intact.

---

[93]*Id.* & note 98, *citing* Raden v. Azusa, 47 Cal. App. 3d 336, 158 Cal. Rptr. 689 (1979).

[94]*See* HOLLOWAY & LEECH, EMPLOYMENT TERMINATION, *supra* note 2, at 149 note 101, *citing* McGee v. McNally, 119 Cal. App. 3d 891, 174 Cal. Rptr. 253 (1981); Renteria v. County of Orange, 182 Cal. App. 3d 833, 147 Cal. Rptr. 447 (1978); Ritter v. Allied Chem. Corp., 295 F. Supp. 1360 (D.S.C. 1968).

CHAPTER IV

California

It is ironic that California, a state that has been most progressive in eroding the employment-at-will doctrine, is among those states which have statutorily codified the traditional at-will rule. Section 2922 of the California Labor Code provides, in relevant part, that: "An employment, having no specified term, may be terminated at the will of either party on notice to the other."[1] Indeed, several cases have been decided in adherence to this statutory policy.[2] But the majority of wrongful discharge cases brought in California have limited application of the statute in a number of ways, creating broad exceptions to the general at-will rule. As one California appellate court explained: "Three distinct theories [of wrongful discharge] have been developed [in California]: (1) a tort cause of action for wrongful discharge in violation of public policy; (2) a cause of action for employer's breach of the implied covenant of good faith and fair dealing, which sounds both in tort and contract; and, (3) a cause of action for employer's breach of an implied-in-fact covenant to terminate only for good cause."[3]

The development of the employment-at-will doctrine in California has been marked by confusing and contradictory rulings from lower state courts since the California Supreme Court issued its last major employment-at-will decision in 1980. Presently there is a case before the California Supreme Court which many practitioners hope will provide clarification of wrongful discharge law in California.[4] "The case before the court, *Foley v. Interactive Data Corp.*, presents several employment at will questions," including whether a "cause of action exist[s] for violation of a substantive public policy that is not

[1]Cal. Lab. Code § 2922 (West 1971).

[2]*See* K. McCulloch, Termination of Employment (1986) at ¶ 20,051 & note 2, *citing* Swaffield v. Universal Ecsco Corp., 271 Cal. App. 2d 147, 76 Cal. Rptr. 680 (1969); Marin v. Jacuzzi, 24 Cal. App. 2d 549, 36 Cal. Rptr. 880 (1964); Mallard v. Boring, 182 Cal. App. 2d 390, 6 Cal. Rptr. 171 (1960) [hereinafter cited as McCulloch, Termination].

[3]*See* Shapiro v. Wells Fargo Realty Advisors, 152 Cal. App. 3d 467, 475-76, 199 Cal. Rptr. 613, 617 (2d Dist. 1984) (citations omitted).

[4]*See* Foley v. Interactive Data Corporation, 179 Cal. App. 3d 282, 219 Cal. Rptr. 866 (1985), *review granted*, 222 Cal. Rptr. 740 (Jan. 30, 1986).

grounded in statute" and whether "a plaintiff [must] show a certain length of employment to allege a breach of the covenant of good faith and fair dealing."[5] As the *Daily Labor Report* notes, "[t]his is the second time that *Foley* has been argued before the court."[6] "Reargument was ordered after three justices who heard the case in June, 1986, lost reconfirmation elections in November."[7] Although most attorneys are not sure how the change in the bench will affect the case's final outcome, most commentators agree that the *Foley* decision should provide some long-awaited guidance on the issues that have arisen since *Tameny v. Atlantic Richfield Co.*,[8] in 1980.[9]

LEGISLATIVE ACTIVITY

During the 1985 legislative session, the California legislature enacted a whistleblower protection statute.[10] This statute provides that: "No employer shall retaliate against any employee for disclosing information to a government or law enforcement agency, where the employee has reasonable cause to believe that the information discloses a violation of state or federal statute . . . or regulation.[11] In particular, section 1102.5 prohibits the retaliatory discharge of any employee for disclosure.[12]

The veritable flood of wrongful discharge litigation in California led to the introduction of several bills addressing the wrongful discharge issue in both houses of the state legislature during the 1986 session. The state senate proposal, SB 2317, required "that an employee must prove that the discharge was for the purpose of denying the employee benefits of an express or implied agreement."[13] An employer would not violate the proposed law if the termination decision was based on a good faith belief by the employer that the discharge was related to the lawful interests of the business.[14] A noteworthy provision of the Senate proposal was its express exclusion of tort relief, such as punitive damages, for violations of the law.[15] Fur-

---

[5] 72 DAILY LAB. REP. at A-3 (April 16, 1987).
[6] *Id.* at A-4.
[7] *Id.*
[8] 27 Cal.3d 167, 164 Cal. Rptr. 839 (1980).
[9] 72 DAILY LAB. REP. at A-4 (April 16, 1987).
[10] *See* CAL. LAB. CODE § 1102.5 (West 1982).
[11] *Id.* at § 1102.5 (b).
[12] *See id.*
[13] Green, *An Ounce of Prevention: Avoiding Liability by Lawfully Terminating Employees*, at 16 (unpublished paper presented at the American Financial Services Association, May 13-14, 1986) [hereinafter cited as Green, *Prevention*].
[14] *Id.*
[15] *Id.*

thermore, in an effort to deter frivolous lawsuits, SB 2317 entitled the prevailing party to attorneys' fees.[16] Finally, the bill did not provide a cause of action for "bona fide" executives, which is defined to include policymakers earning more than $50,000 per year.[17] The policy-makers exclusion is noteworthy since it is these individuals who tend to be most litigious because they have the knowledge and resources to file wrongful discharge claims.

In the California Assembly, delegates introduced AB 1400, which is essentially a legislative attempt to codify the wrongful discharge cause of action. The Assembly proposal provided, in relevant part, that an employee who has five years of consecutive service (each year working at least 1000 hours) is entitled to equitable relief if the court determines that the employer discharged its employee without a good faith belief that the discharge was for good cause.[18] Like the Senate proposal, no punitive damages are available under the Assembly bill.[19] Assembly Bill 1400 permitted the parties to submit the dispute to binding arbitration.[20]

IMPLIED CONTRACT EXCEPTIONS

California courts have recognized in several cases that a contract limiting the employer's right to discharge an at-will employee may be implied from certain written or oral assurances from the employer or other employer conduct.

Employee Handbooks and Policy Statements

One of the first cases in California to find an implied contract arising from an employer's policy statements was *Hepp v. Lockheed California Co.,*[21] involving an employee discharged from his job in the aerospace industry. Here, a California appellate court found that the employer breached its "contract" with its employee when it failed to adhere to its well-established policy that when a job opening occurred, it had to be offered to those persons who had been laid off within the last two years, suitable for rehire and qualified for the position, before it could be filled by promotion or transfer within the company or by a new employee.[22] The appellate court reversed the

---

[16]*Id.*
[17]*Id.*
[18]*Id.*
[19]*Id.*
[20]*Id.* at 17.
[21]86 Cal. App. 3d 714, 150 Cal. Rptr. 408 (2d Dist. 1978).
[22]*Id.* at 716, 150 Cal. Rptr. at 409.

trial court and held that it could be inferred that Lockheed's rehiring policy was not merely a supervisory guideline for the benefit of management, as the employer argued, but a positive inducement for employees to take and continue employment with the company.[23] In sum, the hiring policy was the basis of an implied contract between the employer and the employee which circumscribed the employer's personnel decisions.

Similar binding contracts have been implied by the courts from handbook provisions. In *Walker v. Northern San Diego County Hospital*,[24] for example, the plaintiff, who was summarily discharged from her position as head nurse of the hospital, alleged in her complaint that the hospital breached its employment contract with her by discharging her without a predetermination hearing. After reviewing the employer's documents, particularly those handbook provisions governing the probationary period, the court concluded that the hospital's handbook did constitute the terms of employment for the plaintiff with the hospital.[25] According to the court's reasoning, the probationary period provisions implied that once an employee had completed this probationary period he was eligible for all the benefits of a permanent employee.[26] Among these benefits was the right to intitiate a grievance proceeding, a promise which the court found that the hospital had breached when it did not afford the plaintiff a hearing prior to termination.[27] More recent California cases have continued to support this implied contract line of cases, finding that discipline procedures contained in employee handbooks become part of an implied contract and alter the at-will status of the employee.[28]

One effective way employers in California have found to prevent the finding of an implied contract is the use of "at will disclaimers," (explicit provisions in company literature clearly stating the at-will

---

[23]*Id.* at 719, 150 Cal. Rptr. at 411.
[24]135 Cal. App. 3d 896, 185 Cal. Rptr. 617 (4th Dist. 1982).
[25]*Id.* at 903, 185 Cal. Rptr. at 621.
[26]*Id.*
[27]*Id.* at 903-04, 185 Cal. Rptr. at 623.
[28]*See, e.g.,* Gray v. Superior Court, 181 Cal. App. 3d 813, 226 Cal. Rptr. 570 (2d Dist. 1986).

nature of the employment. Generally, courts interpreting California law have upheld the use of such disclaimers.[29] (See discussion of disclaimers in chapter II, supra, at 22.)

In *Crain v. Burroughs Corp.*,[30] for example, a salesman for Burroughs Corporation claimed that the company breached its contract of employment by discharging him without a just cause determination. The United States District Court, however, granted the employer's motion for summary judgment, holding that because the salesman's employment contract clearly provided that the employment was terminable at any time at Burrough's discretion, the employee had no right to a just cause determination prior to discharge and could not reasonably have had a legitimate expectation of such a right.[31] Moreover, the federal court noted that the preface to the "Field Marketing Manual" expressly stated that the manual's contents were under no circumstances to be construed as describing the conditions of employment or as creating a contract between Burroughs and its employees.[32]

It must be noted, however, that there has been at least one California court which has found that an employer's at-will disclaimer was superseded by a subsequent material understanding between the parties that contract rules would apply to the employment relationship. In that case, *Hillsman v. Sutter Community Hospitals of Sacramento*,[33] a physician who was employed by the hospital was allowed to pursue her wrongful discharge claim based on the breach of an implied contract, despite language in her employment contract which appparently created an at-will relationship. The physician was hired pursuant to a letter of understanding agreement which provided, in part, that "[i]t is further understood that renegotiation or termination of this letter of understanding by *either* party may be accomplished within 30 days' notice."[34] Although the employer contended that this provision created an at-will arrangement, the appellate court concluded that the letter agreement was silent as to the

---

[29]*See* McCulloch, Termination, *supra* note 2, at ¶ 20,032 note 5, *citing* Bohm v. Transworld Airlines, Inc., No. C-84-5004 JPV (N.D. Cal. May 5, 1986); Crain v. Burroughs Corp., 560 F. Supp. 849 (C.D. Cal. 1983); *See also* Shapiro v. Wells Fargo Realty Advisors, 152 Cal. App. 3d 467, 199 Cal. Rptr. 613 (2d Dist. 1984); *But see* Hillsman v. Sutter Community Hospitals of Sacramento, 153 Cal. App. 3d 743, 200 Cal. Rptr. 605 (3d Dist. 1984) (material understanding between parties superseded at-will language contained in letter of agreement) (cited in McCulloch, Termination, *supra* note 2, at ¶ 20,032 note 6).

[30]560 F. Supp. 849 (C.D. Cal. 1983).

[31]*Id.* at 852.

[32]*Id.*

[33]153 Cal. App. 3d 743, 200 Cal. Rptr. 605 (3d Dist. 1984).

[34]*Id.* at 747 & note 2, 200 Cal. Rptr. at 607 & note 2 (emphasis added).

grounds and procedures by which termination could be effected.[35]
And, in light of this silence, the court permitted the plaintiff's argument that she was entitled to a predetermination hearing in accordance with the hospital's regular bylaws.[36]

Oral Promises

California courts have generally held that oral promises made by an employer to terminate an employee only for good cause or to employ as long as performance is satisfactory are unenforceable if such promises, by their terms, cannot be performed within one year.[37] This statute of frauds bar to a wrongful discharge cause of action based on an oral promise was recently illustrated in *Miller v. Indasco, Inc.*[38] In that case, a California appellate court held that: "When the terms of an oral agreement make it evident by clear implication from the subject matter of the contract that a period longer than one year was contemplated by the parties, the statute of frauds applies to bar the action."[39]

Written Contracts

"An express written contract may limit an employer's right to terminate at will."[40] *Drzewiecki v. H. & R. Block, Inc.*, involved an employment contract which stated that: "This agreement shall be for a period of two years ... First party may give notice of termination only in the case of Second party improperly conducting business [or] ... if any law were passed to make the operation of the business illegal."[41] The state appeals court found that this wording of the employment contract barred the employer from terminating

---

[35]*Id.* at 755, 200 Cal. Rptr. at 612-13.

[36]*Id.*, 200 Cal. Rptr. at 613.

[37]*See, e.g.,* Miller v. Indasco, Inc., 178 Cal. App. 3d 296, 223 Cal. Rptr 551 (2d Dist. 1986); Sorosky v. Burroughs Corp., 119 L.R.R.M. 2785, 37 Fed.Empl.Prac. 1510 (C.D. Cal. 1985); Santa Monica Hospital v. Superior Court, 172 Cal. App. 3d 698, 218 Cal. Rptr. 543 (1985); Newfield v. Ins. Co. of the West, 156 Cal. App. 3d 965, 203 Cal. Rptr. 9 (1st Dist. 1984); Munoz v. Kaiser Steel Corp., 156 Cal. App. 3d 965, 203 Cal. Rptr. 345 (4th Dist. 1984). *Contra* Rabago-Alvarez v. Dart Industries, Inc., 55 Cal. App. 3d 91, 127 Cal. Rptr. 222 (1976) (employer bound by an oral promise made to employee at hiring to terminate only for good cause or to employ as long as performance was satisfactory).

[38]178 Cal. App. 3d 296, 223 Cal. Rptr. 551 (2d Dist. 1986).

[39]*Id.* at 299, 223 Cal. Rptr. at 553, *quoting* Newfield v. Ins. Co. of the West, 156 Cal. App. 3d 440, 447, 203 Cal. Rptr. 9, 13, *citing* Lacy v. Bennett, 207 Cal. App. 2d 796, 800, 24 Cal. Rptr. 806 (2d Dist. 1962); Tostevin v. Douglas, 160 Cal. App. 2d 321, 327, 325 P.2d 130 (1958).

[40]McCulloch, Termination, *supra* note 2, at ¶ 20,032.

[41]24 Cal. App. 3d 695, 700, 101 Cal. Rptr. 169, 171 (1972).

its employee except for cause.[42] In comparison, another case found that a written contract stating that employment would continue "at such compensation and for such length of time as shall be mutually agreeable to employer and employee" to be terminable at will.[43]

Promises to Discharge for Cause Only

California courts have afforded plaintiffs a wrongful discharge cause of action on the basis that the employer, through various actions, impliedly promised its employees to discharge for cause only. The leading California case in this area of wrongful discharge law is *Pugh v. See's Candies, Inc.*[44]

The *Pugh* case involved an employee who had worked for See's Candies for thirty-two years, during which time he had worked his way up the corporate ladder from dishwasher to vice-president in charge of production and a member of the board of directors. Suddenly, upon returning from vacation, Pugh was terminated. The company president gave no specific reason for the discharge. Pugh subsequently brought charges against his former employer, alleging breach of an implied contract to discharge for cause only and violation of public policy.[45]

In deciding the implied contract claim, the court of appeals first acknowledged that an employment contract is presumed to be terminable at will.[46] But, like any presumption of law, the court continued, it is subject to rebuttal by contrary evidence.[47] The evidence which the court found to rebut the at-will presumption included: "the duration of appellant's employment, the commendations and promotions he received, the apparent lack of any direct criticism of his work, the assurances he was given, and the employer's acknowledged policies."[48] In light of this evidence, the court held that it was reversible error for the trial court to grant nonsuit to See's and permitted Pugh's contract claim to proceed.[49]

Later cases have refined the teaching of the *Pugh* decision. For instance, a federal court applying California law concluded that four and one-half years of service did not constitute evidence of adequate

---

[42]*Id.* at 705, 101 Cal. Rptr. at 175.

[43]McCULLOCH, TERMINATION, *supra* note 2, at ¶ 20,032 & note 10, quoting Baker v. Kaiser Aluminium & Chemical Corp., 608 F. Supp. 1315 (N.D. Cal. 1984).

[44]116 Cal. App. 3d 311, 171 Cal. Rptr. 917 (1st Dist. 1981).

[45]*Id.* The court dismissed Pugh's public policy claims.

[46]*Id.*

[47]*Id.*

[48]*Id.* at 329.

[49]*Id.*

longevity to rebut the at-will presumption.[50] More recently, in *Wilson v. Vlasic Foods, Inc.,*[51] a court held that where an employee fails to allege *specific* policies or statements that would give rise to a legitimate expectation of a good cause standard, no claim for the breach of an implied contract will be recognized.

An employee's contract claim that the employer promised to discharge for cause only has arisen in the context of corporate reorganizations. In these instances, an employee who was terminated pursuant to a downsizing plan may allege that the employer breached its promise to discharge only for good cause. California courts have uniformly held that an employer's dismissal of an employee because of depressed economic conditions and relocation as part of a corporate reorganization does constitute termination for good cause.[52]

The leading case in this area is *Clutterham v. Coachmen Industries,*[53] where a California appellate court granted summary judgment to an employer faced with such a wrongful discharge claim. The plaintiff in *Clutterham* was in a sales position for a recreational vehicle company. Due to the extremely depressed market in this industry during 1979, the company transferred all operations for six of its facilities from California back to its Indiana-based headquarters in an effort to reduce overhead costs at these facilities.[54] In connection with this reorganization, the plaintiff's position was eliminated, at which time the plaintiff brought charges against his former employer claiming breach of the implied promise to discharge for cause only. In rejecting the plaintiff's wrongful discharge claim, the court concluded that "courts must take care not to interfere with the legitimate exercise of managerial discretion."[55] The court granted

[50]*See* Green, *Prevention, supra* note 13, at 19, *citing* Scopas v. Armstrong World Industries, Inc., 114 L.R.R.M. 2933 (C.D. Cal. 1983). *See also* Comerio v. Beatrice Foods Co., 600 F. Supp. 765 (E.D. Mo. 1985) (employer granted summary judgment where employee's length of service was three years and no evidence of express policies by employer that employee would be discharged for cause only).

[51]116 L.R.R.M. 2419 (D. Cal. 1984).

[52]*See, e.g.,* Gianaculus v. Trans World Airlines, Inc., 761 F.2d 1391 (9th Cir. 1985) (elimination of plaintiff's position as part of corporation's general reduction in force necessitated by economic circumstances constituted good cause for discharge); Sorosky v. Burroughs Corp., 119 L.R.R.M. 2785, 37 Fed.Empl.Prac. 1510 (C.D. Cal. 1985) (employer's motion for summary judgment granted where employee failed to establish that company's proffered legitimate business justifications for layoff were pretextual); Clutterham v. Coachmen Industries, 169 Cal. App. 3d 1223, 215 Cal. Rptr. 795 (2d Dist. 1985). *See also* Green, *Prevention, supra* note 13, at 20-21.

[53]169 Cal. App. 3d 1223, 215 Cal. Rptr. 795 (2d Dist. 1985).

[54]*Id.* at 1226, 215 Cal. Rptr. at 796.

[55]*Id.* at 1227, 215 Cal. Rptr. at 797.

the employer's motion for summary judgment since Clutterham did not claim that Coachmen's reason for discharge was pretextual and therefore failed to raise a triable issue of fact.[56]

Implied Covenant of Good Faith and Fair Dealing

The concept of the implied covenant of good faith and fair dealing was first formulated by the California courts in the context of insurance contracts. The doctrine was explained in *Comunale v. Traders & General Ins. Co.* as follows: "There is an implied covenant of good faith and fair dealing in *every* contract that neither party will do anything which will injure the right of the other to receive the benefits of the agreement."[57] Since *Comunale,* however, the doctrine of the implied covenant has spread to employment law cases.[58]

The seminal case involving the implied covenant in a wrongful discharge action is *Cleary v. American Airlines, Inc.,*[59] in which a state appellate court recognized the existence of the implied covenant where certain particular facts are present. *Cleary* involved an employee who alleged that American Airlines breached the implied covenant of good faith and fair dealing when it arbitrarily discharged him, "accusing him of theft, leaving his work area without authorization, and threatening a fellow employee with bodily harm, all in violation of American Airlines' regulations."[60] In determining that the plaintiff had pleaded a viable cause of action, the court found two factors to be of paramount importance. First, the court examined the plaintiff's length of service, eighteen years of apparently satisfactory service, and noted that "[t]ermination of employment without legal cause after such a period offends the implied-in-law covenant of good faith and fair dealing *contained in all contracts, including employment contracts.*"[61] The second factor of significance was the expressed policy of the employer contained in its Regulation 135-4. This policy involved the adoption of specific procedures for adjudicating employee disputes, such as the one at bar.

With these two factors before it, the court concluded that "we hold that the longevity of the employee's service, together with the express policy of the employer, operate as a form of estoppel, pre-

---

[56]*Id.*

[57]50 Cal. 2d 654, 658 (1958) (emphasis added).

[58]For a criticism of the expansion of the implied covenant of good faith and fair dealing by the courts, *see generally* Note, *Defining Public Policy Torts in At-Will Dismissals,* 34 Stan. L. Rev. 153 (1981).

[59]111 Cal. App. 3d 443, 168 Cal. Rptr. 722 (2d Dist. 1980).

[60]*Id.* at 447, 168 Cal. Rptr. at 724.

[61]*Id.* at 455, 168 Cal. Rptr. at 729 (emphasis added).

cluding any discharge of such an employee by the employer without good cause."[62] Moreover, since the employee's claim alleged bad faith action by the employer, the court found that if the plaintiff met his burden of proof, he would be entitled to both contract and tort relief.[63] The availability of tort relief for a plaintiff alleging bad faith breach of the implied covenant can be particularly crippling to employers. In one case, for instance, a plaintiff who successfully alleged such a bad faith breach was awarded more than $2 million in punitive damages, although that award was later reduced by the court.[64]

The trend among the California courts to permit a plaintiff to sue in contract and to recover both in contract and tort relief flies in the face of legal precedent. The California cases find "support for their analysis in a line of insurance cases . . . the only context in which courts had treated the breach of an implied covenant of good faith and fair dealing as a public policy tort."[65] As one commentator notes, the "courts cannot assume that the same factors that justify treating an insurer's breach of the implied covenant as a public policy tort exist when employers fail to deal fairly and in good faith with their employees."[66] By doing so, "the courts may invoke the punitive damage sanction in a circumstance where it is inappropriate."[67]

What precisely constitutes "good faith" on the part of the employer is uncertain. In *Crosier v. United Parcel Service*,[68] a managerial employee with UPS was discharged after twenty-five years of service for violating the employer's policy against fraternization with non-managerial employees. UPS had an unwritten rule proscribing social relationships between management and non-

---

[62]*Id.* at 456, 168 Cal. Rptr. at 729.

[63]*Id.*

[64]*See* Smithers v. Metro-Goldwyn-Mayer Studios, Inc., 139 Cal. App. 3d 643, 189 Cal. Rptr. 20 (2d Dist. 1983). As Green explains:

Smithers was an actor on an MGM television series whose contract included a provision stating that no other performer would receive greater compensation or more prominent billing. An executive at MGM allegedly threatened to blacklist Smithers and to encourage others to blacklist him unless he would forego his contractual rights. The jury found this to be a breach of the covenant of good faith and good dealing and awarded him $300,000 on this count alone. Plaintiff was also awarded $500,000 for breach of contract, $200,000 for fraud and $2,000,000 in punitive damages, although the court reduced all damages.

Green, *Prevention, supra* note 13, at 18-19.

[65]Note, *Defining Public Policy Torts in At Will Dismissals,* 34 STAN. L. REV. 153, 154 (1981).

[66]*Id.*

[67]*Id.*

[68]150 Cal. App. 3d 1132, 198 Cal. Rptr. 361 (2d Dist. 1983).

management employees. "The purposes of the rule [are] to avoid misunderstandings, complaints of favoritism, and possible claims of sexual harassment."[69] Although recognizing that Crosier had a strong interest in preserving the stability of his employment, the court held that "UPS is legitimately concerned with appearances of favoritism, possible claims of sexual harassment and employee dissension created by romantic relationships between management and non-management employees."[70] Furthermore, "the public also has an interest in the prevention of sexual harassment and favoritism."[71] So, the court concluded, UPS's dismissal of Crosier was not a breach of the implied covenant of good faith and fair dealing.

Moreover, it is important to note the *Crosier* court's appreciation of the employer's discretion over its workforce. In particular, the appellate court stated that "we are sensitive to the difficulties presented by undue restrictions on the ability of an employer to discipline its staff and concur with the statement in *Pugh* that an employer 'must of necessity be allowed substantial scope for the exercise of subjective judgment where an employee has a managerial position.'"[72]

A court in a subsequent case attempted to clear up some of the uncertainty surrounding the elements of the duty of good faith and fair dealing. In *Rulon-Miller v. IBM*,[73] a marketing manager was dismissed because of her romantic involvement with the manager of a rival firm. Although IBM had a legitimate policy permitting it to discharge employees for conflicts of interest, the plaintiff successfully argued that the supervisor did not have any belief that her relationship was in violation of this policy. More importantly, the plaintiff highlighted the fact that the company also had a policy ensuring to all employees both a right of privacy and a right to hold a job even though their off-the-job behavior might not be approved by the manager.[74]

---

[69]*Id.* at 1135, 198 Cal. Rptr. at 362.

[70]*Id.* at 1140, 198 Cal. Rptr. at 366.

[71]*Id.* The court cited federal regulations that require an employer to act to prevent sexual harassment. *See* 29 CFR § 1604.11 (f), which provides in part that: "An employer should take all steps necessary to prevent sexual harassment from occurring ..."

[72]*Crosier,* 150 Cal. App. 3d at 1139-40, 198 Cal. Rptr. at 366, *quoting* Pugh v. See's Candies, Inc., 116 Cal. App. 3d 311, 330, (1st Dist. 1981).

[73]162 Cal. App. 3d 241, 208 Cal. Rptr. 524, *modified,* 162 Cal. App. 3d 1181b (1st Dist. 1984).

[74]*Id.* at 249, 208 Cal. Rptr. at 530.

In its discussion of the duty of good faith and fair dealing, the court reasoned that "[t]he duty of fair dealing by an employer is, simply stated, a requirement that like cases be treated alike."[75] Thus, the court continued, "the fair dealing portion of the covenant of good faith and fair dealing is at least the right of an employee to the benefit of the rules and requirements adopted for his or her protection."[76] Since IBM had afforded its employees privacy rights, its subsequent discharge of Ms. Rulon-Miller was held by the court to be a breach of the implied covenant.[77]

The California court of appeals further refined the necessary elements for a breach of the implied covenant claim in *Shapiro v. Wells Fargo Realty Advisors*.[78] That case involved the treasurer of Wells Fargo Bank who claimed that the bank breached its implied covenant of good faith and fair dealing when it denied him the opportunity to obtain maximum employee benefits.[79] In holding that the employee did not have a viable cause of action, the court reviewed the elements necessary to sustain a plaintiff's action based on a breach of the implied covenant. First, the court upheld the *Cleary* factors—employee's longevity of service and the company's established practices—finding that Shapiro had not adequately established either factor.[80] The court went on to observe that the bad faith breach of the implied covenant of good faith and fair dealing entitling a claimant to tort relief had only been well developed in the insurance field.[81] Citing *Sawyer v. Bank of America*,[82] the court held that a plaintiff seeking tort relief for an employer's alleged breach of the covenant must establish that a bad faith action by the employer,

---

[75]*Id.* at 247-48, 208 Cal. Rptr. at 529.
[76]*Id.* at 248, 208 Cal. Rptr. at 529.
[77]*Id.* at 253, 208 Cal. Rptr. at 533.
[78]152 Cal. App. 3d 467, 199 Cal. Rptr. 613 (2d Dist. 1984).
[79]*Id.* at 473, 199 Cal. Rptr. at 615.
[80]*Id.* at 478-79, 199 Cal. Rptr. at 619.
[81]*Id.* at 478 note 6, 199 Cal. Rptr. at 619 note 6:
"The pioneering cases, Comunale v. Traders & General Insurance Co. (1958) 50 Cal. 2d 654, and Crisci v. Security Ins. Co. (1967) 66 Cal. 2d 425, 58 Cal. Rptr. 13, 426 P.2d 173 have been followed by noteworthy bad faith tort cases including: Egan v. Mutual of Omaha Ins. Co. (1979) 24 Cal. 3d 809, 169 Cal. Rptr. 691, 620 P.2d 141; Royal Globe Ins. Co. v. Superior Court (1979) 23 Cal. 3d 880, 153 Cal. Rptr. 842, 592 P.2d 329; Silberg v. California Life Ins. Co. (1974) 11 Cal. 3d 452, 113 Cal. Rptr. 711, 521 P.2d 1103; Gruenberg v. Aetna Ins. Co. (1973) 9 Cal. 3d 566, 108 Cal. Rptr. 480, 510 P.2d 1032; and Fletcher v. Western National Life Ins. Co. (1970) 10 Cal. App. 3d 376, 89 Cal. Rptr. 78.
[82]83 Cal. App. 3d 135, 145 Cal. Rptr. 623 (1978).

which is extraneous to the contract, was combined with the employer's intent to frustrate the employee's enjoyment of the contract rights.[83]

Despite the clear approach taken by the *Shapiro* court, subsequent decisions in California have once again clouded the implied covenant cause of action. In one case, a California appellate court held that the factors relied on in *Cleary* are not the *sine qua non* of establishing a breach of the implied covenant of good faith and fair dealing in every employment contract.[84] And in another recent case, the California Supreme Court implied that tort relief may be available simply by establishing a breach of the implied covenant without any bad faith action by the employer.[85]

PUBLIC POLICY EXCEPTIONS

Since 1959 the California courts have recognized exceptions to the employment-at-will rule where it is determined that an employee's termination violates an important public policy.[86] Over the years there has been much controversy over the definition of "public policy." Some courts and commentators advocate a broad interpretation extending to any judicially conceived public policy. Others, however, argue for a more narrow reading which would limit public policy to statutorily enacted policy. As the discussion below illustrates, it now seems clear under California law that a public policy wrongful discharge claim must rest upon statutorily enacted policy. As mentioned at the beginning of this chapter, the California Supreme Court's decision in *Foley* should address this issue.

It is well established under California law that an employee can maintain a tort action for retaliatory discharge when the employee is terminated for refusing to commit a crime, or for exercising a constitutional or statutory right. The foundations of this cause of action lie in two cases, *Petermann v. International Brotherhood of Teamsters,*[87] and *Tameny v. Atlantic Richfield Co.*[88]

---

[83]*See Shapiro,* 152 Cal. App. 3d at 478-79, 199 Cal. Rptr. at 619.

[84]*See* Khanna v. Microdata Corp., 170 Cal. App. 3d 250, 262, 215 Cal. Rptr. 860, 867 (1985).

[85]*See* Seaman's Direct Buying Service, Inc. v. Standard Oil Co. of Calif., 36 Cal. 3d 752 note 6 (1984).

[86]*See* Petermann v. International Brotherhood of Teamsters, 174 Cal. App. 2d 184 (1959) (first public policy exception to at will rule recognized where employee discharged for refusing to commit perjury).

[87]174 Cal. App. 2d 184 (1959).

[88]27 Cal. 3d 167, 164 Cal. Rptr. 839 (1980).

In *Petermann* a union business agent was discharged for refusing his supervisor's demand that he perjure himself before a legislative committee. The court specifically recognized a cause of action for retaliatory discharge in violation of public policy, but did not state whether the cause of action was in contract or tort. *Petermann* contains language which can be read to suggest an extremely broad reading of the term "public policy."[89] The actual holding, however, rests firmly on the fact that the discharge violated public policy which was specifically embodied in statute:

> It would be obnoxious to the interests of the state and contrary to public policy and sound morality to allow an employer to discharge any employee, whether the employment be for a designated or unspecified duration, on the ground that the employee declined to permit perjury, an act specifically enjoined by statute . . . . The public policy of this state as reflected in the Penal Code would be seriously impaired if it were to be held that one could be discharged by reason of his refusal to commit perjury.[90]

In 1980 the California Supreme Court in *Tameny* specifically recognized a tort cause of action for wrongful discharge in violation of public policy.[91] In that case, the plaintiff alleged that he had been discharged for his refusal to participate in a scheme to fix gasoline prices in violation of the antitrust laws. Like *Petermann*, the decision contains hints of an expansive definition of "public policy." The court cites a number of non-employment cases, two of which clearly apply judicially conceived public policy,[92] holding that "[i]n light of the foregoing authorities, we conclude that an employee's action is *ex delicto* and subjects an employer to tort liability."[93]

The holding of *Tameny*, however, rests on a narrower view of *statutorily enacted* public policy. The majority of the cases cited in this opinion rest upon public policy embodied in statute.[94] Moreover, Justice Manuel narrows the decision with a two sentence concurrence, stating that "the cause of action here in question flows from a clear statutory source. . . . Accordingly, I see no reason to search further for it among the vague and ill-defined dictates of 'fundamental public policy.'"[95]

[89]*See Petermann*, 174 Cal. App. 2d at 188.
[90]*Id.* at 189.
[91]*See Tameny*, 27 Cal. 3d at 1178, 164 Cal. Rptr. at 846.
[92]*See, e.g.*, Eads v. Marks, 39 Cal. 2d 807 (1952); Aweeka v. Bonds, 20 Cal. App. 3d 278, 97 Cal. Rptr. 650 (1971).
[93]*Tameny*, 27 Cal. 3d at 176, 164 Cal. Rptr. at 844.
[94]*See id.* at 175, 164 Cal. Rptr. at 843-44 and cases cited therein.
[95]*Id.* at 179, 164 Cal. Rptr. at 846 (Manuel, J. concurring).

Thus, both *Petermann* and *Tameny* suggest a broad interpretation of the public policy definition, which could easily be extended to any case including a well-recognized or easily identified public policy. In the final analysis, however, both cases rest clearly on public policy embodied in statute and subsequent cases have clarified this narrower reading.

Decisions since *Tameny* leave little doubt that judges are not free to declare a tort cause of action on the basis of public policy notions which are not embodied in statute. In *Hentzel v. Singer Co.,*[96] the plaintiff alleged he was discharged in retaliation for exercising his statutory right to express dissatisfaction with his working conditions as provided by the California Labor Code. The Court of Appeals upheld his tort cause of action, but stated that "[w]e are mindful of the restraint which courts must exercise in this arena, lest they mistake their own predilections for public policy which deserves recognition at law."[97]

Several other cases echo this same theme.[98] In *Shapiro v. Wells Fargo Realty Advisors,*[99] Justice Arabian of the Second Appellate District recognized that "courts have no power to declare public policy in wrongful discharge cases without statutory support."[100] More recently, the Fourth Appellate District stated that "[t]he discharge to be actionable on this theory must reflect a violation of a strong public policy; generally, violation of a statute must be involved, as when the discharge is because the employee would not violate the law."[101] In light of these recent pronouncements by courts interpreting California law, it seems clear that a public policy wrongful discharge claim must rest upon statutorily enacted public policy.

---

[96]138 Cal. App. 3d 290, 188 Cal. Rptr. 159 (1982).

[97]*Id.* at 297.

[98]*See* Baker v. Kaiser Aluminum & Chemical Corp., 608 F. Supp. 1315, 1322 (N.D. Cal. 1984) ("job security is not, in itself, a substantial public policy" sufficient to support a cause of action under *Tameny*). *See also* Tyco Industries, Inc. v. Superior Court, 164 Cal. App. 3d 148, 211 Cal. Rptr. 540 (1985).

[99]152 Cal. App. 3d 467, 199 Cal. Rptr. 613 (1984).

[100]*Id.* at 477, 199 Cal. Rptr. at 618. *See also* Foley v. InterActive Data Corp., 174 Cal. App. 3d 282, 219 Cal. Rptr. 866 (1985), *rev. granted,* 712 P.2d 891, 22 Cal. Rptr. 740 (1986).

[101]Gray v. Superior Court, 181 Cal. App. 3d 813, 819, 226 Cal. Rptr. 570, 572 (1986). *See also* Sorosky v. Burroughs Corp., 119 L.R.R.M. 2785, 2788 (C.D. Cal. 1985).

PREEMPTION

In many cases California courts have held that an employee may not recover under state tort or contract law theories of wrongful discharge where the claim is preempted by a federal, state, or local statute or regulation.

Employees Covered By Collective Bargaining Agreements

Generally, courts interpreting California law have held that federal labor laws preempt a union employee's state law claim for wrongful discharge based on implied contract and public policy theories.[102] In one important case, however, the Ninth Circuit Court of Appeals allowed an employee's wrongful discharge action, despite the fact that he was covered by a collective bargaining agreement.[103] In that case the plaintiff alleged that his employer had ordered him to deliver a load of spoiled milk in violation of local health regulations. When the plaintiff refused to make the delivery, he was discharged and subsequently filed suit against his former employer. The federal court held that Sections 301 and 301(a) of the Labor Management Relations Act, as amended (LMRA)[104] do not preempt a state tort action to enforce local regulations, such as the one at bar, since the suit addressed solely local concerns and did not interfere with federal labor policy.[105] The court went on to hold that "where an employee" under a collective bargaining agreement "asserts ... that he was discharged for reasons illegal under federal labor stat-

---

[102]*See* McCulloch, Termination, *supra* note 2, at ¶ 20,076 note 3, *citing* Friday v. Hughes Aircraft Co., 179 Cal. App. 3d 947, 225 Cal. Rptr. 89 (1986); Miller v. United Airlines, Inc., 174 Cal. App. 3d 878, 220 Cal. Rptr. 684 (1985); Williams v. Caterpillar Tractor Co., 786 F.2d 928 (9th Cir. 1986), *cert. granted*, No. 86-526 (Nov. 11, 1986); Bale v. General Telephone Co. of California, 795 F.2d 775 (9th Cir. 1986); Truex v. Garrett Freightlines, Inc., 784 F.2d 1347 (9th Cir. 1986); Buscemi v. McDonnell Douglas Corp., 736 F.2d 1348 (9th Cir. 1984); Olguin v. Inspiration Consolidated Copper Co., 740 F.2d 1468 (9th Cir. 1984). *See also* Green, *Prevention, supra* note 13, at 24, *citing* Harper v. San Diego Transit Corp., 764 F.2d 663 (9th Cir. 1985) (tort claim for breach of the implied covenant of good faith and fair dealing preempted by the LMRA); Schroeder v. Trans World Airlines, Inc., 702 F.2d 189 (9th Cir. 1983) (Railway Labor Act preempts wrongful discharge cause of action); Fristoe v. Reynolds Metal Co., 615 F.2d 1209 (9th Cir. 1980).

[103]*See* Garibaldi v. Lucky Food Stores, Inc., 726 F.2d 1367 (9th Cir. 1984), *cert. denied*, 105 S.Ct. 2319 (1985).

[104]29 U.S.C.A. §§ 185, 185 (a) (1982).

[105]*Garibaldi*, 726 F.2d at 1372-74.

utes, that employee is not acting on behalf of a state law or policy and the applicable federal statute preempts the state common law cause of action."[106]

Indeed, subsequent decisions demonstrate that most claims brought by union employees do implicate federal labor law interests and result in preemption of the state law claim. For example, in *Buscemi v. McDonnell Douglas Corp.*,[107] the Ninth Circuit found that the National Labor Relations Act (NLRA)[108] preempted an employee's wrongful discharge cause of action based on his retaliatory discharge "for passing out petitions and voicing employee complaints."[109] Likewise, a federal district court denied an employee's public policy claim where it was alleged that the supervisor had acted illegally in connection with a union election because the complaint involved a possible unfair labor practice.[110]

Nonetheless, some recent cases highlight the fact that there remains uncertainty on the preemption issue for union employees. In *Scott v. New United Motor Manufacturing*,[111] a federal district court rejected an employer's preemption defense in a case involving the dismissal of a probationary employee who was not allowed to file a grievance under the union contract.[112] Since the employee did not yet have adequate contractual protection, the court permitted the common law wrongful discharge claim to proceed.[113] Moreover, California courts apparently agree that tort claims for breach of the implied covenant of good faith and fair dealing by a union employee are not preempted "where the emotional distress arises from conduct not itself subject to exclusive federal jurisdiction."[114] For instance, in the *Garibaldi* case discussed above, the court permitted the plaintiff's emotional distress claim because the distress arose from the delivery of spoiled milk, a subject not embraced exclusively by federal legislation. "In a case remanded by the United States Supreme Court, a California appeals court reaffirmed its earlier

[106]Green, *Prevention, supra* note 13, at 23-24.
[107]736 F.2d 1348 (9th Cir. 1984).
[108]29 U.S.C. SS. 158 (a) (3), 158 (a) (4) (1982).
[109]Green, *Prevention, supra* note 13, at 24.
[110]*See* McCulloch, Termination, *supra* note 2, at ¶ 20,076 notes 5 & 6, *citing* Basset v. Atteberry, 180 Cal. App. 3d 288, 225 Cal. Rptr. 399 (1986); *see also* Mathieson v. Auto Club of S. Calif., 212 Cal. Rptr. 575 (App. 1985) (employee's state law claim of retaliatory discharge for union organizing activities preempted by NLRB's prior dismissal of a retaliation claim under federal law). *See also* note 102, *supra,* and cases cited therein.
[111]632 F. Supp. 891 (N.D. Cal. 1986).
[112]*See* McCulloch, Termination, *supra* note 2, at ¶ 20,076.
[113]*Id.*
[114]Green, *Prevention, supra* note 13, at 24.

position that a union employee's claim for emotional distress damages was not preempted."[115] In that case, "the distress had allegedly resulted from a pattern of harassment inflicted on the employee by her managers."[116] "[S]ince the claim did [not] concern the employee's discharge and no protected activity or unfair labor practice was involved," the court concluded that the issue represented simply "the state's purely local interest in protecting its citizens from abusive behavior" and rejected the preemption defense.[117]

Worker's Compensation Claims

With the addition of Section 132a to the California Labor Code,[118] which prohibits the retaliatory discharge of any employee filing a worker's compensation claim, it is now clear that this statutory provision preempts common law wrongful discharge claims.[119] Moreover, California courts generally agree that Sections 3600 and 3601 of the state Labor Code provide the exclusive remedy "where the injury occurs within the scope and course of employment and where physical illness and disability accompany the emotional distress," thereby preempting an employee's common law action for emotional distress damages.[120] Some courts, however, have held that a cause of action for emotional distress, absent physical injury compensable under the Workers Compensation Act, constitutes an implied exception to Section 3601's exclusive remedy provision.[121]

---

[115]McCulloch, Termination, *supra* note 2, at ¶ 20,076 & note 9, *citing* Alpha Beta, Inc. v. Superior Ct., 160 Cal. App. 3d 1049, 207 Cal. Rptr. 117 (1980), *rev'd and remanded,* 105 S. Ct. 2696 (1985), *decision on remand,* 180 Cal. App. 3d 324, 225 Cal. Rptr. 551 (1986).

[116]McCulloch, Termination, *supra* note 2, at ¶20,076.

[117]*Id.*

[118]Cal. Lab. Code § 132a (West 1980).

[119]*See, e.g.,* Portillo v. G. T. Price Products, Inc., 131 Cal. App. 3d 285, 182 Cal. Rptr. 291 (1982). Prior to the enactment of this non-retaliation provision, a court did permit an employee to bring a civil action against his former employer for his discharge for filing a worker's compensation claim. *See* Meyer v. Byron Jackson, Inc., 174 Cal. Rptr. 428 (1981).

[120]Green, *Prevention, supra* note 13, at 25, *citing* Hollywood Refrigeration Sales Co. v. Superior Ct., 164 Cal. App. 3d 754, 210 Cal. Rptr. 619 (2d Dist. 1985); Gates v. Transvideo Corp., 93 Cal. App. 3d 196, 155 Cal. Rptr. 486 (2d Dist. 1979). *See also* Ankeny v. Lockheed Missiles & Space Co., 88 Cal. App. 3d 531, 151 Cal. Rptr. 828 (1979).

[121]*See* Green, *Prevention, supra* note 13, at 26-27, *citing* Renteria v. County of Orange, 82 Cal. App. 3d 833, 147 Cal. Rptr. 447 (4th Dist. 1978). *See also* McCulloch, Termination, *supra* note 2, at ¶ 20,075 note 5 *citing* Russell v. Massachusetts Mutual Life Ins. Co., 722 F.2d 482 (9th Cir. 1983); Young v. Libby-Owens Ford Co., 168 Cal. App. 3d 1037, 214 Cal. Rptr. 400 (1985); McGee v. McNally, 119 Cal. App. 3d 891, 174 Cal. Rptr. 253 (1981).

Age Discrimination Claims

It is clear under California law that the state law against age discrimination preempts all common law wrongful discharge claims based on age discrimination.[122] This rule has been consistently upheld by courts applying California law.[123] Moreover, one California court has held that the state law prohibiting age discrimination not only preempts any common law wrongful discharge claim, but provides the exclusive remedy for any discharge claim based on age.[124]

Employee Retirement Income Security Act (ERISA)[125] Claims

Where an employee alleges that he was discharged for the purpose of denying him benefits arising from a pension plan governed by ERISA, courts applying California law have generally held that the common law wrongful discharge claim is preempted by ERISA.[126] Of course, there are exceptions to this general rule. In *Presti v. Connecticut General Life Insurance Co., Inc.,*[127] for example, an employee brought suit against Connecticut General, the company which administered his company's ERISA-governed pension plan. In his suit, the plaintiff alleged that Connecticut General "violated state insurance laws, breached the implied covenant of good faith and fair dealing, and caused him to suffer emotional distress" by denying him long-term disability benefits.[128] The federal district court rejected the preemption defense, finding that the plaintiff's claims were purely local in nature because they concerned "the state's interest in regulating the insurance industry" within California.[129]

---

[122]*See* CAL. FAIR EMPL. AND HOUSING ACT, CAL. GOVT. CODE § 12940 *et seq.* (West 1980).

[123]*See, e.g.,* Commodore Home Systems, Inc. v. Superior Ct., 32 Cal. 3d 211, 185 Cal. Rptr. 270 (1982); Wilson v. Vlasic Foods, Inc., 116 L.R.R.M. 2419 (D. Cal. 1984); Mahoney v. Crocker National Bank, 571 F. Supp. 287 (N.D. Cal. 1983); Strauss v. A.L. Randall Co., 114 Cal. App. 3d 514, 194 Cal. Rptr. 520 (1983).

[124]*See* Wilson v. Vlasic Foods, Inc., 116 L.R.R.M. 2419 (D.Cal. 1984).

[125]29 U.S.C. § 1140 (1982).

[126]*See* Green, *Prevention, supra* note 13, at 25, *citing* Johnson v. Trans World Airlines, Inc., 149 Cal. App. 3d 518, 196 Cal. Rptr. 896 (1983); Provience v. Valley Clerks Trust Fund, 209 Cal. Rptr. 276 (App. 1984); Ziskind v. Retail Clerks Int'l Assoc., 3 Empl. Ben. Cas. 1012 (E.D. Cal. 1982). *See also* Baker v. Kaiser Aluminum & Chemical Corp., 608 F. Supp. 1315 (N.D. Cal. 1984).

[127]605 F. Supp. 163 (N.D. Cal. 1985).

[128]McCULLOCH, TERMINATION, *supra* note 2, at ¶ 20,076.

[129]*Id.*

In another case, the Ninth Circuit held that ERISA preemption was not applicable in a case involving accrued vacation pay.[130] In that case, the circuit court reasoned that vacation pay coming out of an employer's "general revenues rather than from a special fund is merely a 'payroll practice'" and therefore exempted from ERISA coverage.[131]

CONCLUSION

It is already clear that at-will employment is one of the fastest changing areas of employment law; and, within this context, California is the jurisdiction most active in restructuring the at-will doctrine. California courts are inundated with wrongful discharge cases and opinions are handed down daily which alter the employment-at-will doctrine in some way. This deluge of cases, however, has rendered the state's codification of the at-will rule riddled with pigeonhole exceptions which prescribe the circumstances in which an employee becomes vested with a "right" to his job.

Operating from a contract analysis, California courts have recognized in several cases that a contract limiting an employer's right to discharge an at-will employee may be implied from certain oral or written assurances from the employer or other employer conduct, including employee handbooks, policy statements, and discipline procedures. Furthermore, California courts have gone far in advancing a cause of action for wrongful discharge based on the employer's breach of the implied covenant of good faith and fair dealing which the California judiciary finds implied in all employment contracts. What constitutes "good faith" on the part of the employer, however, remains a source of dispute among courts applying California law. More importantly, California courts have permitted plaintiffs to recover tort relief for the breach of the implied covenant and have further implied, in one case, that tort relief may be available in any contract breach action.

In the public policy tort analysis, the California courts have recognized a cause of action where an employee is terminated for refusing to commit a crime or for exercising a constitutional or statutory right. It appears from the case law that under California law a public policy wrongful discharge claim must rest upon statutorily enacted public policy rather than mere judicial notions of public fairness.

---

[130]*Id.* at ¶ 20,062 & note 3, *citing* Calif. Hospital Assoc. v. Henning, 730 F.2d 856 (9th Cir. 1985), *cert. denied,* 106 S. Ct. 3273 (1986).
[131]McCulloch, Termination, *supra* note 2, at ¶ 20,062.

Lastly, in many areas, ranging from worker's compensation claims to claims alleging age discrimination, California courts have held that federal or state laws may preempt common law wrongful discharge claims.

CHAPTER V

Michigan

In comparison to the California courts' derogation of the employment-at-will doctrine discussed in the previous chapter, Michigan courts appear to have followed a different path in their erosion of the at-will rule. Specifically, California jurisdictions have made inroads into the at-will rule by carving out expansive tort-based exceptions resting on concepts of public policy. In Michigan, on the other hand, the courts have circumscribed the rule's application most significantly through contract theory. The Supreme Court of Michigan, in handing down the *Toussaint v. Blue Cross & Blue Shield*[1] decision, led the way for courts in other jurisdictions to develop the implied contract exception. Also notable in Michigan is the presence of one of the first Whistleblower Protection Acts, designed to protect employees from discharge for reporting unlawful acts. Both of these aspects of Michigan law will be discussed in greater detail below.

Historically, the traditional employment-at-will doctrine stating that an employment contract for an indefinite period is terminable at will by either party for any or no reason, has never been codified in Michigan[2] and exists only as a rule of the state's common law. The at-will rule was first enunciated by the Michigan Supreme Court in *Lynas v. Maxwell Farms*[3] where the justices held that "[i]n general, it may be said that in the absence of distinguishing features or provisions or a consideration in addition to the services to be rendered, such contracts are indefinite hirings, terminable at the will of either party."[4] Although many exceptions have been carved out of this gen-

---

[1] 408 Mich. 579, 292 N.W.2d 880 (1979).

[2] The employment-at-will doctrine has, however, been codified in several states, such as California and Montana. The Montana statute, enacted in 1885, states that an employment having no specified term may be terminated at the will of either party on notice to the other. MONT. CODE ANN. § 39-2-503 (1979). The California Labor Code similarly provides that "[a]n employment having no specified term may be terminated at the will of either party on notice to the other." CAL. LAB. CODE § 2922 (West 1971).

[3] 279 Mich. 684, 273 N.W. 315 (1937).

[4] *Id.* at 687, 273 N.W. at 316.

eral rule,[5] Michigan courts have "uniformly refused to enforce indefinite term employment contracts," following the at-will rule set out in *Lynas.*[6] Federal courts, applying Michigan law, have also consistently applied this common law rule.[7]

Over the years, the Michigan courts and legislature have recognized three exceptions to the traditional common law employment-at-will doctrine. The general rule does not apply in each of the following instances: (1) when "the employment contract specifies a specific term"[8]; (2) when "the employment was offered for special consideration, such as release from a claim which the individual held against the prospective employer, other than the services to be performed"[9]; and (3) when "the discharge is in retaliation for the employee's claim of a benefit to which (s)he is entitled by law or refusal to perform an unlawful act."[10]

---

[5]Some cases argue that the "general" rule set forth in *Lynas* concerning the terminability of a hiring for an indefinite duration is not a substantive limitation on the enforceability of employment contracts, but is merely a rule of construction. *See, e.g., Toussaint,* 408 Mich. at 600, 292 N.W.2d at 885.

[6]Parets v. Eaton Corp., 479 F. Supp. 512, 518 (E.D. Mich. 1979), *citing* Ambrose v. Detroit Edison Co., 367 Mich. 334, 116 N.W.2d 726 (1962); Adolph v. Cookware Co. of America, 283 Mich. 561, 278 N.W. 687 (1938); Schipani v. Ford Motor Co., 102 Mich. App. 606, 302 N.W.2d 307 (1981); Salisbury v. McLough Steel Corp., 93 Mich. App. 248, 287 N.W.2d 195 (1979); Milligan v. Union Corp., 87 Mich. App. 179, 274 N.W.2d 10 (1978); McMath v. Ford Motor Co., 77 Mich. App. 721, 259 N.W.2d 140 (1977); Hernden v. Consumers Power Co., 72 Mich. App. 349, 249 N.W.2d 419 (1976).

[7]*See Parets,* 479 F. Supp. at 518, *citing* McLaughlin v. Ford Motor Co., 269 F.2d 120 (6th Cir. 1959); Percival v. General Motors Corp., 539 F.2d 1126 (8th Cir. 1976); Giocosa v. Sony Corp., Civil No. 6-71173 (E.D. Mich. 1978); Schroeder v. Dayton-Hudson Corp., 448 F. Supp. 910 (E.D. Mich. 1977), *reh'g granted in part on other grounds,* 456 F. Supp. 650 and 456 F. Supp. 652 (1978).

[8]Schroeder v. Dayton-Hudson Corp., 448 F. Supp. 910, 916 (E.D. Mich. 1978), *citing* McClain v. Township of Royal Oak, 276 Mich. 185, 267 N.W. 613 (1936); Brown v. Chris Nelsen & Son, Inc., 10 Mich. App. 95, 158 N.W.2d 818 (1968) (where written contract for a specific term does not call for service to employer's satisfaction, employee may only be discharged for cause). One caveat to this exception is that if an employment contract for a specific term states that the employee's work be to the employer's satisfaction, a court will not substitute its opinion for that of the employer as to whether the employee has performed satisfactorily. *See* Lynas v. Maxwell Farms, 279 Mich. 684, 689, 273 N.W. 315, 319 (1937).

[9]*Schroeder,* 448 F. Supp. at 916, *citing* Lynas v. Maxwell Farms, 279 Mich. 684, 688, 273 N.W. 315, 319 (1937).

[10]*Schroeder,* 448 F. Supp. at 916, *citing* Sventko v. Kroger Co., 69 Mich. App. 644, 647-649, 245 N.W.2d 151, 154-155 (1976).

TORT EXCEPTIONS

Public Policy Torts

Overall, Michigan courts appear to have acted with circumspection in creating public policy tort exceptions to the employment-at-will doctrine.[11] "Each recognized exception involves either an employee's exercise of a statutorily or constitutionally granted right or an employee's refusal to violate a law."[12] Accordingly, "each public policy exception is grounded on a clearly articulated, well-accepted public policy."[13] As one court observed, "the public policy of any state is neither easily defined nor by any means static. Nor is it always precisely located in the laws and judicial opinions of the state."[14] As the Michigan Supreme Court observed more than half a century ago:

> What is the meaning of "public policy?" A correct definition, at once concise and comprehensive, of the words "public policy" has not yet been formulated by our courts ... In substance, it may be said to be the community common sense and common conscience, extended and applied throughout the state to matters of public morals, public health, public safety, public welfare and the like. It is that general and well-settled public opinion relating to man's plain, palpable duty to his fellow men, having due regard to all the circumstances of each particular relation and situation.
>
> Sometimes such public policy is declared by Constitution; sometimes by statute; sometimes by judicial decision. More often, however, it abides only in the customs and conventions of the people—in their clear consciousness and conviction of what is naturally and inherently just and right between man and man. It regards the primary principles of equity and justice and is sometimes expressed under the title of social and industrial justice, as it is conceived by our body politic.[15]

Naturally, such an expansive definition of public policy could give the courts freedom to legislate under the guise of defending the state's public policy. Over the years, however, the Michigan courts at both the state and federal levels have more narrowly construed the parameters of public policy which will support a tort action for wrongful discharge.

---

[11]*See* Clifford v. Cactus Drilling Corp., 419 Mich. 356, 367, 353 N.W.2d 469, 474 (1984) (Williams, C.J., dissenting).
[12]*Id.*
[13]*Id.*
[14]*Id.* at 366 note 4, 353 N.W.2d at 473-74 note 4.
[15]Skutt v. Grand Rapids, 275 Mich. 258, 264-265, 266 N.W. 344, 346 (1936), *quoting* Pittsburgh, C.C. & St. L. R. Co. v. Kinney, 95 Ohio St. 64, 115 N.E. 505 (1918).

The recognized public policy exceptions fall into three categories. Most often, an articulation of public policy stems from a legislative provision granting employees some protection from discharge but no specific remedy. Therefore, a cause of action may be permitted so that the employee is not without any avenue of redress. For example, an employee may not be discharged under Michigan law on the basis of religion, race, color, national origin, sex,[16] because of a physical handicap,[17] or in retaliation for filing a complaint under the Michigan Occupational Safety and Health Act.[18] "In these specific instances," the Michigan Supreme Court has held that "the policy of ensuring employee job security against an improperly motivated discharge curtails the employer's prerogative to terminate the employment."[19] Moreover, "the plight of employees forced to choose between their jobs and an employer's direction to act in violation of the law has been recognized" as permissible grounds for a public policy exception to the employment-at-will doctrine.[20] Lastly, Michigan "courts have shown some willingness to recognize a public policy exception despite the lack of a statutory provision explicitly guaranteeing employees protection from discharge."[21] Each of these categories is examined below.

Before discussing each of the recognized public policy exceptions, it should be noted that in any case based on a public policy exception to the employment-at-will rule, three elements must be established.[22] First, the plaintiff must be engaged in an activity which falls within the protection of the state's public policy.[23] That is, "[t]he activity's protection may stem either from a constitutional or statutorily granted right or from an obligation favored by statutory policy."[24]

---

[16]MICH. COMP. LAWS ANN. § 37.2101 *et seq.* (West 1985)[hereinafter cited as M.C.L.A.].

[17]M.C.L.A. § 37.1202.

[18]M.C.L.A. § 408.1065 (1).

[19]*Clifford,* 419 Mich. at 364, 353 N.W.2d at 472.

[20]*Id.* at 365, 353 N.W.2d at 473. *See also* Trombetta v. Detroit, Toledo & Ironton R. Co., 81 Mich. App. 489, 495-96, 265 N.W.2d 385, 392 (1978) (employer's discharge of an at-will employee for refusing to falsify state required pollution control reports held to be in contravention of state public policy). *See also, infra,* notes 26-34 and accompanying text.

[21]*Clifford,* 419 Mich. at 364, 353 N.W.2d at 472. *See also* Sventko v. Kroger Co., 69 Mich. App. 644, 245 N.W.2d 151 (1976) (discharge for filing claim under the Workers' Disability Compensation Act found to contravene strong public policy, despite lack of any provision in the statute prohibiting retaliatory discharge.) *See also, infra,* notes 35-64 and accompanying text.

[22]*Clifford,* 419 Mich. at 368, 353 N.W.2d at 474, *citing* Schlei & Grossman, Employment Discrimination Law, ch. 15, at 534 (1983).

[23]*Clifford,* 419 Mich. at 368, 353 N.W.2d at 474.

[24]*Id.* at 368-69, 353 N.W.2d at 474.

Second, the plaintiff must establish that he was discharged. And, "[t]hird, a causal connection must exist between the plaintiff's protected activity and the discharge."[25]

Refusal To Commit Unlawful Acts. The earliest and most clearly defined public policy exception to the employment-at-will doctrine involves situations where the employer discharges a worker for refusing to violate the law.[26] Michigan courts recognize such terminations as contraventions of public policy sufficient to abrogate the at-will rule. In *Trombetta v. Detroit, Toledo & Ironton R. Co.,*[27] for example, the plaintiff alleged that he was discharged for refusing to manipulate sampling results used for pollution control reports which were filed with the state pursuant to the statute. It was clear that such tampering violated state law.[28] The court concluded, then, that the plaintiff had set forth a cause of action based on a public policy exception since: "[i]t is without question that the public policy of this state does not condone attempts to violate its duly enacted laws."[29]

One of the more interesting aspects of Michigan law is the presence of the state's Whistleblower Protection Act which is designed to prohibit the discharge of employees who report a violation of the law.[30] The statute provides, in part, that an employer can not discharge or threaten to discharge any employee because that employee reports, or is about to report, a violation of the law or regulation of the state or nation, unless, of course, the employee knows the report is false.[31] Punitive damages and jury trial are not provided for by the statute, although civil fines, compensatory damages and attorney's fees are authorized.[32]

A recently decided case, *Watassek v. Michigan Department of Mental Health*[33] applied the statute retroactively to permit a public policy cause of action. In *Watassek,* a former employee filed suit against the state department of mental health alleging that he was

---

[25]*Id.* at 369, 353 N.W.2d at 474.

[26]*See, e.g.,* Tameny v. Atlantic Richfield Co., 27 Cal. 3d 167, 164 Cal. Rptr. 839 (1980) (California Supreme Court found contravention of state public policy where employee discharged for refusing to participate in an illegal price-fixing scheme); Petermann v. International Brotherhood of Teamsters, Local 396, 174 Cal. App. 2d 184 (1959) (public policy violation recognized where employee discharged for refusing to commit perjury).

[27]81 Mich. App. 489, 491, 265 N.W.2d 385, 388 (1978).

[28]M.C.L.A. § 323.10 (1)- (2).

[29]*Trombetta,* 81 Mich. App. at 495, 265 N.W.2D at 388.

[30]M.C.L.A. § 15.361-15.369.

[31]M.C.L.A. § 15.362.

[32]M.C.L.A. § 15.363 (3); §§ 15.364-5.

[33]143 Mich. App. 556, 372 N.W.2d 617 (1985).

terminated from his position as a nurse at a mental health facility in retaliation for reporting incidents of patient abuse to his superior. The court observed that:

> Although this statute (the Whistleblower Protection Act) took effect in 1981, well after the action complained of in this case, we nevertheless find that the statute is evidence of a recognized public policy preexisting its actual enactment. Therefore, we hold that it was contrary to public policy in 1976 for an employer to discharge an employee in retaliation for reporting abuses committed on patients in the Plymouth Center for Human Development. For that reason, the complaint does state a claim upon which relief may be granted.[34]

Theoretically, the Whistleblower Protection Act may afford a new avenue on which wrongful discharge suits may advance. At this time, however, invocation of the Act is still infrequent.

Exercise of Statutory Rights or Privileges: Retaliatory Discharge. Another well-defined area on which public policy exceptions rest involves the situation where the plaintiff's activity is statutorily protected from the employer's general right to discharge. Throughout the years, federal and state legislatures have created explicit exceptions to the employment-at-will doctrine that protect workers who would otherwise be classified as at-will employees based upon certain common characteristics or collective activities. For example, the National Labor Relations Act (NLRA) of 1935 prohibits discharges for union organizing activity.[35] Additionally, Title VII of the Civil Rights Act of 1964[36] and the Federal Age Discrimination in Employment Act[37] (among other federal employment discrimination statutes[38]) forbids employee terminations which discriminate on the basis of race, color, religion, sex, national origin, age, handicap, or other "protected" characteristics. There are also several specific provisions against retaliatory dismissals based on an individual's invocation of rights guaranteed under these stat-

---

[34]*Id.* at 564, 372 N.W.2d at 621.
[35]29 U.S.C. §§ 157, 158 (a) (3) (1982).
[36]42 U.S.C. § 2000e-2 (1982).
[37]29 U.S.C. § 623 (a) (1982).
[38]*See, e.g.,* Consumer Credit Protection Act, 15 U.S.C. § 1674 (a) (1982) (forbids discharge of those whose wages are garnished for indebtedness); Fair Labor Standards Act, 29 U.S.C. § 215 (a) (3) (1982) (prohibits the discharge of those exercising rights under the Act); Occupational Safety and Health Act of 1970, 29 U.S.C. § 660 (c) (1982) (prohibits the discharge of anyone exercising rights under the Act); Vietnam Era Veterans Readjustment Act, 38 U.S.C. § 2021 (1976) (grants returning veterans the right to their former job and prohibits discharge for one year).

utes.[39] State legislatures have created additional protection for various at-will employees. Several states, for instance, have statutes prohibiting discharges based upon political activity or affiliation.[40]

Where a statute creates a right not previously recognized under common law, the Michigan courts have generally held that the plaintiff's exclusive remedy is with the administrative agency enforcing the statute and does not include a civil action for the tort of retaliatory discharge.[41] In *Ohlsen v. DST Industries, Inc.*,[42] for instance, the plaintiff filed a complaint alleging that his discharge was in retaliation for his exercise of rights afforded him under the Michigan Occupational Safety and Health Act (MIOSHA),[43] specifically the right to protest an unsafe place to work.[44] The *Ohlsen* court reasoned that an employee has no common law right to refuse to work upon alleging an unsafe workplace.[45] "Therefore," the court concluded, "the remedies provided in the MIOSHA statute are exclusive and not cumulative."[46]

Looking to the statute, then, the court found that:

> Nowhere in the statute, in its legislative history, nor in its statutory declaration of purpose and policy is there any provision that a private litigant can bring a civil action under the statute.
>
> In addition, there is no Michigan appellate court authority for allowing a private litigant to bring a civil action under the MIOSHA statute.
>
> To allow a private litigant to bring a civil action under the statute would circumvent the apparent legislative desire to channel claims under the Act through the Department of Labor as provided under M.C.L.A. § 408.1065; M.S.A., Section 17.50(65).

---

[39]Specific protections against retaliatory discharge include: Consumer Credit Protection Act, § 304 (a), 15 U.S.C. § 1674 (a) (1982); Fair Labor Standards Act, § 15 (a) (3), 29 U.S.C. § 215 (a) (3) (1982); Age Discrimination in Employment Act of 1967, § 4 (a), 29 U.S.C. § 623 (a) (1982); Occupational Health and Safety Act, § II (c), 29 U.S.C. § 660 (c) (1982); Vietnam Era Veterans Readjustment Act, 38 U.S.C. § 2021 (1982).

[40]*See, e.g.,* MASS. GEN. LAWS ANN. ch. 56, § 33 (1976); CAL. LAB. CODE § 1102 (West 1971).

[41]*See, e.g.,* Covell v. Spengler, 141 Mich. App. 76, 366 N.W.2d 76 (1985); Ohlsen v. DST Industries, Inc., 111 Mich. App. 580, 583, 314 N.W.2d 699, 701 (1982); Schroeder v. Dayton-Hudson Corp., 456 F. Supp. 652 (E.D. Mich. 1978) (plaintiff's claim of intentional infliction of emotional distress held to be exclusively covered by the Michigan Worker's Compensation Act).

[42]111 Mich. App. 580, 314 N.W.2d 699 (1982).

[43]M.C.L.A. § 408.1001 *et seq.*

[44]M.C.L.A. § 408.1011 (a).

[45]*Ohlsen,* 111 Mich. App. at 583, 314 N.W.2d at 701. The court did recognize that there was a common law remedy for a violation of the right to a safe place to work, but the common law right was exercisable only when a physical injury occurred (not upon mere allegation), giving rise to damages, and then the breach of the employer's duty to provide a safe place to work was argued to prove negligence. *Id.*

[46]*Id.* at 583, 314 N.W.2d at 701.

> Consistent with the language of M.C.L.A. § 408.1065; M.S.A. §
> 17.50(65), the Court finds that the language of M.C.L.A. §
> 408.1002(2); M.S.A. § 17.50(2)(2) does not evidence any statutorily
> stated public policy for allowing a private litigant to bring a civil
> action under the MIOSHA statute.
>
> Since Plaintiff cannot pursue a private civil action in this Court, he
> has failed to state a claim upon which relief can be granted. Accord-
> ingly, Defendant's Motion for Summary Judgment is granted.[47]

The federal courts, too, when applying Michigan law, generally
decline to permit a public policy wrongful discharge action where
statutory remedies exist. For instance, in *Parets v. Eaton Corp.,*[48]
the district court declined to extend the public policy exception to a
plaintiff who alleged that he was discharged due to his national origin. "Although in the total absence of such remedies, Michigan
courts might well apply such an exception," the court reasoned,
"plaintiff here had available to him adequate remedies. A remedy
was available to plaintiff under Title VII, Civil Rights Act of 1964
and also under Ohio law."[49]

Such a judicial stance was also evident in *Schroeder v. Dayton-
Hudson, Corp.,*[50] where the district court for the Eastern District of
Michigan refused to recognize the plaintiff's public policy cause of
action stemming from an allegation of age and/or sex discrimination. As the court observed:

> she [plaintiff] claims that she was fired because of her age and/or sex.
> While it would be against public policy if either of these reasons were
> the basis for her termination, statutory remedies have been provided
> to protect employees from discharge on the basis of sex or age, and it
> is not necessary to expand the public policy exception to provide pro-
> tection for employees for discharges based on status rather than
> affirmative conduct.[51]

Judicial curtailment of the possible grounds for a wrongful discharge lawsuit is welcomed by employers who are already facing litigation for employment decisions which were previously beyond the
courts' purview.

A recent case adds one qualifying footnote to the courts' general
denial of wrongful discharge actions where statutory remedies are
provided. In *Watassek v. Michigan Department of Mental Health,*[52]
the Michigan Court of Appeals held that the plaintiff could bring a

---

[47]*Id.* at 582-83, 314 N.W.2d at 700-701 (quoting trial judge with approval).

[48]479 F. Supp. 512, 518 (E.D. Mich. 1979).

[49]*Id.*

[50]448 F. Supp. 910 (E.D. Mich. 1978).

[51]*Id.* at 917.

[52]143 Mich. App. 556, 372 N.W.2d 617 (1985).

suit for retaliatory discharge, even though he had failed to exhaust administrative remedies, since he had been advised by the facility's personnel director that as a probationary employee he had no griev- ance rights, thereby effectively making any attempt to pursue administrative relief futile.[53] The *Watassek* decision permitting the retaliatory discharge suit despite the availability of adminstrative remedies, it should be noted, turns predominantly on the particular facts of the case, namely that the plaintiff's supervisor had misled the plaintiff as to his grievance rights. As such, one would expect its precedential value to be confined to the particular fact situation.

Implied Statutory Obligations. In the final category, Michigan courts have demonstrated a proclivity in some instances to recog- nize a public policy exception despite the lack of statutory provision explicitly guaranteeing employees protection from discharge. For example, in *Sventko v. Kroger Co.,*[54] the plaintiff alleged that she had been discharged solely in retaliation for filing a lawful claim for workers' compensation. Although the workers' compensation act did not at that time specifically prohibit retaliatory discharges,[55] the court nonetheless found that the act conferred upon the plaintiff a right to receive compensation. "The court reasoned that the well- recognized legislative policy underlying the workers' compensation act was an equitable compromise: employees exchanged their specu- lative tort suits arising out of work-related injuries for guaranteed and expeditiously provided financial and medical benefits; employ- ers exchanged their unpredictable negligence liability for more cer- tain statutory liability under the act."[56] As the *Sventko* court explained:

> The function of the workers' compensation act is to place the finan- cial burden of industrial injuries upon the industries themselves, and spread that cost ultimately among the consumers.
> This humane legislation was developed because the industrializa- tion of our civilization had left in its wake a trail of broken bodies.

---

[53]*Id.* at 563, 372 N.W.2d at 620.

[54]69 Mich. App. 644, 245 N.W.2d 151 (1976).

[55]The Act was amended in 1981 by prohibiting discharges in retaliation for exercis- ing rights established by the Act. The statute now provides:

> A person shall not discharge an employee or in any manner discriminate against an employee because the employee filed a complaint or instituted or caused to be instituted a proceeding under or because of the exercise by the employee on behalf of himself or herself or others of a right afforded by this act.

M.C.L.A. § 418.301 (11).

[56]*Clifford,* 419 Mich. at 365, 353 N.W.2d at 473 (Williams, C.J., dissenting).

Employers were absolved from general liability for negligence, in exchange for the imposition of more certain liability under the act.[57]

So, the *Sventko* court found that the public policy expressed in this compromise would be contravened if employers were allowed to take advantage of their exemption from general liability and yet circumvent their statutorily imposed duty to provide benefits.[58] Therefore, the plaintiff's allegation that she was discharged in retaliation for exercising the statutorily granted right to compensation benefits was found by the court to state a cause of action.[59]

Later, in *Goins v. Ford Motor Co.,*[60] the Michigan Court of Appeals reaffirmed that it was contrary to the public policy of the state for an employer to discharge an employee in retaliation for filing a workers' compensation claim and extended this exception to cover an employer's retaliatory discharge because the worker filed a claim against *any* employer:

> We find no reason, as defendant suggests, to limit this rule only to employers who fire employees who file claims against them rather than against previous employers. The public policy extends to situations such as this where the employee argues an unlawful or retaliatory discharge because he or she filed a workers' compensation claim against *any employer, including a previous employer.*[61]

Procedurally, it should be noted that the *Goins* court affirmed the trial court's holding concerning the plaintiff's burden of proof in a workers' compensation public policy exception. Specifically, the court held that where the plaintiff claims that he was wrongfully discharged for filing a workers' compensation claim, he "has the burden of proving that the filing of the worker's compensation claim was a significant factor in defendant's decision to discharge the plaintiff."[62] It is not necessary then that the plaintiff establish that the filing of the claim was the sole, or even the motivating factor, but only that it was a significant element. Obviously, this burden of proof invites the court to set the threshold of meeting this burden very low, thereby allowing a flood of possible litigation.

---

[57]*Sventko,* 69 Mich. App. at 648, 245 N.W.2d at 153, *quoting* Whethro v. Awkerman, 383 Mich. 235, 249, 174 N.W.2d 785, 787 (1970).

[58]*See Sventko,* 69 Mich. App. at 648, 245 N.W.2d at 153-154.

[59]Protection against discharge in retaliation for the exercise of constitutional and statutory rights was also extended in Pilarowski v. Brown, 76 Mich. App. 666, 257 N.W.2d 211 (1977) (employee wrongfully discharged for exercising right to free speech); Hrab v. Hayes Albion Corp., 103 Mich. App. 90, 302 N.W.2d 606 (1981) (employee discharged for filing workers' compensation claim).

[60]131 Mich. App. 185, 347 N.W.2d 184 (1983).

[61]*Id.* at 194, 347 N.W.2d at 189 (emphasis added).

[62]*Id.* at 198, 347 N.W.2d at 191.

In discussing the public policy exception as related to workers' compensation claims, it is important to compare those cases in which the courts have not recognized the plaintiff's attempt to establish a public policy cause of action. Most important in this area is the recent Michigan Supreme Court case, *Clifford v. Cactus Drilling Co.*[63] In *Clifford*, the state supreme court reversed a court of appeals decision and held that the plaintiff's allegation that he was discharged as a result of an absence from work because of a work-related injury (for which he received workers' compensation) did *not* state a cause of action under any public policy exception to the employment-at-will doctrine.[64]

As the court reasoned, the plaintiff's claim did not fall within the public policy umbrella created by *Sventko:*

> Certainly an employer's power to discharge an employee at will should not prevail when that power is exercised to prevent an employee from asserting his statutory rights under the Worker's Disability Compensation Act. The case before us presented no evidence or reason to infer that plaintiff's statutorily conferred right to claim workers' disability compensation benefits was chilled in any way. Plaintiff made no claim that he was deprived of his legal rights under the Worker's Disability Compensation Act. Plaintiff did not allege that he was discharged in retaliation for filing a claim for compensation. Plaintiff alleged that he was fired because he missed work because of a work-related injury for which he had already received workers' disability compensation benefits.[65]

Miscellaneous Cases. As the above cases indicate, any concept as nebulous as public policy can pose problems of definition. In order to gauge more accurately the boundaries of public policy, it is necessary to review briefly several incidents where the Michigan courts have refused to recognize novel attempts to expand the limits of the public policy exception.

In *Suchodolski v. Michigan Consolidated Gas Co.,*[66] the Michigan Supreme Court was unable to find a contravention of the state's public policy. In that case the plaintiff alleged that he had been discharged in retaliation for reporting improper accounting practices and poor internal management of defendant public utility to his superiors. The plaintiff proffered two sources of public policy: the Code of Ethics of the Institute of Internal Auditors and the exten-

---

[63] 419 Mich. 356, 353 N.W.2d 469 (1984).

[64] *Id.* at 361, 353 N.W.2d at 470.

[65] *Id.* at 360-61, 353 N.W.2d at 471. *See also* Schroeder v. Dayton-Hudson Corp., 448 F. Supp. 910, 917 (E.D. Mich. 1978).

[66] 412 Mich. 692, 696-97, 316 N.W.2d 710, 715 (1982).

sive regulations of the accounting systems of public utilities.[67] The court rejected both grounds, holding first that "[t]he code of ethics of a private association does not establish public policy," and second that "[t]he regulation of the accounting systems of utilities is not, as is the worker's compensation statute, directed at conferring rights on the employees."[68] Thus, the court concluded that the case "involve[d] only a corporate management dispute and lack[ed] the kind of violation of a clearly mandated public policy that would support a cause of action for retaliatory discharge."[69]

Similarly, in *Percival v. General Motors Corp.*,[70] the federal district court for the Eastern District of Missouri, applying Michigan law, found that the plaintiff in that case did not state a cause of action where he alleged that his discharge resulted from his attempt to correct misleading information. In *Percival*, the plaintiff claimed that "he was forced out in retaliation for trying to correct misleading information given out by GM regarding its work on alternative power plants," going to such efforts as writing letters to corporate superiors and even notifying the Securities Exchange Commission.[71] The court distinguished this case from those such as *Trombetta*, where the plaintiff was discharged for refusing to commit an illegal act. "The mere fact that the discharge was unjustified," the court held, "does not give rise to a cause of action in the absence of contractual, statutory or public policy considerations."[72] For, as the court viewed the fact situation:

> Even if the plaintiff were to prove that he was discharged in retaliation for his efforts as a responsible corporate employee to correct false impressions given by the corporation to outside business associates and to urge corporate management itself to correct misleading information conveyed to the public in possible violation of the securities laws, it is in the opinion of this court that his discharge did not involve a breach of public policy sufficient to state a cause of action for wrongful or retaliatory discharge.[73]

---

[67]*Id.* at 696, 316 N.W.2d at 712, *citing* M.C.L. § 483.113; M.S.A. § 22.1323.

[68]*Suchodolski*, 412 Mich. at 696-97, 316 N.W.2d at 712.

[69]*Id.* at 696, 316 N.W.2d at 712.

[70]400 F. Supp. 1322 (E.D. Mo. 1975) (applying Michigan law).

[71]*Id.* at 1324.

[72]*Id.*

[73]*Id. See also* Ledl v. Quik Pik Food Stores, Inc., 133 Mich. App. 583, 588, 349 N.W.2d 529, 532 (1984) (general manager of a store, who, with all other store employees, was discharged for failure to correct inventory shortages, failed to allege actionable claim for wrongful discharge on theory that the discharge violated state public policy).

The cases involving the evolution of the public policy exception to the employment-at-will doctrine in Michigan reveal that several important competing interests are at stake.[74] "An employer's ability to make and act upon independent assessments of an employee's abilities and job performance as well as business needs is essential to the free enterprise system."[75] The courts, however, are "also cognizant that social conditions have changed since the development of the employment-at-will doctrine."[76] And, "although a large sector of the workforce is protected against discharge without just cause, the majority of today's workforce does not enjoy the protection of a collective bargaining agreement or civil service regulation."[77]

"Of course, it is not the courts' function to legislate employee job security."[78] "Nonetheless," as Michigan Supreme Court Chief Justice Williams reasons, "the employee does have an interest in protection from discharge based solely on refusal to act in an unlawful manner or attempt to exercise a statutorily or constitutionally conferred right," and "society has an interest in ensuring that its laws and important public policies are not contravened."[79] As the Michigan case law illustrates, "[t]hese interests can be equitably balanced by recognizing an action for retaliatory discharge only when important and concretely articulated public policies are contravened."[80] Otherwise, to the extent that amorphous and undefined public policy exceptions are permitted to be the basis for litigation and potential recovery, the courts will be performing the role reserved for the elected legislature.

CONTRACT EXCEPTIONS

"Although Michigan has followed several other states in its construction of the public policy exception, it has substantially departed from the weight of authority in its approach to implied contracts" arising from handbooks, personnel policies, and other representations.[81] "Michigan does recognize the theory of implied contract as an exception to the general rule of termination at will by

---

[74]*See Clifford*, 419 Mich. at 367, 353 N.W.2d at 474 (Williams, C.J., dissenting).
[75]*Id.*
[76]*Id.*
[77]*Id.*
[78]*Id.* at 368, 353 N.W.2d at 474.
[79]*Id.*
[80]*Id. citing with approval* Adler v. American Standard Corp., 291 Md. 31, 432 A.2d 464 (1981).
[81]Bureau of National Affairs (BNA), *The Employment-At-Will Issue: A BNA Special Report*, DAILY LAB. REP. No.225, at 48 (Nov. 19, 1982).

either party."[82] As the case law indicates, "[r]ules and understandings promulgated and fostered by the employer may justify a legitimate claim to continued employment" under Michigan law.[83]

Employee Handbooks and Personnel Policies

The seminal case recognizing the implied contract exception in Michigan is *Toussaint v. Blue Cross and Blue Shield of Michigan*,[84] where the Supreme Court of Michigan held in a 4-3 decision that "employers may have an implied contractual obligation not to discharge employees without just cause, based on expressed terms of an employment agreement or an employee's legitimate expectations derived from the employer's policy statement."[85] In addition, the *Toussaint* court found that "oral statements made during a hiring interview to the effect that an employee would remain at work as long as he did his job," could also form the source of an employee's legitimate expectations of definite employment.[86]

In *Toussaint*, the plaintiff was discharged from Blue Cross after being employed with the company for five years in a middle management position.[87] Plaintiff Toussaint commenced the action against his former employer, claiming that the discharge breached his employment agreement which permitted discharge only for just cause.[88] As Toussaint testified at trial, he had been assured by an officer of Blue Cross at his hiring interview that "as long as I did my job, I would be with the company" until the mandatory retirement age.[89] The officer then gave him a Supervisory Manual. When Toussaint asked about his job security, the officer responded that "if . . . [he] came to Blue Cross . . . [he] wouldn't have to look for another job because he knew of no one ever being discharged."[90] Then, on cross-examination, when Toussaint was asked whether he had an employ-

---

[82]K. McCulloch, Termination of Employment (1983), at ¶ 20,032 [hereinafter cited as McCulloch, Termination].
[83]*Id.*
[84]408 Mich. 579, 292 N.W.2d 880 (1980).
[85]D. Cathcart, *et al.*, The Developing Law of Wrongful Terminations (1983) at 88 [hereinafter cited as Cathcart, *et al.*, Wrongful Terminations].
[86]*Id. See* Farrell v. Automobile Club of Michigan, 31 Daily Lab. Rep. at A-9 (Feb. 18, 1987) where a Michigan appellate court held that oral promises may modify the written terms of an employment contract.
[87]*Toussaint*, 408 Mich. at 595, 292 N.W.2d at 883.
[88]*Id.*
[89]*Id.* at 597 note 5, 292 N.W.2d at 884 note 5.
[90]*Id.*

ment contract, he responded, "'I certainly felt I did,' and that the pertinent sections of the Supervisory Manual were part of ... [his] 'contract'."[91]

The Supreme Court reasoned that the traditional employment-at-will rule set out in *Lynas* was useful only as a rule of construction, rather than as a principle of substantive contract law.[92] The Court focused instead on the employer's actions in this case and the environment they created in the working relationship, noting that:

> It is enough that the employer chooses, presumably in his own interest, to create an environment which the employee believes, whatever the personnel policies and practices, they are established and official at any given time, purport to be fair, and are applied consistently and uniformly to each employee. The employer has then created a situation 'instinct with obligation'.[93]

Furthermore, once the employer has acted to create such a situation "instinct with obligation," the actions of the employee appear in the court's eye to be largely irrelevant since:

> [W]here an employer chooses to establish such policies and practices and makes them known to its employees, the employment relationship is presumably enhanced. The employer secures an orderly, cooperative and loyal workforce, and the employee the peace of mind associated with job security and the conviction that he will be treated fairly. *No pre-employment negotiations need take place and the parties' minds need not meet on the subject;* nor does it matter that the employee knows nothing of the particulars of the employer's policies and practices or that the employer may change them unilaterally.[94]

Under such reasoning, then, it was "unnecessary for Toussaint to prove reliance on the policies set forth in the manual."[95]

Naturally, the expansive employer liability arising from personnel handbooks established by the *Toussaint* court made many companies wary. Subsequent cases, however, defined some of the outer boundaries of employers' liability under *Toussaint*. For instance, in *Schwartz v. Michigan Sugar Company,*[96] the Michigan Court of Appeals held that "a mere subjective expectancy on the part of an employee" will not create a legitimate expectation capable of sustaining a breach of contract claim.

---

[91]*Id.*

[92]*See Toussaint*, 408 Mich. at 600, 292 N.W.2d at 885.

[93]*Id.* at 613, 292 N.W.2d at 892, *quoting* Wood v. Lucy, Lady Duff-Gordon, 222 N.Y. 88, 118 N.E. 214 (1917); McCall Co. v. Wright, 133 A.D. 62, 117 N.Y.S. 775 (1909).

[94]*Toussaint*, 408 at 613, 292 N.W.2d at 892 (emphasis added).

[95]*Id.* note 25, 292 N.W.2d at 892 note 5.

[96]106 Mich. App. 471, 478, 308 N.W.2d 459, 462 (1981).

In *Schwartz*, the plaintiff based his implied contract claim on his belief that "the company was originally a closely-knit family operation ... with virtually no employee turnover."[97] Furthermore, "literature on the company's pension plan indicated that all employees would be eligible unless the particular employee 'was injurious or detrimental to the interests of the company.'"[98] From this, then, the "plaintiff concluded that it was a 'foregone conclusion that if you perform your job competently and are an asset to the company, the natural expectation is that you will continue to be employed by the company.'"[99]

The *Schwartz* court, however, distinguished these circumstances from *Toussaint*, holding that they did not meet the requirements of a contract implied in fact. Quoting earlier Michigan cases, the court noted that:

> A contract implied in fact arises under circumstances which, according to the ordinary course of dealing and common understanding of men, show a mutual intention to contract. A contract is implied in fact where the intention as to it is not manifested by direct or explicit words between the parties, but is to be gathered by implication or proper deduction from the conduct of the parties, language used or things done by them, or other pertinent circumstances attending the transaction.[100]

Therefore, although rules and understandings promulgated and fostered by the employer may justify a legitimate claim to continued employment, as in *Toussaint*, it is clear under Michigan law that a mere subjective expectancy on the part of the employee will not create such a legitimate claim.[101] The *Schwartz* decision's limitation of *Toussaint* has been followed by federal courts applying Michigan law.[102]

---

[97]*Id.*

[98]*Id.*

[99]*Id.*

[100]*Id.* at 477, 308 N.W.2d at 461, *quoting* Erickson v. Goodell Oil Co., Inc., 384 Mich. 207, 211-12, 180 N.W.2d 798 (1970) (citations omitted).

[101]*Schwartz*, 106 Mich. App. at 478, 308 N.W.2d at 462.

[102]*See, e.g.,* Wickes v. Olympic Airways, 745 F.2d 363 (6th Cir. 1984) where the Sixth Circuit affirmed the district court's granting of summary judgment against the plaintiff on his breach of implied contract claim, holding that:

> [i]t appears that Olympic made no representations, oral or written, from which plaintiff could derive a legitimate expectation that he could be terminated only for good cause. Therefore, plaintiff cannot maintain a cause of action for breach of an implied employment contract based on *Toussaint*.

Id. at 370; *see also* Katch v. Speidel Div. of Textron, Inc., No. 80-74383 (E.D. Mich. 1982).

"The Michigan Supreme Court re-emphasized the limited nature of the *Toussaint* holding in *Valentine v. General American Credit, Inc.*"[103] Justice Levin, who wrote the court's opinion in *Toussaint*, made it clear in writing the Valentine decision that: "The only right held in *Toussaint* to be enforceable was the right that arose out of the promise not to terminate except for cause."[104] In other words, *Toussaint* did not create a "new special right."[105] Even before *Valentine*, the Michigan courts interpreted the *Toussaint* holding narrowly.[106] In *Wickes v. Olympic Airways*,[107] for example, the Sixth Circuit Court of Appeals upheld a lower court's rejection of the plaintiff's claims to a just cause dismissal. The court stressed that *Toussaint* held "that oral representations and written policy statements, ensuring termination only for good cause, can sustain a breach of contract claim."[108] As the *Wickes* court held *Toussaint* is of limited applicability since it provides only "the at-will presumption to be overcome by evidence of oral representations or written policy statements *on which the employee based a legitimate expectation that he would be terminated only for cause.*"[109]

When plaintiffs have based their implied contract claims solely on oral representations made with their employers, the Michigan courts have been hesitant to apply the expansive *Toussaint* rule unless there is a showing of sufficient evidence that the oral contract was other than at-will. In *Crownover v. Sears, Roebuck and Co.*,[110] for example, former full-time employees of Sears, who had been hired under oral employment contracts, sued the corporation for breach of a contract of continued employment upon their discharge following the company's restructuring. Applying Michigan law, the United States Court of Appeals for the Sixth Circuit concluded simply that "the law of the State of Michigan to date appears to be settled that oral employment contracts are terminable at will by either party,"[111] and that there was no legal basis for the employees' "reliance upon

---

[103] Amicus Brief of the Equal Employment Advisory Council in Support of Defendant, Boynton v. TRW, Inc., No. 83-1773 (E.D. Mich. June 1986) at 22, *citing* Valentine v. General American Credit, Inc., 420 Mich. 256, 362 N.W.2d 628 (Mich. 1984).

[104] *Valentine*, 362 N.W.2d at 629.

[105] *Id.*

[106] Amicus Brief in Support of Defendant, at 23.

[107] 745 F.2d 363 (6th Cir. 1984).

[108] *Id.* at 369.

[109] *Id.* (emphasis added).

[110] 594 F.2d 565 (6th Cir. 1979) (applying Michigan law).

[111] *Id.* at 566, *citing* Lynas v. Maxwell Farms, 279 Mich. 684, 273 N.W. 315 (1937); Dunn v. Goebel Brewing Co., 357 Mich. 693, 99 N.W.2d 380 (1959); McLaughlin v. Ford Motor Co., 269 F.2d 120 (6th Cir. 1959).

their prior participation in the Savings and Profit Sharing Fund of Sears Employees as having any effect upon creating continuing rights to employment."[112]

Later, in *Hollowell v. Career Decisions, Inc.*,[113] a plaintiff claimed she was not an at-will employee because of her employer's representations alleging that her employment relationship with Career Decisions was an "ongoing affiliation," and that her employment was to be "indefinite, but with a minimum of terms of one year or more."[114] The court found that it was questionable that this allegation alone would constitute a legal claim upon which relief could be granted since "a term of 'one year or more' is hardly definite."[115] Furthermore, the plaintiff's own admissions in her deposition that there was "no specific time involved at any point" led the court to conclude that a breach of contract claim relying on the *Toussaint* reasoning could not be sustained.[116]

Disclaimers

Courts at both the state and federal levels interpreting Michigan law have upheld the use of disclaimers by employers to protect themselves from wrongful discharge litigation. Employment applications and personnel manuals providing that employment can be terminated by either party with or without notice and with or without cause, effectively bar the employee's claim that he had a right to a just cause determination prior to his severance under Michigan law.[117]

Novosel v. Sears, Roebuck & Co.[118] is illustrative of the cases in this area of at-will law. In *Novosel,* the employment relationship between the plaintiff and the defendant was expressly set out in the employment application, which governed the rights and duties of the parties. The contract, which was signed by the plaintiff, stated in relevant part that:

---

[112]*Crownover,* 594 F.2d at 566.

[113]100 Mich. App. 561, 298 N.W.2d 915 (1980).

[114]*Id.* at 568, 298 N.W.2d at 919.

[115]*Id.*

[116]*Id.* at 568-69, 298 N.W.2d at 919. *See also* Crownover v. Sears, Roebuck & Co., 594 F.2d 565 (6th Cir. 1979) (oral employment contracts are terminable at will by either party in Michigan).

[117]*See, e.g.,* Ledl v. Quik Pik Food Stores, Inc., 133 Mich. App. 583, 349 N.W.2d 529 (Mich. App. 1984); Novosel v. Sears, Roebuck & Co., 495 F. Supp. 344 (E.D. Mich. 1980).

[118]495 F. Supp. 344 (E.D. Mich. 1980).

In consideration of my employment, I agree to conform to the rules and regulations of Sears, Roebuck and Co., and my employment and compensation can be terminated, with or without cause, and with or without notice, at any time, at the option of either the Company or myself. I understand that no store manager or representative of Sears, Roebuck and Co., other than president or vice-president of the Company, has any authority to enter into any agreement for employment for any specified period of time, or to make any agreement contrary to the foregoing.[119]

As the *Novosel* court noted, this type of contract, limiting the employment relationship to an at-will arrangement, was "expressly provided for by *Toussaint.*"[120]

So, as the *Novosel* court concluded, the plaintiff had no right to a just cause determination prior to his dismissal.[121] Moreover, Sears did not abridge any legal duty owed to the plaintiff by terminating his employment.[122] Based on the agreement set forth in the application, the court reasoned that "there ... [was] no way that the plaintiff could reasonably have had a legitimate expectation of a right to a just cause determination prior to termination."[123] And, for this reason, the court dismissed the plaintiff's wrongful discharge cause of action.[124]

---

[119]*Id.* at 346.

[120]*Id.* In particular, the *Novosel* court noted that the Supreme Court of Michigan in *Toussaint v. Blue Cross & Blue Shield of Michigan,* 408 Mich. 579, 292 N.W.2d 880 (1980), had expressly recognized that employers may limit the nature of the employment relationship via contract:

Employers are assuredly free to enter into employment contracts terminable at will without assigning cause. We hold only that an employer's express agreement to terminate only for cause, or statements of company policy and procedure to that effect, can give rise to rights enforceable in contract....

If Blue Cross or Masco had desired, they could have established a company policy of requiring prospective employees to acknowledge that they served at the will or the pleasure of the company and, thus, have avoided the misunderstandings that generated this litigation...

Where the employer has not agreed to job security, it can protect itself by entering into a written contract which explicitly provides that the employee serves at the pleasure or at the will of the employer or as long as his services are satisfactory to the employer.

Novosel, 495 F. Supp. at 346, *quoting Toussaint v. Blue Cross,* 408 Mich. at 610, 612, 612 note 24, 292 N.W.2d at 890, 891, 891 note 24.

[121]*Novosel,* 495 F. Supp. at 346.

[122]*Id.*

[123]*Id.*

[124]*Id.* The court in *Novosel* also dismissed plaintiff's tort claims that the employer's action in discharging his employee gave rise to a cause of action for the intentional infliction of emotional distress. *Id.* at 347.

Later, the Michigan Court of Appeals in *Ledl v. Quik Pik Food Stores, Inc.*,[125] held that employers are able to place disclaiming language in the employment contract even *during* the course of employment. In *Ledl*, the plaintiff was discharged from her position as a general manager in the defendant's store for failing to correct inventory shortages.[126] Plaintiff brought a breach of contract claim against her former employer, claiming that she had been told when she accepted employment that she would continue to be employed so long as her performance was satisfactory and cited *Toussaint* in support of her argument.[127]

Approximately seven and one-half years after the plaintiff in *Ledl* was hired by the defendant, she signed an employment agreement which contained language almost identical to that discussed in *Novosel* above. Specifically, the agreement which the plaintiff signed, stated in relevant part that:

> Our Quik Pik Store Employee Policies are the basis of our operations. They are central to the agreement you are undertaking with Quik Pik. They clarify for everyone exactly what is acceptable job performance and employee conduct and what is not.
>
> You will be held fully accountable for abiding by the Policies expressed in your store copy of Quik Pik Policies/Procedures manual. Abiding by these Policy statements is a job requirement. In no fashion does this material or anything else presented to you in written or verbal form serve as a guarantee of your future employment with Quik Pik.
>
> In consideration of my employment with Quik Pik, I agree to conform to the rules and policies of Quik Pik, and that my employment and compensation can be terminated, with or without cause, and with or without notice at any time at the option of the Company or myself. I understand that no Supervisor or representative of Quik Pik Food Stores, Inc., other than the President of the Company, has any authority to enter into any agreement contrary to the foregoing.[128]

Although the plaintiff alleged that such an agreement was an adhesion contract, was not supported by consideration, and, therefore, should not be given effect, the Court of Appeals disagreed, basing the decision on rationale found in *Toussaint*.[129] The *Ledl* court cited *Tousssaint* for the proposition that:

---

[125]133 Mich. App. 583, 588, 349 N.W.2d 529, 531 (1984).
[126]*Id.* at 586, 349 N.W.2d at 530.
[127]*Id.*, 349 N.W.2d at 531.
[128]*Id.* at 586-87, 349 N.W.2d at 531.
[129]*Id.* at 587-88, 349 N.W.2d at 531.

Employers can make known to their employees that personnel policies are subject to unilateral changes by the employer. Employees would then have no legitimate expectation that any particular policy will continue to remain in force. Employees could, however, legitimately expect that policies in force at any given time will be uniformly applied to all.[130]

The *Ledl* court concluded that since the "[p]laintiff does not allege, and the record does not indicate that defendant's employment policy was less than uniformly applied," it could "find no grounds for invalidating the employment agreement signed by plaintiff at defendant's request some six months prior to her termination."[131] Accordingly, the court dismissed the breach of contract claim.[132]

Promissory Estoppel

Michigan courts have recognized the use of the equitable principle of promissory estoppel as a means to limit an employer's right to terminate its at-will employees. According to Michigan case law, "[t]he elements of equitable or promissory estoppel are: (1) a promise; (2) that the promisor should reasonably have expected to induce action of a definite and substantial character on the part of the promisee; (3) which in fact produced reliance or forbearance of that nature; and (4) in circumstances such that the promise must be enforced if injustice is to be avoided."[133]

The leading Michigan case recognizing the promissory estoppel argument is *Rowe v. Noren Pattern & Foundry Co.*[134] In that case, the Michigan Court of Appeals considered the breach of oral contract claim of a maintenance worker who had given up a virtually assured position and pension for the rest of his life at his former job in exchange for the promise of a new job which would provide the protection of union membership.[135] According to the oral agreement between the parties, the plaintiff was to become a member of the union after he had worked for the defendant for forty-five days, after

---

[130]*Id.* at 588, 349 N.W.2d at 531, *quoting Toussaint,* 408 Mich. at 613, 619.

[131]*Ledl,* 133 Mich. App. at 588, 349 N.W.2d at 531.

[132]*Id.*, 349 N.W.2d at 531-32.

[133]Schipani v. Ford Motor Co., 102 Mich. App. 606, 612-13, 302 N.W.2d 307, 310 (1981), *citing* McMath v. Ford Motor Co., 77 Mich. App. 721, 725, 259 N.W.2d 140, 142 (1977).

[134]91 Mich. App. 254, 283 N.W.2d 713 (1979).

[135]*Id.* at 256-57, 283 N.W.2d at 717.

which time he could be dismissed only for just cause.[136] Plaintiff's
employment, however, was summarily terminated just two days
prior to the end of his 45-day probation period.[137]

Although the court noted that this was a hiring for an indefinite
period and could be classified as an at-will employment relationship,
it recognized that an exception to the rule existed, stating:

> [A]n exception to the [employment-at-will] rule is recognized where it
> is clear that the employer knew at the time of the hiring that the
> employee would not have left his former position except for the offer of
> a permanent position. Thus, where the job which is given up is "ten-
> ured" or permanent and the new job offer is also tenured or perma-
> nent, special consideration is found to exist.[138]

Moreover, the court concluded that this exception did apply to the
instant case since the court found that the plaintiff "would not have
switched jobs without coming under the protective umbrella of
union membership."[139] So, here, to alleviate the harsh result otherwise inflicted upon the plaintiff, the court held that contract for new
employment was *not* terminable at will by either party, even though
it was a contract for an indefinite period.[140] "Absent this type of
special circumstance, however," it is generally the rule that the
Michigan "courts will not find an exception to the ... [employment-
at-will] rule."[141]

CONCLUSION

The employment-at-will rule has never been codified by the Michigan legislature and exists in the state as a rule of common law. Over
the years, courts at both the state and federal levels have carved out
exceptions to the rule based on tort and contract theories.

On the tort side, Michigan does recognize a public policy tort
exception to the general at-will rule, but it is a limited one, requiring
the public policy to be statutorily defined. Public policy exceptions
recognized by the courts include such employer actions as discharge
following the filing of a worker's compensation claim and termination of an employee for his refusal to falsify state-required pollution
control reports. Michigan has enacted a Whistleblower's Protection
Act, designed to prohibit the discharge of employees who report a

---

[136]*Id.* at 256, 283 N.W.2d at 715.
[137]*Id.* at 254, 283 N.W.2d at 717-18.
[138]*Id.* at 259, 283 N.W.2d at 716 (citations omitted).
[139]*Id.* at 262, 283 N.W.2d at 717-18.
[140]*Id.* at 263-64, 283 N.W.2d at 718.
[141]McCulloch, Termination, *supra* note 82, at ¶ 20,035.

violation of the law. The Act may afford a new avenue on which wrongful discharge suits may advance; however, at this time invocation of the Act is still infrequent. In addition, Michigan has permitted a tort action for negligent discharge, applying a comparative negligence standard.[142] Furthermore, the Michigan courts have recognized a tort claim for the intentional infliction of emotional distress, but to date, no court has found sufficient evidence to allow such a claim to succeed.[143]

As noted earlier, Michigan does recognize the theory of implied contract as an exception to the employment-at-will doctrine. Statements of policy in handbooks and manuals can give rise to contractual rights even where there is no evidence that the parties agreed to such rights. That is, such policies need not be the subject of specific negotiations between the parties in order for them to be binding and enforceable in Michigan courts. The theory rests on the reasoning that wherever an employer engenders expectation among its employees of continued employment—either through oral or written assurances—a discharged employee is entitled to a jury's determination as to whether the discharge was for good cause. Furthermore, the Michigan courts have gone so far as to hold that under certain circumstances, oral promises made by the employer may negate the effect of a clause in the employment contract which expressly allows at-will discharge. The employer, however, is not bound by an employee's private, personal, or subjective expectations where there is no evidence of any employer assurances.

In the next chapter, discussion will focus on the status of the employment-at-will doctrine in Pennsylvania, a state in which the courts have generally permitted fewer exceptions to the at-will rule.

---

[142]*See id.* at ¶ 20,034, *citing* Chamberlain v. Bissell, Inc., 547 F. Supp. 1067 (W.D. Mich. 1982) (company's failure to inform employee at performance review that his job was in jeopardy held negligent).

[143]*See* McCulloch, Termination, *supra* note 82, at ¶ 20,034, *citing* Novosel v. Sears, Roebuck & Co., 495 F. Supp. 344 (E.D. Mich. 1980) (standard applied in order to sustain tort claim is that stress inflicted is so severe that no reasonable person could be expected to endure it).

CHAPTER VI

Pennsylvania

Although Pennsylvania has never codified the traditional employment-at-will rule into law, the doctrine was recognized by the state supreme court as early as 1891 in *Henry v. Pittsburgh & Lake Erie R.R. Co.*[1] In *Henry* the plaintiff ticket seller was discharged based on false allegations concerning the performance of his duties. Henry sought reinstatement with the railroad company but was refused and subsequently brought an action in trespass for damages claiming that the railroad supervisor "maliciously and without probable cause suspended the plaintiff from the position of traveling passenger-agent."[2] The court refused to recognize the suit, supporting its holding with the traditional employment-at-will rationale that "an employee may be discharged with or without probable cause at pleasure, unless restrained by contract, so that ... questions of malice and want of probable cause have ... [nothing] to do with the case."[3] This holding formed the foundation of Pennsylvania's judicial response to the employment-at-will question for the next eighty years.[4]

---

[1]139 Pa. 289, 21 A. 157 (1891).

[2]*Id.* at 290, 21 A. at 158.

[3]*Id.* at 297, 21 A. at 157, *quoted* in Note, *Public Policy Limitations to the Employment-At-Will Doctrine Since Geary v. United States Steel Corporation,* 44 U. Pitt. L. Rev. 1115, 1118 (1983) [hereinafter cited as Note, *Public Policy Limitations*].

[4]*See* Note, *Public Policy Limitations, supra* note 3, at 1118-19. For cases applying the traditional employment-at-will doctrine *see* Comment, *The Role of the Federal Courts in Changing State Law: The Employment-At-Will Doctrine in Pennsylvania,* 133 U. Pa. L. Rev. 227, 247 notes 109-110 [hereinafter cited as Comment, *The Role of Federal Courts*], *citing* Cummings v. Kelling Nut Co., 368 Pa. 448, 451, 84 A.2d 323, 325 (1949) (representations of anticipated success do not create promise of employment over period of time); Polk v. Steel Workers Organizing Committee, 360 Pa. 631, 634, 62 A.2d 850, 852 (1949) (employee may be discharged for refusing to join union); Trainer v. Laird, 320 Pa. 4414, 415, 183 A.40, 40 (1936) (contract fixing compensation annually does not defeat employment-at-will presumption).

TORT EXCEPTIONS

In *Geary v. United States Steel Corp.*,[5] decided in 1974, the Pennsylvania Supreme Court for the first time considered imposing common law "restrictions on an employer's power to discharge an at-will employee."[6] One of the plaintiff's main arguments in seeking recovery rested on a public policy limitation to the employer's power to terminate at will.[7]

Plaintiff Geary sold tubular products to the oil and gas industry. He claimed that his termination resulted from a disagreement concerning one of the company's new products which he believed had not been adequately tested and posed a serious danger to consumers.[8] Geary expressed to his superiors his apprehension about the product's potential danger, and was ordered to follow directions, which he agreed to do.[9] Nonetheless, he continued to voice his misgivings about the product and took his concerns to a vice president in charge of sales.[10] Following this, the product was reexamined and withdrawn from the market; soon after the product's removal, Geary was summarily removed from his job.[11] Geary brought suit against U.S. Steel alleging that he was discharged for expressing his concern beyond his immediate superiors and that such termination was "wrongful, malicious and abusive" since his primary interest at all times was the well-being of the company and the general interest of the public.[12]

In affirming the case's dismissal by the trial court, the Pennsylvania Supreme Court found that Geary had bypassed the employer's chain of command and created a nuisance.[13] Although the court acknowledged the possibility of employer abuse "where an employee must exercise independent, expert judgment in matters of product safety," the justices noted that Geary did not hold himself out as that sort of employee.[14] More importantly, the court declined to cre-

---

[5]456 Pa. 171, 319 A.2d 174 (1974).

[6]Note, *Public Policy Limitations, supra* note 3, at 1119.

[7]*See Geary,* 456 Pa. at 174, 319 A.2d at 175. Plaintiff also advanced a claim for tort relief based on an unjustified interference with prospective advantage. *Id.* at 178, 319 A.2d at 177. This claim was ultimately dismissed, as the court held that plaintiff did not establish defendant's specific intent which is necessary to succeed on a claim of alleged interference with a prospective relationship. *Id.* at 179, 319 A.2d at 177-78.

[8]*Id.* at 173, 319 A.2d at 175.

[9]*Id.*

[10]*Id.*

[11]*Id.* at 173-74, 319 A.2d at 175.

[12]*Id.* at 174, 319 A.2d at 175.

[13]*Id.* at 180, 319 A.2d at 178.

[14]*Id.* at 181, 319 A.2d at 178.

ate an overall nonstatutory cause of action, warning against "the possible impact of such suits on the legitimate interests of the employers in hiring and retaining the best personnel available" and fearful that suits of this nature "could well be expected to place a heavy burden upon our judicial system in terms of both an increased case load and thorny problems of proof."[15]

Despite the *Geary* court's rigid endorsement of the traditional employment-at-will rule, the justices did leave open what has now become a significant legal avenue for growth of the public policy argument. In dictum, the *Geary* court recognized that there are "areas of an employee's life in which his employer has no legitimate interest."[16] Intrusions into this domain, the court continued, might give rise to a legal cause of action where some "recognized facet of public policy is threatened."[17] Finally, the court concluded that:

> [W]here the complaint itself discloses a plausible and legitimate reason for terminating an at-will employment relationship and no clear mandate of public policy is violated thereby, an employee at-will has no right of action against his employer for wrongful discharge.[18]

It is important to note that the Pennsylvania Supreme Court's "holding in *Geary* is couched in negative terms."[19] That is, the "employee will have *no* cause of action for wrongful discharge on public policy grounds if a plausible and legitimate reason for the termination is disclosed in the complaint *and* no clear mandate of public policy is violated."[20]

Several claims have since been filed in state and federal courts in Pennsylvania attempting to fall within *Geary's* exception to the at-will rule. *Geary* implies that two different types of tort claims for wrongful discharge exist: a claim based on public policy and a claim based on a specific intent to harm the employee. Pennsylvania state appellate courts and the federal courts applying Pennsylvania law under diversity jurisdiction have found in varying factual circumstances instances of manifest public policy entitling the at-will employee an opportunity to pursue a cause of action for wrongful discharge.

---

[15]*Id.* at 181-82, 319 A.2d at 179 (citations omitted).
[16]*Id.* at 184, 319 A.2d at 179 (*quoted* in Note, *Public Policy Limitations, supra* note 3, at 1120).
[17]*Id.* (*quoted* in Note, *Public Policy Limitations, supra* note 3, at 1120).
[18]*Id.* at 184-85, 319 A.2d at 180 (*quoted* in Note, *Public Policy Limitations, supra* note 3, at 1120).
[19]Note, *Public Policy Limitations, supra* note 3, at 1123.
[20]*Id.*

In *Reuther v. Fowler & Williams, Inc.,* [21] for instance, "the Superior Court of Pennsylvania recognized the vital role the jury system plays in a democratic society and afforded it the necessary protection against infringement by employers."[22] In *Reuther,* "the employer ... allegedly acted maliciously, wrongfully, injuriously and intentionally in discharging the plaintiff in retaliation for exercising his duty to perform jury service."[23] Reversing the lower court's grant of nonsuit, the *Reuther* court relied on the dictum of *Geary,* interpreting it to mean that even where public policy has been violated, termination is proper *if* the employer has "a separate, plausible, and legitimate reason for the discharge."[24] In this case, the corporate defendant presented evidence that "the dismissal had been issued because Reuther had failed to inform the company of his absence due to jury service."[25] The court "intimated that this would be a sufficient justification for dismissal and that no liability would ensue" to the employer.[26]

Although no manifest public policy was found to exist in *Yaindl v. Ingersoll-Rand, Co.,* [27] the Pennsylvania Superior Court demonstrated a clear shift in the method by which it defined public policy. In the new test, courts "must weigh several factors, balancing against the appellant's interest in making a living, his employer's interest in running its business, its motive in discharging appellant and its manner of effecting the discharge, and any social interests or public policies that may be implicated in the discharge."[28]

The *Yaindl* balancing test, however apparently equitable, rests on an expansive interpretation of public policy. "A discharge motivated by bad faith or malice," the court held, "or [one] based on retaliation is not in the best interest of the economic system."[29] Furthermore,

---

[21]255 Pa. Super. 28, 386 A.2d 119 (1978).

[22]Note, *Public Policy Limitations, supra* note 3, at 1122.

[23]*Id.*

[24]*Id.* at 1123.

[25]*Id.*

[26]*Id.* Several critics have commented that the relative ease with which some courts accept the employer's justification for dismissal as sufficient to preclude liability is one of the major weaknesses of the *Geary* standard. *See id.* As one legal journalist noted, "[g]enerally tort law permits recovery where a tortious act is a substantial factor in causing injury, *even* if it is not the *only* factor. The *Geary* language should not be interpreted to limit the normal rules of proximate cause. *See* Bannon, *A Tort of Wrongful Discharge?: Geary v. U.S. Steel Revisited,* 3 PA. L. J. 1, 3 (Nov. 10, 1980) (emphasis added).

[27]281 Pa. Super. 560, 422 A.2d 611 (1980).

[28]*Id.* at 577, 422 A.2d at 620 (*quoted* in Comment, *The Role of the Federal Courts, supra* note 4, at 250-51).

[29]*Id.* at 573 note 5, 422 A.2d at 618 note 5 (*quoted* in Comment, The Role of the Federal Courts, *supra* note 4, at 251).

when assessing the weight of each factor, "the law ... accords *great* weight to the individual's right to earn a living."[30] As some have noted, *Yaindl* effectively established a just cause requirement for termination of an employee since "any discharge other than for just cause should tip the balance of the *Yaindl* test in favor of the employee."[31]

In other cases, Pennsylvania courts have recognized the public policy exception where discharge of an employee was the result of his refusal to take a polygraph test,[32] where discharge was the result of an employee's refusal to participate in an allegedly illegal price fixing scheme,[33] where discharge resulted from the filing of a worker's compensation claim,[34] where the discharge resulted from the employee's willingness to cooperate in a district attorney's investigation of the employer,[35] and where termination resulted from the employee's complaints of occupational hazards to a state agency.[36]

Overall, case history shows that the public policy exception in Pennsylvania applies only when a *clear* statutory mandate exists, consistent with the Pennsylvania Supreme Court's ruling in *Geary.* This general rule has been seriously undercut, however, by a recent case, *Novosel v. Nationwide Insurance Co.*[37] The plaintiff in *Novosel* had been employed by Nationwide for more than fifteen years and was summarily discharged when he refused to aid his employer's lobbying effort for the elimination of no-fault auto insurance. The United States Court of Appeals for the Third Circuit held that a discharged employee states a cause of action under Pennsylvania

---

[30]*Id.* at 584, 422 A.2d at 623-24 (*quoted* in Comment, *The Role of the Federal Courts, supra* note 4, at 251 note 137).

[31]Note, *The Role of Federal Courts, supra* note 4, at 230.

[32]*See, e.g.,* Molush v. Orkin Exterminating Co, Inc., 547 F. Supp. 54 (E.D. Pa. 1982); Perks v. Firestone Tire & Rubber Co. 611 F.2d 1363 (3d Cir. 1979).

[33]*See, e.g.,* McNulty v. Borden, Inc., 474 F. Supp. 1111 (E.D. Pa. 1979); Shaw v. Russell Trucking Line, Inc., 542 F. Supp. 776 (W.D. Pa. 1982) (court found no public policy tort under the federal antitrust laws for a discharge, but plaintiff allowed to sue directly under the Clayton Act).

[34]*See, e.g.,* Michelson v. Exxon Research & Engineering Co., 629 F. Supp. 418 (W.D. Pa. 1986); Rettinger v. American Can Co., 115 L.R.R.M. 3011 (M.D. Pa. 1984); Bonham v. Dresser Industries, Inc., 569 F.2d 187 (3d Cir. 1977), *cert. denied,* 439 U.S. 821 (1978). *But see* Rogers v. International Business Machines, 500 F. Supp. 867 (W.D. Pa. 1980) (alleged invasion of plaintiff's privacy in connection with an investigation leading to discharge does not violate public policy to such an extent as to permit a tort claim for wrongful discharge).

[35]*See* McLaurin v. Glen Mills School, No. 85-0146, slip op. (E.D. Pa. May 17, 1985).

[36]*See* Kilpatrick v. Delaware County Society for the Prevention of Cruelty to Animals, 632 F. Supp. 542 (E.D. Pa. 1986) (OSHA provides sufficient source of public policy under Pennsylvania law to support cause of action).

[37]721 F.2d 894 (3d Cir. 1983).

law "where the employment termination abridges a significant and recognized public policy."[38] The court proceeded to define public policy as follows:

> [A]n important public policy is in fact implicated wherever the power to hire and fire is utilized to dictate the terms of employee political activities. In dealing with public employees, the cause of action arises directly from the Constitution rather than from common law developments ... The inquiry before us is whether the concern for the rights of political expression and association which animated the public employee cases is sufficient to state a public policy under Pennsylvania law. While there are no Pennsylvania cases squarely on this point, we believe that the clear direction of the opinions promulgated by the state's courts suggests that this question be answered in the affirmative.[39]

The public policy theory recognized by the *Novosel* court is significant for two reasons. First, a *constitutional* right was the predicate of the decision, even though the case involved a private employer, and there was, therefore, no state action. Second, no "clear" *statutory* mandate was violated.[40] Moreover, the practical significance of the *Novosel* holding is enormous. Despite the absence of any legislative or constitutional protection of political speech in private-sector employment, the *Novosel* court prohibits employers from discharging employees who either refuse to support business-related political causes or who actively seek political changes detrimental to the employer's continued business operations.[41] Indeed, it is likely that the *Novosel* holding—were it to be given literal, unimpeded application in other cases—would eventually lead to the following situation feared by the *Geary* court:

> Given the rapidity of change in corporate personnel in the areas of employment not covered by labor agreements, suits like the one at bar could well be expected to place a heavy burden on our judicial system in terms of both an increased case load and the thorny problems of proof which would inevitably be presented. We agree with appellant, however, that these considerations do not in themselves justify denying a legal forum to a plaintiff with a justiciable claim ... Of greater concern is the possible impact of such suits on the legitimate interests

---

[38]*Id.* at 898.

[39]*Id.* at 900.

[40]*See* Perritt, *Employee Dismissal Law in Pennsylvania,* 1984 Pa. Bar Assoc. Quart., 212, 217-18 (October, 1984)[hereinafter cited as Perritt, *Pennsylvania Dismissal Law*].

[41]*See* Amicus Brief in Support of Appellee's Petition for Rehearing and Suggestion for Rehearing *en banc,* at 8, Novosel v. Nationwide Insurance Company.

of employers in hiring and retaining the best personnel available. The ever-present threat of suit might well inhibit the making of critical judgments by employers concerning employee qualifications.[42]

When the appellate court remanded the case for trial, it instructed the federal district court to consider several factors set forth for wrongful discharge cases by the Pennsylvania Superior Court in an earlier case, including: (i) the nature and motive of employer's conduct; (ii) the employee's interest in earning a living; (iii) the employer's interest in conducting a business; and (iv) society's interest in protecting both employer's and employee's interests.[43] The *Novosel* case ultimately was settled before the district court, prior to opening statements being presented to the jury. The entire proceedings surrounding settlement, as well as the actual settlement in the case, have been subjected to an order of confidentiality from the judge, and the record has been sealed.

Many view *Novosel* as an aberration in Pennsylvania law because in its attempt to apply state law the appellate court lost sight of the limitations of previous Pennsylvania decisions and was improperly influenced by changes in the at-will doctrine that courts in other states had adopted.[44] Indeed, as the panel in *Novosel* recognized, federal courts sitting in diversity are "not free to follow ... [their] own inclinations as to the manner in which the common law should develop,"[45] or "to decide whether creation of a common law remedy ... would be a wise and progressive social policy."[46] Furthermore, "[t]he Internal Operating Procedures of the Third Circuit do not allow one panel to reverse a prior panel's interpretation of state law unless an intervening state supreme court decision has clearly announced the change."[47] Moreover, "because district courts are

---

[42]*Geary*, 456 Pa. at 181-82, 319 A.2d at 179 (citations and footnotes omitted).

[43]*See Novosel*, 721 F.2d at 901 [*citing* Yaindl v. Ingersoll-Rand Co., 281 Pa. Super. 560, 574, 422 A.2d 611, 618 (1980)].

[44]Some commentators, however, argue that *Novosel* is a proper reflection of Pennsylvania at-will law in keeping with the spirit of *Erie R.R. v. Tompkins*, 304 U.S. 64 (1938). *See generally* Note, *The Role of Federal Courts, supra* note 4, at 259.

[45]*Novosel*, 721 F.2d at 897, *quoting* Bruffett v. Warner Communications, Inc., 692 F.2d 910, 918 (3d Cir. 1982). *See also* McKenna v. Ortho Pharmaceutical Corp., 622 F.2d 657 (3d Cir. 1980), *cert. denied,* 449 U.S. 976 (1981).

[46]*Bruffet*, 692 F.2d at 918.

[47]Comment, *The Role of Federal Courts, supra* note 4, at 228 note 6, *citing* Wolk v. Saks Fifth Avenue, Inc., 728 F.2d 221, 224 note 3 (3d Cir. 1984) [*citing* Third Cir. Internal Operating P. VIII (C) ("[N]o subsequent panel overrules a published opinion of a previous panel."), *reprinted in* 28 U.S.C.A. 78 (West Supp. 1984)].

bound by Third Circuit decisions, no change in the state law may be recognized by federal courts within the Third Circuit unless it is first announced by the state's supreme court."[48]

Several of the cases cited by Judge Adams in *Novosel* to support the public policy claim are not even Pennsylvania cases. For example, in support of the discussion of public policy torts, the court cited with approval *Palmateer v. International Harvester Co.*[49] This case, however, was expressly disavowed by a previous Third Circuit panel in *Bruffett v. Warner Communications, Inc.*[50] as being contrary to the reasoning of *Geary*. In addition, the court effectively substituted its own convictions concerning the constitutional free speech rights of private-sector employees by citing Pennsylvania cases involving free speech rights of public-sector employees and completely side-stepping any analysis of the state action requirement.[51] In short, it appears that the *Novosel* court derived its own interpretation of the proper direction of Pennsylvania wrongful discharge law instead of limiting its analysis to a prediction of how the Pennsylvania Supreme Court would decide the case.[52]

The suspicion that *Novosel* might represent a judicial overstep by the Third Circuit has been supported by subsequent federal and state cases which retreat from *Novosel's* expansive holding. In *Wolk v. Saks Fifth Avenue, Inc.*,[53] for instance, Judge Adams stepped back significantly from his *Novosel* stance, stressing instead the "gradual emergence" of change in the common law and stating that:

> *Novosel* must be understood against the backdrop of the limited role of a federal court sitting in diversity jurisdiction. While a federal court must be sensitive to the doctrinal trends of the jurisdiction whose law it applies, it is beyond the authority of a federal court in such circumstances to create entirely new causes of action.[54]

The *Wolk* court affirmed the lower court's dismissal of plaintiff's allegations that she was discharged for refusing her supervisor's sexual advances. The possible existence of an alternative remedy under the Pennsylvania Human Relations Act (PHRA), the court

[48]Comment, *The Role of Federal Courts, supra* note 4, at 228 note 6.
[49]*Novosel*, 721 F.2d at 899, *citing* Palmateer v. International Harvester Co., 95 Ill. 2d 124, 421 N.E.2d 876 (1981).
[50]692 F.2d 910, 918 (3d Cir. 1984).
[51]Amicus Brief in Support of Appellee's Motion for Rehearing *en banc, supra* note 39, at 12.
[52]*Id.* at 11.
[53]728 F.2d 221 (3d Cir. 1984).
[54]*Id.* at 223, *citing* Becker v. Interstate Properties, 569 F.2d 1203, 1206 (3d Cir. 1977), *cert. denied,* 436 U.S. 906 (1978) (*quoted* in Comment, *The Role of Federal Courts, supra* note 4, at 259 note 175).

reasoned, precluded the recognition of a wrongful discharge action under Pennsylvania state law.[55] Absent a pronouncement of change by the state supreme court, Judge Adams believed he could not depart from the holdings of federal precedent and concluded:

> [T]here is no indication that the Pennsylvania courts have as yet fashioned or indicated their intention to fashion a uniform just cause requirement for all discharges. Absent such a declaration on the part of the state courts, a federal tribunal sitting in diversity is not empowered to take this step for the state courts.[56]

In the Pennsylvania courts, *Martin v. Capital Cities Media, Inc.,*[57] demonstrated the limited nature of the public policy exception announced in *Novosel.* In *Martin,* an employee was discharged for placing an advertisement in a rival newspaper and claimed that his discharge was wrongful because of violations of his first amendment rights. The superior court dismissed the plaintiff's claim, however, holding that although free speech rights are guaranteed to all those who advertise, such rights cannot be extended to all aspects of life. Accordingly, the court held that the employer had legitimate business reasons which justified the employee's discharge.[58]

In several other cases, plaintiffs have attempted to transform allegations of age, sex, race, or handicap discrimination into wrongful discharge claims. Generally, these claimants maintain that the public policy against discrimination is statutorily defined, and violations of this policy, therefore, should be actionable under the tort exception to the employment-at-will rule. Federal courts, interpreting Pennsylvania case law, have rejected such reasoning, holding that the absence of an alternative remedy is a prerequisite for recognizing a wrongful discharge action under Pennsylvania law.[59] Since

---

[55]*Id.* at 224.

[56]*Id.* at 225 (*quoted* in Comment, *The Role of Federal Courts, supra* note 4, at 260).

[57]Slip op. (Pa. Super. June 12, 1986).

[58]*See also* Ferguson v. Freedom Forge Corp., 604 F. Supp. 1157 (W.D. Pa. 1985) (plaintiff's claim based on freedom of association dismissed); Veno v. Meredith, No. 00133, slip op. (Pa. Super. Sept. 22, 1986).

[59]*Wolk,* 728 F.2d at 224. *See also* Braun v. Kelsey-Hayes Co., No. 85-2377, slip op. (E.D. Pa. March 14, 1986) (OSHA provides exclusive remedy and preempts plaintiff's common law tort action).

the PHRA provides remedies for acts stemming from age, race, sex, or handicap discrimination, such wrongful discharge claims are barred.[60]

Pennsylvania courts have also decided several cases which argue that tort recovery can be based on a separate claim of "specific intent to harm employees without legitimate business justification."[61] In *Harrison v. Fred S. James, Inc.*,[62] for example, "the court stated in dictum that allegations of specific intent to harm may state a claim of wrongful discharge, while finding no claim made out on the facts of the case."[63] Recently, in *Tourville v. Inter-Ocean Insurance Co.*,[64] the superior court elaborated on the specific intent requirement. Specific intent, according to the court, can be successfully alleged if there is no other basis for the employer's action other than pure, unadulterated malevolence, or if the action was motivated by an ulterior purpose to harm the employee.[65] In *Lekich v. International Business Machines*,[66] however, the court held that "no tort claim exists unless a public policy is violated by the discharge."[67]

Pennsylvania does recognize the tort of intentional infliction of emotional distress. In order for a claim to be allowed, Pennsylvania law follows the general rule that the employer's conduct must be "particularly egregious."[68] In *Shaffer v. National Can Corp.*,[69] for example, a claim was permitted where the employer used his "position of authority to gain sexual favors and to intimidate."[70] In contrast, "no cause of action was found where an employee was induced

[60]PA. STAT. ANN. tit. 43, §§ 951-963 (Purdons 1964 & Supp. 1986-87). *See also* Murray v. Commercial Union Insurance Co., 782 F.2d 432 (3d Cir. 1986); Lofton v. Wyeth Laboratories, Inc., No. 84-2581 (E.D. Pa. June 18, 1986); Rettinger v. American Can Co., 574 F. Supp. 306 (M.D. Pa. 1983); Bruffett v. Warner Communications, Inc., 534 F. Supp. 375 (E.D. Pa. 1982), *aff'd*, 69 F.2d 910 (3d Cir. 1982); Bonham v. Dresser Indus., Inc., 569 F.2d 187 (3d Cir. 1977), *cert. denied*, 439 U.S. 821 (1978); Wehr v. Burroughs Corp., 438 F. Supp. 1052 (E.D. Pa. 1977).
[61]Perritt, *Pennsylvania Dismissal Law*, *supra* note 38, at 217, *citing* Keddie v. Pennsylvania State University, 412 F. Supp. 1264 (M.D. Pa. 1976); O'Neill v. ARA Services, Inc., 457 F. Supp. 182 (E.D. Pa. 1978); Boreson v. Rohm & Haas, Inc., 526 F. Supp. 1230 (E.D. Pa. 1981). *Compare* Yaindl v. Ingersoll-Rand Co., 281 Pa. Super. 560, 573 note 5, 422 A.2d 611, 618 note 5 (1981) (specific intent tort theory merely a variant of the public policy tort theory).
[62]558 F. Supp. 438 (E.D. Pa. 1983).
[63]Perritt, *Pennsylvania Dismissal Law*, *supra* note 38, at 217.
[64]Slip op. (Pa. Super. March 4, 1986).
[65]*Id.* at 8.
[66]469 F. Supp. 485 (E.D. Pa. 1979).
[67]Perritt, *Pennsylvania Dismissal Law*, *supra* note 40, at 217.
[68]K. McCulloch, TERMINATION OF EMPLOYMENT (1984) at ¶ 20,034 [hereinafter cited as McCulloch, TERMINATION].
[69]565 F. Supp. 909 (E.D. Pa. 1983).
[70]McCulloch, TERMINATION, *supra* note 68, at ¶ 20,034.

to continue employment although the employer knew the employee might be forced to relocate,"[71] or "where the employee was harassed by being excluded and ignored."[72]

CONTRACT EXCEPTIONS

Pennsylvania state courts have been extremely unclear in their recognition of a cause of action for wrongful discharge based on implied contract theory. In fact, two panels of the Pennsylvania Superior Court have recently given conflicting signals regarding the application of the same legal theory, as will be discussed below. This judicial uncertainty has led employers, employees, and attorneys to pay special attention to this potentially explosive area of employment law.

Pennsylvania state and federal courts both permit recovery for wrongful discharge based on contract theory. Indeed, courts have provided much room for an employee to bring a cause of action on implied contract grounds. The Third Circuit, writing recently in *Novosel v. Nationwide Insurance Co.*,[73] held that an allegation that an employer's "custom, practice or policy created either a 'just cause' requirement or contractual procedures by which defendant failed to abide is a factual matter that should survive a motion to dismiss."[74] Earlier cases confirm the courts' leniency towards contract-based claims. For instance, in *Wagner v. Sperry Univac*,[75] a federal court "denied the employer's motion for summary judgment, holding that the plaintiff was entitled to prove an implied promise of employment tenure arising from the employer's written personnel policies establishing seniority as the criteria to be used in layoffs."[76]

Despite a clear history of case law revealing the courts' general openness to allowing contract-based claims to proceed, the judiciary's stance becomes increasingly difficult to decipher when interpreting the parties' intentions from surrounding circumstances. The case law will be reviewed along the three lines of contract doctrine upon which Pennsylvania courts have decided cases.

---

[71]*Id.* note 2, *citing* Cantilli v. GAF Corp., 531 F. Supp. 71 (E.D. Pa. 1982).

[72]McCulloch, Termination, *supra* note 62, at ¶ 20,034 note 3, *citing* Beidler v. W.R. Grace, Inc., 461 F. Supp. 1013 (E.D. Pa. 1978).

[73]721 F.2d 894 (3d Cir. 1983).

[74]*Id.* at 896.

[75]458 F. Supp. 505 (E.D. Pa. 1978).

[76]Perritt, *Pennsylvania Dismissal Law, supra* note 40, at 216.

At-Will Employment Doctrine

Express or Oral Guarantees

"Under Pennsylvania case law, vague promises of continued employment are ordinarily insufficient to overcome the employment-at-will doctrine. Thus, employment contracts for broad, unspecified durations, such as 'until retirement' or 'so long as you live,' do not generally constitute an implied contract for a reasonable period of time."[77] Factual circumstances can be used by the employee, however, to show that the parties intended a contractual relationship other than at-will.[78] For example, in *Lacacher v. Kerson*[79] the Superior Court found that oral promises of "permanent employment" made by the employer were sufficient to rebut the presumption of an at-will arrangement. More recently, the jury in *Forman v. BRI Corp.*[80] found that the employer's five-year business plan for the plaintiff's work, coupled with assurances made to the employee that the job was one in which to "stay and grow," was sufficient to establish an enforceable promise of employment security.[81]

Employee Handbooks and Personnel Policies

The use of employee handbooks or personnel policies as the basis of implied contract claims is one of the most dynamic and uncertain areas of employment-at-will law in Pennsylvania. The first Pennsylvania case to address the issue of the contractual force of employee manuals was *Richardson v. Charles Cole Memorial Hospital.*[82] In *Richardson*, a panel of the Superior Court expressly rejected the possibility that an enforceable promise of employment security could arise from a personnel handbook. The court reasoned that the policies in the hospital's manual providing for continued employment as long as work performed was satisfactory were gratuitous benefits and did not constitute part of the employment contract.[83] Soon after,

---

[77]McCULLOCH, TERMINATION, *supra* note 68, at ¶ 20,032, *citing* Adams v. Budd, No. 83-1080 (E.D. Pa. 1984); Forman v. BRI Corp., 532 F. Supp. 49 (E.D. Pa. 1982).
[78]*See* McCULLOCH, TERMINATION, *supra* note 68, at ¶ 20,032.
[79]158 Pa. Super. 437, 45 A.2d 245, *aff'd*, 355 Pa. 79, 48 A.2d 857 (1946).
[80]532 F. Supp. 49 (E.D. Pa. 1982).
[81]*Id.* at 50. *See also* discussion of *Forman* in Perritt, *Pennsylvania Dismissal Law*, *supra* note 40, at 216.
[82]466 A.2d 1084 (Pa. Super. 1983). Federal courts in Pennsylvania, however, had already decided handbook claims three times prior to *Richardson. See* Comment, *The Role of Federal Courts*, *supra* note 4, at 252 note 141, *citing* Rogers v. International Business Machines Corp., 500 F. Supp. 867 (W.D. Pa. 1980); Beidler v. W. R. Grace, Inc., 461 F. Supp. 1013 (E.D. Pa. 1978); Wagner v. Sperry Univac, 458 F. Supp. 505 (E.D. Pa. 1978).
[83]*Richardson*, 466 A.2d at 1090.

in *Banas v. Matthews International Corp.*,[84] another panel of the same court held that "a manual published or authorized by an employer and distributed to an at-will employee becomes part of the parties' employment contract," and such contract could be breached by dismissing the employee in contravention of the manual.[85] The *Banas* panel's decision attaching contractual significance to employee manuals, in direct contradiction of the *Richardson* holding, rests on non-Pennsylvania precedent. In arriving at its final holding, the *Banas* panel cited precedent from nine other states with only cursory regard for Pennsylvania law.[86] Although the court in *Banas* was careful to leave *Richardson* intact, noting that the facts in *Richardson and the precedents cited were "readily distinguishable" from* Banas, *the distinction has eluded the majority of commentators.*[87]

Whether Pennsylvania law concerning the contractual importance of employee manuals lies more with *Banas* or with *Richardson* is difficult to determine. *Banas* does, however, stand in contrast to several other Pennsylvania cases in which courts have held that employee handbooks or personnel policies do not give rise to enforceable contract promises under Pennsylvania law.[88] Although these cases form federal precedent, the judges are bound to accurately predict and apply state law and, therefore, represent the most accurate source of the law in this unsettled area. In *Beidler v. W. R. Grace, Inc.*,[89] the court held that the company's procedures regarding exit interviews, performance evaluations, and progressive discipline did not create an implied contract of employment. And, in *Rogers v. International Business Machines Corp.*,[90] "the court held that

---

[84]348 Pa. Super. 464, 502 A.2d 637 (1984).

[85]*Id.* at 475, 502 A.2d at 645 (*quoted* in Comment, *The Role of Federal Courts, supra* note 4, at 251-52).

[86]*See id.* at 473 note 5, 502 A.2d at 643.

[87]*See Employee Handbook Is Contract*, 3 PA. L. J. REP. at 9 (June 25, 1984).

[88]*See* Comment, *The Role of Federal Courts, supra* note 4, at 252 note 141, *citing* Rogers v. International Business Machines, Corp., 500 F. Supp. 867 (W.D. Pa. 1980) (manual too vague); Beidler v. W.R. Grace, Inc., 461 F. Supp. 1013, 1016 (E.D. Pa. 1978) ("[F]ailure to adhere to company personnel policy does not create a cause of action for breach of an employment contract."), *aff'd mem.*, 609 F.2d 500 (3d Cir. 1979); Wagner v. Sperry Univac, 458 F. Supp. 505, 519-21 (E.D. Pa. 1978) (summary judgment precluded by genuine issue of fact regarding whether employer actually breached contract), *aff'd mem.*, 624 F.2d 1092 (3d Cir. 1980).

[89]461 F. Supp. 1013 (E.D. Pa. 1978).

[90]500 F. Supp. 867 (W.D. Pa. 1980).

the employer's promote-from-within policy, combined with statements contained in a personnel manual and other communications to employees, did not give rise to an enforceable promise."[91]

The superior court, however, has recently issued two decisions which suggest that Pennsylvania law will follow the *Richardson* stance on handbooks. In *Darlington v. General Electric,*[92] the court rejected all of the plaintiff's attempts to argue that the employer was contractually bound by the provisions contained in the handbook and granted judgment in favor of the defendant company, notwithstanding a lower court's ruling in favor of the plaintiff. And, in the *Capital Cities* case discussed earlier, the superior court, per Judge Cavanaugh, held that handbook provisions will not be presumed to alter an otherwise at-will employment relationship unless there is a clear statement of intent by the employer to do so.[93]

Promissory Estoppel

There have been instances in Pennsylvania case law where plaintiffs have succeeded in wrongful discharge claims by arguing that because of an employee's detrimental reliance on an employer's promise, the employer is estopped from discharging the employee without just cause. In *Caldwell v. American Components, Inc.,*[94] the Third Circuit "approved a jury verdict finding an implied contract based on an employer's request to relocate, employee rejection of other job offers under urging by employer, and oral assurances by the employer of a 'career'."[95] Similarly, promissory estoppel arguments have been successfully used to make employer promises enforceable in *O'Neill v. ARA Services, Inc.*[96] and *DeFrank v. County of Greene.*[97]

---

[91]Perritt, *Pennsylvania Dismissal Law, supra* note 40, at 216. *See also* Boreson v. Rohm & Haas, Inc., 526 F. Supp. 1230 (E.D. Pa. 1981); Wells v. Thomas, 569 F. Supp. 426 (E.D. Pa. 1983).

[92]504 A.2d 306 (Pa. Super. 1986).

[93]Slip op. (Pa. Super. June 12, 1986). *See also* Muscarella v. Milton Shoe Manufacturing Co., 507 A.2d 430 (Pa. Super. 1986) (employer's failure to follow policy procedures does not support cause of action for breach of implied contract).

[94]Civ. No. 81-0361 (E.D.Pa. Aug. 2, 1982), *aff'd mem.,* 707 F.2d 1400 (3d Cir. 1983).

[95]Perritt, *Pennsylvania Dismissal Law, supra* note 40, at 216.

[96]457 F. Supp. 182 (E.D. Pa. 1978) (cited in Perritt, *Pennsylvania Dismissal Law, supra* note 40, at 216).

[97]50 Pa. Cmmw. 30, 412 A.2d 663 (1980) (cited in Perritt, *Pennsylvania Dismissal Law, supra* note 40, at 216).

CONCLUSION

In the decade after *Geary* opened the door to erosion of the employment-at-will doctrine, both state and federal courts in Pennsylvania have seen a flood of attacks on the common law rule. Since *Geary,* federal courts in Pennsylvania have adjudicated wrongful discharge actions thirty-seven times, upholding a cause of action only nine times,[98] while in contrast, state courts have recognized a

---

[98]*See* Comment, *The Role of Federal Courts, supra* note 4, at 253 note 142, *citing* the following federal cases which have dismissed wrongful discharge actions or granted summary judgment for defendant: Wolk v. Saks Fifth Avenue, Inc., 728 F.2d 221 (3d Cir. 1984) (sexual harassment claim preempted by statutory remedy); Bruffett v. Warner Communications, Inc., 692 F.2d 910 (3d Cir. 1982) (termination allegedly because of physical handicap that did not affect job performance); Bonham v. Dresser Indus., Inc., 569 F.2d 187 (3d Cir. 1977) (age discrimination), *cert. denied,* 439 U.S. 821 (1978); Kamens v. Summit Stainless, Inc., No. 83-3644 (E.D. Pa. Mar. 29, 1984) (age discrimination claim preempted by statute); Buckmon v. Wilmington Dry Goods Store, No. 82-1167 (E.D.Pa. Feb. 6, 1984) (alleged violation of public policy); Adams v. Budd Co., 583 F. Supp. 711 (E.D. Pa. 1984) (implied contract and public policy claims); Ruch v. Strawbridge & Clothier, Inc., 567 F. Supp. 1078 (E.D. Pa. 1983) (alleged breach of terms of personnel manual); Shaffer v. National Can Corp., 565 F. Supp. 909 (E.D. Pa. 1983) (sexual harassment claim preempted by statutory remedy); Harrison v. Fred Jones, P.A., Inc., 558 F. Supp. 438 (E.D. Pa. 1983) (alleged breach of implied contract); Madreperla v. Willard Co., No. 82-3505 (E.D. Pa. Dec. 17, 1982) (public policy violation); Shaw v. Russell Trucking Line, 542 F. Supp. 776 (W.D. Pa. 1982) (discharge for refusing to drive overloaded trucks; motion to dismiss allowed, but plaintiff given leave to amend complaint); Callahan v. Scott Paper Co., 541 F. Supp. 49 (E.D. Pa. 1982) (discharge for refusal to participate in price fixing); Wood v. Burlington Indus., 536 F. Supp. 56 (E.D. Pa. 1981) (alleged oral contract for permanent employment); Boreson v. Rohm & Haas, 526 F. Supp. 1230 (E.D. Pa. 1981) (discharge for unsatisfactory conduct), *aff'd,* 729 F.2d 1445 (3d Cir. 1984); Huff v. County of Butler, 524 F. Supp. 751 (W.D. Pa. 1981) (discharge for alleged sexual harassment); Fleming v. Mack Trucks, Inc., 508 F. Supp. 917 (E.D. Pa. 1981) (alleged discharge for disclosing embezzlement); Moorhouse v. Boeing Co., 501 F. Supp. 390 (E.D. Pa.) (alleged oral contract for permanent employment), *aff'd,* 639 F.2d 774 (3d Cir. 1980); Rogers v. Int'l Business Machines Corp., 500 F. Supp. 867 (E.D. Pa. 1980) (discharge contrary to employee manual); Lekich v. Int'l Business Machines Corp., 469 F. Supp. 485 (E.D. Pa. 1979) (bad faith discharge); Beidler v. W.R. Grace, Inc., 461 F. Supp. 1013 (E.D. Pa. 1978) (discharge contrary to personnel manual), *aff'd mem.,* 609 F.2d 500 (1979); Walker v. Univ. of Pittsburgh, 457 F. Supp. 1000 (W.D. Pa. 1978) (discharge allegedly for exercising right to free speech); O'Neill v. A.R.A. Sers., Inc., 457 F. Supp. 182 (E.D. Pa. 1978) (discharge in bad faith and contrary to public policy); Wehr v. Burroughs Corp., 438 F. Supp. 1052 (E.D. Pa. 1977) (age discrimination); Geib v. Alan Wood Steel Co., 419 F. Supp. 1205 (E.D. Pa. 1976) (implied contract); Keddie v. Penns. State. Univ., 412 F. Supp. 1264 (M.D. Pa. 1976) (public policy and first amendment); Green v. Medford Knitwear Mills, 408 F. Supp. 577 (E.D. Pa. 1976) (implied contract).

Only the following federal cases have recognized wrongful discharge actions: Novosel v. Nationwide Ins. Co., 721 F.2d 894 (3d Cir. 1983) (public policy and implied

cause of action five out of the seven times they were presented with a claim.[99] This disparate adjudication of the at-will issue between the two court systems has riddled the doctrine of employment-at-will with exceptions and exemptions depending on the jurisdiction and focus of each individual case.

In many ways Pennsylvania illustrates the problems caused, even in a relatively "restrained" state, by uncertainty and the lack of effective guidelines in the law. In particular, potential plaintiffs, defendants and attorneys in Pennsylvania have been plagued by the pervasive ambiguities in the Pennsylvania Supreme Court's *Geary* decision, by the Third Circuit's anomolous application of Pennsylvania law in *Novosel,* and by the Pennsylvania Supreme Court's failure to provide any meaningful guidance in the employment-at-will area for more than thirteen years. The absence of meaningful Supreme Court guidance has resulted in conflicting and, to a certain extent, irreconcilable results among various lower courts in Pennsylvania, which is exemplified in the *Banas* and *Richardson* decisions.[100]

Moreover, the courts have left many critical questions unresolved. In particular, in the tort area, ambiguity surrounds "the specificity with which public policy must be shown before an employee can proceed to trial."[101] In some instances, the judges have gone far beyond the boundaries set by the elected lawmakers and have assumed a quasi-legislative function in deciding what they feel are the proper remedies to be afforded discharged employees. In the contract analysis, the Supreme Court of Pennsylvania has yet to resolve the basic question concerning the breach of an implied contract. Most likely, the high court will follow the path of other jurisdictions and explain that the "traditional unilateral contract doctrine requires that the

contract); Perks v. Firestone Tire & Rubber Co., 611 F.2d 1363 (3d Cir. 1979) (discharge on basis of polygraph test); Karr v. Township of Lower Merion, 582 F. Supp. 410 (E.D. Pa. 1983) (public policy); Rettinger v. American Can Co., 574 F. Supp. 306 (M.D. Pa. 1983) (discharge because of disability and filing of worker's compensation claim); Molush v. Orkin Extermination Co., 547 F. Supp. 54 (E.D. Pa. 1982) (discharge on basis of polygraph test); Forman v. BRI Corp., 532 F. Supp. 49 (E.D. Pa. 1982) (alleged hiring for reasonable time); McNulty v. Borden, Inc., 474 F. Supp. 1111 (E.D. Pa. 1979) (discharge for refusing to participate in price fixing); Wagner v. Sperry Univac, 458 F. Supp. 505 (E.D. Pa. 1978) (discharge contrary to employment manual); McGinley v. Burroughs Corp., 407 F. Supp. 903 (E.D. Pa. 1976) (rationale unrelated to Geary reasoning).
[99]*See* Comment, *The Role of Federal Courts, supra* note 4, at 253.
[100]Letter from Philip A. Miscimarra, Esq. to Andrew D. Hill (May 29, 1987).
[101]Perrit, *Pennsylvania Dismissal Law, supra* note 40, at 218.

employee prove that the promise alleged was communicated to him under circumstances that the employer should have known would induce reliance ... [to the employee's] detriment."[102]

In the next chapter, this study will examine the limited abrogation of the at-will rule that has occurred in New York.

---

[102]*Id.*

CHAPTER VII

New York

New York, unlike some states,[1] has been generally reluctant to carve out broad exceptions to the traditional employment-at-will doctrine. As a result, employees who feel they have been unfairly dismissed "have had little success in the New York courts."[2] It is the "long-settled rule [in New York] that where an employment is for an indefinite term it is presumed to be a hiring at will which may be

---

[1]The California courts, for example, have been very aggressive in their attack on the employment-at-will doctrine, permitting exceptions on both public policy and implied contract grounds. The seminal case denying an employer's right to terminate an at-will employee is *Petermann v. Teamsters Local 396,* 174 Cal. App. 2d 184, 344 P.2d 25 (1959). In *Petermann,* plaintiff was discharged for refusing to commit perjury at employer's request at a legislative hearing. Although the California Court of Appeals recognized Petermann as an at-will employee, the court held that the rule could be limited by statute:

> It would be obnoxious to the interests of the state and contrary to public policy and sound morality to allow an employer to discharge any employee ... on the ground that the employee declined to commit perjury, an act specifically enjoined by statute ... [I]n order to more fully effectuate the state's declared policy against perjury, the civil law, too, must deny the employer his generally unlimited right to discharge an employee whose employment is for an unspecified duration, when the reason for the dismissal is the employee's refusal to commit perjury.

Id. at 188-89, 344 P.2d at 27. The public policy argument has since grown beyond the boundaries set by the legislature. The expansive view of public policy now prevalent in California courts is most evident in *Tameny v. Atlantic Richfield Co.,* 27 Cal. App. 3d 167, 164 Cal. Rptr. 839 (1980) where the California Supreme Court held that where an employee's discharge violates public policy, there is also a concurrent violation by the employer of the duty he assumed upon entering into the employment relationship, thereby giving rise to a cause of action in tort.

The leading case involving the implied contract exception to the employment-at-will doctrine is *Pugh v. See's Candies, Inc.,* 116 Cal. App. 3d 311, 171 Cal. Rptr. 917 (1981) where the California Supreme Court found that plaintiff's regular bonuses and wage increases created an obligation by employer to discharge only for just cause. *See also Cleary v. American Airlines, Inc.,* 111 Cal. App. 3d 443, 168 Cal. Rptr. 722 (1980) (employee's tenure of eighteen years created a covenant of good faith and fair dealing for employer). *See generally* discussion of California employment-at-will, *supra* chapter IV, at 55-75.

[2]Comment, *Weiner v. McGraw-Hill, Inc.: Is Employment in New York Still at Will?,* 3 PACE L. REV. 245, 247 & note 11 (1983) [hereinafter cited as Comment, *Is New York Still at Will?*], *citing* Edwards v. Citibank, N.A., 100 Misc.2d 59, 418 N.Y.S.2d 269

freely terminated by either party at any time for any reason or even for no reason."[3] Neither implied contract nor tort-based exceptions to the at-will rule has developed significantly in the Empire State. "Tort claims have failed because New York, unlike some states, has not yet recognized the tort of abusive discharge"[4] in contravention of public policy, "and because the elements of a *prima facie* tort usually cannot be established in an employment situation."[5] Similarly, the courts' "unwillingness to recognize contractual rights as being created by documents such as employee handbooks and policy manuals"[6] and their rigid application of the state's statute of frauds have erected barriers to contract claims.[7]

After the court of appeals issued its opinion in *Murphy v. American Home Products Corp.*[8] in 1983, it appeared that efforts seeking to create judicial exceptions to the employment-at-will doctrine were dead. Judge Jones, delivering the opinion of the court, recognized the trend in other jurisdictions to adopt protections for at-will

---

(Sup. Ct. 1979), *aff'd*, 74 A.D.2d 553, 425 N.Y.S.2d 327 (App. Div.), *appeal dismissed*, 51 N.Y.2d 875, 414 N.E.2d 400, 433 N.Y.S.2d 1020 (1980); Marinzulich v. National Bank of N. America, N.Y.L.J., May 10, 1979, at 10, col. 2 (Sup. Ct. May 8, 1979), *aff'd*, 73 A.D.2d 886, 423 N.Y.S.2d 1014 (App. Div. 1980); Chin v. American Tel. & Tel. Co., 96 Misc.2d 1070, 410 N.Y.S.2d 737 (Sup. Ct. 1978), *aff'd*, 70 A.D.2d 791, 416 N.Y.S.2d 160 (App. Div.), *appeal denied*, 48 N.Y.2d 603, 421 N.Y.S.2d 1028 (1979).

[3]Murphy v. American Home Products Corporation, 58 N.Y.2d 293, 300, 448 N.E.2d 86, 89, 461 N.Y.S.2d 232, 235, *citing* Martin v. New York Life Insurance Co., 148 N.Y. 117, 42 N.E. 416 (1895); Parker v. Borock, 5 N.Y.2d 156, 156 N.E.2d 297, 182 N.Y.S.2d 577 (1959). *See also* Watson v. Gugino, 204 N.Y. 535, 98 N.E. 18 (1912); Grozek v. Ragu Foods, Inc., 63 A.D.2d 858, 406 N.Y.S.2d 213 (App. Div. 1978).

[4]Comment, *Is New York Still At Will?*, *supra* note 2, at 249. *See Murphy*, 58 N.Y.2d 293, 448 N.E.2d 86, 461 N.Y.S.2d 232 (1983) which concluded that "recognition in New York of tort liability for what has become known as abusive or wrongful discharge should await legislative action." *Id.* at 236.

[5]Comment, *Is New York Still at Will?*, *supra* note 2, at 249 & note 21, *citing* Marinzulich v. National Bank of N. America, N.Y.L.J., May 10, 1979, at 10, col. 2 (Sup. Ct. May 8, 1979), *aff'd*, 73 A.D.2d 886, 423 N.Y.S.2d 1014 (App. Div. 1980); Chin v. American Tel. & Tel. Co., 96 Misc.2d 1070, 410 N.Y.S.2d 737 (Sup. Ct. 1978), *aff'd*, 70 A.D.2d 791, 416 N.Y.S.2d 160 (App. Div.), *appeal denied*, 48 N.Y.2d 603, 421 N.Y.S.2d 1028 (1979).

[6]Comment, *Is New York Still At Will?*, *supra* note 2, at 249 & note 23, *citing* Edwards v. Citibank, N.A., 100 Misc.2d 59, 418 N.Y.S.2d 269 (Sup. Ct. 1979), *aff'd*, 74 A.D.2d 553, 425 N.Y.S.2d 327 (App. Div.), *appeal dismissed*, 51 N.Y.2d 875, 414 N.E.2d 400, 433 N.Y.S.2d 1020 (1980); Chin v. American Tel. & Tel. Co., 96 Misc.2d 1070, 410 N.Y.S.2d 737 (Sup. Ct. 1978), *aff'd*, 70 A.D.2d 791, 416 N.Y.S.2d 160 (App. Div.), *appeal denied*, 48 N.Y.2d 603, 421 N.Y.S.2d 1028 (1979).

[7]*See* Comment, *Is New York Still At Will?*, *supra* note 2, at 249 & note 22, *citing* Weisse v. Engelhard Minerals and Chem. Corp., 571 F.2d 117 (2d Cir. 1978); Savodnik v. Korvettes, Inc., 488 F. Supp. 822 (E.D.N.Y. 1980); Edwards v. Citibank, N.A., 100 Misc.2d 59, 418 N.Y.S.2d 269 (Sup. Ct. 1979), *aff'd*, 74 A.D.2d 553, 425 N.Y.S.2d 327 (App. Div.), *appeal dismissed*, 51 N.Y.2d 875, 414 N.E.2d 400, 433 N.Y.S.2d 1020 (1980).

[8]58 N.Y.2d 293, 448 N.E.2d 86, 461 N.Y.S.2d 232 (1983).

employees,[9] but stated that the court was not prepared to create similar protection since such judicial legislating would have tremendous impact on the entire employment area.[10] To recognize a cause of action for the tort of abusive or wrongful discharge would be contrary to New York common law's adherence to the employment-at-will doctrine.[11] Based on this concern, the court concluded that "such a significant change in our law is best left to the Legislature."[12]

Despite the *Murphy* court's directive that modifications to the common law employment-at-will doctrine must come from the legislature, elected officials in Albany have not yet voted on any bills designed to alter the at-will rule. In 1984, the chairman of the New York Senate's Labor Committee introduced an act to protect all employees at will from unjust dismissal.[13] The Unjust Dismissal Act, however, was adamantly opposed by both organized labor concerns and management lobbyists and died in committee, never reaching the floor of the state legislature. No other unjust dismissal bill has since been introduced and, according to experts in this area, the likelihood of any such measures being enacted in the near future is minimal.[14]

Although New York has never codified the traditional employment-at-will doctrine into law, the doctrine was recognized by the state as early as 1895 in *Martin v. New York Life Insurance Co.*[15] "In *Martin,* the plaintiff had been hired at a yearly salary to be paid monthly. After being discharged before the year's end, he claimed that he was entitled to a full year's pay."[16] The court held that this was not a contract of employment for a year and quoted Wood's famous rationale that: "a contract to pay one $2500 a year for services is not a contract for a year, but a contract to pay at the rate of $2500 a year for services actually rendered, and is terminable at will by either party."[17] This holding formed the foundation of New York's

---

[9]*See id.* at 301, 448 N.E.2d at 89, 461 N.Y.S.2d at 235 and cases cited therein.

[10]*Id.* at 302, 448 N.E.2d at 89-90, 461 N.Y.S.2d at 235-36.

[11]*Id.* at 300, 448 N.E.2d at 89, 461 N.Y.S.2d at 235 (emphasis added). *See* note 3, *supra* and cases cited therein.

[12]*Id.* at 301, 448 N.E.2d at 89, 461 N.Y.S.2d at 235.

[13]*See* New York Senate Bill S.8969 (introduced April 10, 1984).

[14]Author's interview with Roger H. Madon, President, National Congress of Employees, November 20, 1985 [hereinafter cited as Madon interview].

[15]148 N.Y. 117, 42 N.E. 416 (1895).

[16]Comment, *Is New York Still At Will?, supra* note 2, at 248 note 17, *citing Martin,* 148 N.Y. at 119, 42 N.E. at 417.

[17]*See* Comment, *Is New York Still At Will?, supra* note 2, at 248 note 17, *citing Martin,* 148 N.Y. at 120, 121, 42 N.E. at 417 (quoting H. Wood, MASTER AND SERVANT § 136 (2d ed. 1884)).

judicial response to the employment-at-will question for nearly the
next century. As recently as 1982, *Martin* was cited as establishing
New York's common law principle that in an at-will employment situation, the ex-employee states no cause of action by simply alleging
that he or she has been discharged.[18]

TORT EXCEPTIONS

When bringing a cause of action for wrongful discharge based on a
tort theory, the plaintiff usually alleges a *prima facie* tort as well as
the specific tort of abusive discharge.[19] A *prima facie* tort, the New
York courts have held, is "the infliction of intentional harm, resulting in damage, without excuse or justification, by an act or a series
of acts which would otherwise be lawful."[20] Courts in New York have
uniformly held that at-will employees may not bring a cause of
action under a *prima facie* tort theory because of the absolute right
of employers to discharge such employees at any time and for any or
no reason.[21]

In *Murphy* the court of appeals relied upon its earlier opinion in
James v. Board of Education,[22] quoting from it as follows:

> Plaintiff cannot, by the device of an allegation that the sole reason
> for the termination of his employment by these public officials acting
> within the ambit of their authority was to harm him without justifica-
> tion (a contention which could be advanced with respect to almost any
> such termination), bootstrap himself around a motion addressed to
> the pleadings.[23]

---

[18]*See* Weiner v. McGraw-Hill, Inc., 57 N.Y.2d 458, 443 N.E.2d 441, 457 N.Y.S.2d
198 (1982) (Wachtler, J., dissenting).

[19]*See* Comment, *Is New York Still At Will?, supra* note 2, at 253. Often wrongful
discharge claims are brought on several legal theories, such as breach of contract,
breach of the duty of good faith and fair dealing, or defamation. In addition, wrongful
discharge actions are often attached to age or sex discrimination charges.

[20]*Id.* & note 59, *citing* Carnival Co. v. Metro-Goldwyn-Mayer, Inc., 23 A.D.2d 75,
78, 258 N.Y.S.2d 110, 113 (App. Div. 1965) (citations omitted).

[21]*See, e.g., Murphy,* 58 N.Y.2d 293, 461 N.Y.S.2d 232, 448 N.E.2d 86 (1983); James
v. Board of Education, 37 N.Y.2d 891, 378 N.Y.S.2d 371, 340 N.E.2d 735 (1975); Cartwright v. Golub, 51 A.D.2d 407, 381 N.Y.S.2d 901 (App. 1976). *See also* Amicus Brief
of the Equal Employment Advisory Council, *Dake v. Tuell,* No. 66541 (Mo. S. Ct.
1985).

[22]37 N.Y.2d 891, 378 N.Y.S.2d 371, 340 N.E.2d 735 (1975).

[23]*Murphy,* 448 N.E.2d at 91 (cited in Amicus Brief at 18).

The *Murphy* court then dismissed the plaintiff's *prima facie* tort claim: "this cause of action cannot be allowed in circumvention of the unavailability of a tort claim for wrongful discharge of an at-will employee."[24]

Lower New York state courts have also denied plaintiffs' attempts to bring a *prima facie* tort claim in relation to a discharge. In *Cartwright v. Golub Corporation,*[25] for instance, the New York Supreme Court, Appellate Division expressly stated that a cause of action for a *prima facie* tort would not lie where "the alleged tortious conduct involves the exercise of an employer's unfettered right to terminate the employment relationship ... "[26] Similarly, in *Kushner v. Ciba-Geigy Corporation,*[27] an appellate court granted the defendant's motion for summary judgment when confronted with a *prima facie* tort claim in a discharge case, again citing the employer's right to terminate at any time and for any or no reason.

"To bring a cause of action successfully in abusive discharge, a plaintiff must persuade the court that there is a public policy of the state and that by firing him the defendant has violated it."[28] In adjudicating these cases, the court engages in a balancing test in which "the interest of the employer in the exercise of his unfettered right to terminate an employee under a contract at will is balanced against the interest of the community in upholding its laws and public policy."[29] To date, New York courts have refused to recognize the tort of abusive discharge, although the New York courts have indicated that they are not averse to recognizing such a cause of action, if the facts so warrant.[30] Unfortunately, the courts have not yet clearly defined the conditions necessary to sustain such a cause of action. A brief review of recent cases in which the abusive discharge tort has been alleged will help delineate the New York courts' posture on this aspect of the employment-at-will controversy.

In *Chin v. American Telephone & Telegraph Co.,*[31] the "plaintiff alleged that he had been discharged by his employer, AT&T, after he was arrested for driving a van into three police officers during a

---

[24]*Id.* (*cited* in Amicus Brief at 18).

[25]51 A.D.2d 407, 381 N.Y.S.2d 901 (App. 1976).

[26]*Cartwright,* 381 N.Y.S.2d at 902 (cited in Amicus Brief at 18).

[27]76 A.D.2d 950, 428 N.Y.S.2d 745, 746 (App. 1980) (cited in Amicus Brief at 18-19).

[28]Comment, *Is New York Still At Will?, supra* note 2, at 250.

[29]*Chin* at 1075, 410 N.Y.S.2d at 741 (Sup. Ct. 1978) (quoted in Comment, *Is New York Still At Will?, supra* note 2, at 250).

[30]*See* Comment, *Is New York Still At Will?, supra* note 2, at 250 and cases cited at note 3, *supra.*

[31]96 Misc.2d 1070, 410 N.Y.S.2d 737 (Sup. Ct. 1978).

political demonstration."[32] In his cause of action, Chin claimed that he was terminated for political reasons, thereby contravening the state's public policy.[33] The state supreme court dismissed Chin's allegation, holding that he had not sustained his burden of showing that a public policy existed in New York which "would restrict the right of a *private* employer to discharge an employee at will due to the employee's political beliefs, activities and associations."[34] Despite the court's dismissal of the tort claim, it did not go on to define what would constitute the "substantial showing" necessary to sustain an abusive discharge tort.[35]

Later the following year, in *Marinzulich v. National Bank of North America*,[36] the state supreme court again dismissed an abusive discharge claim. In *Marinzulich*, "the plaintiff alleged that he was discharged for having uncovered evidence of embezzlement" at the bank and that such termination violated the state's "public policy ... of encouraging the discovery of crimes," or whistleblowing.[37] According to the court's reasoning, New York had not recognized *any* cause of action in abusive discharge and, furthermore, the allegations set forth by the plaintiff "did not warrant such novel recognition."[38] Another case that year, *Edwards v. Citibank, Inc.*,[39] provided a New York supreme court with a fact situation very similar to *Marinzulich*. In *Edwards*, the plaintiff "alleged that he was discharged for having uncovered evidence of illegal foreign currency manipulations" at Citibank.[40] The *Edwards* court quickly dismissed the claim, concluding simply that "abusive discharge is not actionable under New York law."[41]

---

[32]Comment, *Is New York Still At Will?*, supra note 2, at 250 & note 32, *citing Chin*, 96 Misc.2d at 1073, 410 N.Y.S.2d at 739.

[33]*Chin*, 96 Misc.2d at 1072, 410 N.Y.S.2d at 738 (cited in Comment, *Is New York Still At Will?*, supra note 2, at 250).

[34]*Id.* at 1075, 410 N.Y.S.2d at 741 (quoted in Comment, *Is New York Still At Will?*, supra note 2, at 251). Cf. Novosel v. Nationwide Insurance, 721 F.2d 894 (3d Cir. 1983) (employee's allegations of discharge for refusal to participate in private employer's lobbying effort, and his expressed opposition to company's political stand, stated a cause of action for wrongful discharge under Pennsylvania law, despite the absence of any state action). *See generally* discussion in chapter VI, supra, at 105-107.

[35]*See* Comment, *Is New York Still At Will?*, supra note 2, at 251.

[36]N.Y.L.J., May 10, 1979, at 10, col. 2 (Sup. Ct. May 8, 1979), aff'd, 73 A.D.2d 886, 423 N.Y.S.2d 1014 (App. Div. 1980).

[37]Comment, *Is New York Still At Will?*, supra note 2, at 251.

[38]*Marinzulich*, at 10, col. 2. *See also* Comment, *Is New York Still At Will?*, supra note 2, at 251.

[39]100 Misc.2d 59, 418 N.Y.S.2d 269 (Sup. Ct. 1979).

[40]Comment, *Is New York Still At Will?*, supra note 2, at 252.

[41]*Edwards*, 100 Misc.2d at 61, 418 N.Y.S.2d at 271.

Holdings by the state courts which appear to clearly announce that New York does not recognize the tort of abusive discharge find new meaning when interpreted at the federal level. Indeed, the federal courts in New York have been decidedly more lenient towards recognizing a tort of abusive discharge. For example, in *Savodnik v. Korvettes, Inc.*,[42] the plaintiff alleged that after thirteen years of unblemished service he was discharged solely because Korvettes wanted to deprive him of pension benefits. Despite the established New York rule not recognizing a cause of action for abusive discharge, Judge Platt denied the defendant's motion to dismiss, citing *Chin* for the proposition that New York was moving towards recognition of such a tort.[43] According to Judge Platt, the *Chin* court "virtually invited recognition of such law when it stated that 'this court is not averse to recognizing new causes of action ... where clearly warranted.'"[44] The *Savodnik* reasoning presents at best only a tenuous argument for the recognition of a cause of action for abusive discharge. To be sure, the court appears to be reaching in order to advance its own notions of public and social policy.

The following year, in *Hovey v. Lutheran Medical Center*,[45] the federal court for the Eastern District of New York again refused to dismiss an abusive discharge claim. *Hovey* presented the court with facts very similar to *Savodnik*. The plaintiff in *Hovey* was a sixty-two-year-old accountant who was discharged after six and one-half years of employment at the medical center.[46] In his complaint, Hovey alleged that his employer was trying to deprive him of his pension benefits.[47] "The court cited *Chin* as evidence of New York's willingness to recognize a tort of abusive discharge."[48] Although Judge Nickerson admitted that allegations of abusive discharge did not state a claim under New York law,[49] he noted that other states did

---

[42]488 F. Supp. 822 (E.D.N.Y. 1980).

[43]*Id.* at 825.

[44]*Id., quoting Chin*, 96 Misc.2d at 1075, 410 N.Y.S.2d at 741 (quoted in Comment, *Is New York Still At Will?, supra* note 2, at 252).

[45]516 F. Supp. 554 (E.D.N.Y. 1981).

[46]*Id.* at 555 (cited in Comment, *Is New York Still At Will?, supra* note 2, at 253 note 57).

[47]*Id.* at 558 (cited in Comment, *Is New York Still At Will?, supra* note 2, at 253 note 57).

[48]Comment, *Is New York Still At Will?, supra* note 2, at 253 note 57, *citing Hovey*, 516 F. Supp. at 557).

[49]*Hovey*, 516 F. Supp. at 557.

recognize such claims, that there was a great similarity to *Savodnik* (which he thought was a "sound" decision[50]), and concluded that the integrity of pension benefits was a public policy in New York.[51]

That the federal courts have continued to push toward recognition of an abusive discharge tort is evidenced by a recently decided case, *Sherman v. St. Barnabas Hospital.*[52] In *Sherman*, the plaintiff allegedly refused to agree to the union's preferential hiring and scheduling demands. In response, the union threatened an industry-wide work stoppage unless the plaintiff was discharged, a threat to which the hospital succumbed. Subsequently, plaintiff Sherman sued the hospital on abusive discharge and breach of contract theories. The hospital moved to dismiss the claims on the grounds that New York permits employers to terminate at-will employees for any reason.[53] The court denied the motion, however, holding that "*if* the issue had been presented in a state court, New York would have abrogated the employment-at-will rule and adopted the emerging exception."[54] According to the court, the plaintiff was entitled to a trial on the issue "whether, *inter alia*, it was contrary to state public policy for a union to retaliate against an employee for performing his public duty and for the hospital to yield to such retaliation."[55]

The most significant employment-at-will case in New York to date has been *Murphy v. American Home Products Co.*[56] The case's significance lies in the fact that the state court of appeals, the state's highest court, expressly rejected the invitation to follow the trend developing in other jurisdictions and disallowed a cause of action for the tort of abusive or wrongful discharge. Also noteworthy was the court's pronouncement that there exists no implied covenant of good faith and fair dealing with respect to an at-will contract of employment. In sum, the *Murphy* court effectively eliminated two major legal avenues on which exceptions to the at-will rule could proceed by deferring to the legislature.

The "plaintiff, Joseph Murphy, was first employed by the defendant, American Home Products Corporation, in 1957. He thereafter served in various accounting positions, eventually attaining the office of assistant treasurer, but never had a formal contract of employment. On April 18, 1980, when he was fifty-nine years old, he

---

[50]*Id.* at 558.
[51]*Id.*
[52]535 F. Supp. 564 (S.D.N.Y. 1982).
[53]*Id.* at 568.
[54]*Id.* at 571 (emphasis added).
[55]*Id.* at 572.
[56]58 N.Y.2d 293, 448 N.E.2d 86, 461 N.Y.S.2d 232 (1983).

was discharged."[57] Murphy claimed that he was terminated "because of his disclosure to top management of alleged accounting improprieties on the part of corporate personnel and because of his age."[58]

Murphy brought four causes of action before the New York Supreme Court, Special Term, alleging a tort of wrongful or abusive discharge, breach of contract, intentional infliction of emotional distress, and age discrimination. Special Term granted the defendant's motion for summary judgment on the last three causes of action,[59] but allowed Murphy to proceed on the wrongful discharge claim. The court noted that despite the fact that New York had not yet adopted the doctrine of abusive discharge, the plaintiff should be "afforded the opportunity by means of disclosure procedures to elicit evidence which might put his claim on firmer footing."[60] The appellate division on cross appeal granted the defendant's motion to dismiss the wrongful discharge cause of action, and Murphy subsequently appealed to the court of appeals.[61]

Although the court of appeals was sympathetic to the plaintiff's plea for the court to adopt the emerging view permitting the tort of abusive discharge, the court deferred the responsibility of undertaking such a significant change in employment relations to the legislature:

> Those jurisdictions that have modified the traditional at-will rule appear to have been motivated by conclusions that the freedom of contract underpinnings of the rule have become outdated, that individual employees in the modern workforce do not have the bargaining power to negotiate security for the jobs on which they have grown to rely, and that the rule yields harsh results for those employees who do not enjoy the benefits of express contractual limitations on the power of dismissal. Whether these conclusions are supportable or whether for other compelling reasons employers should, as a matter of policy, be held liable to at-will employees discharged in circumstances for which no liability has existed at common law, are issues better left to resolution at the hands of the Legislature. In addition to the funda-

---

[57]*Id.* at 297, 448 N.E.2d at 87, 461 N.Y.S.2d at 233.

[58]*Id.* at 297-98, 448 N.E.2d at 87, 461 N.Y.S.2d at 233.

[59]*See id.* at 299, 448 N.E.2d at 88, 461 N.Y.S.2d at 234. "Special Term held the cause of action for breach of contract barred by the Statute of Frauds. As to the second and third causes of action the court ruled that plaintiff's allegations as to the manner of his dismissal were not sufficient to support causes of action for intentional infliction of emotional distress or for *prima facie* tort." *Id.*

[60]*Id.* at 299, 448 N.E.2d at 88, 461 N.Y.S.2d at 234.

[61]*See id.* at 300, 448 N.E.2d at 88-89, 461 N.Y.S.2d at 234.

mental question whether such liability should be recognized in New York, of no less practical consideration is the definition of its configuration if it is to be recognized.[62]

The *Murphy* court explained in detail the legislature's superior ability to shape the issue and interpret public opinion in this area. "[T]he greater resources of the legislature," the court reasoned, renders it more "capable to examine the considerations involved and [to] elicit constituent opinions ... as well as to assess the impact of imposing liability in this area":[63]

> Both of these aspects of the issue, involving perception and declaration of relevant public policy (the underlying determinative consideration with respect to tort liability in general ...) are best and more appropriately explored and resolved by the legislative branch of our government. The Legislature has infinitely greater resources and procedural means to discern the public will, to examine the variety of pertinent considerations, to elicit the views of the various segments of the community that would be directly affected and in any event critically interested, and to investigate and anticipate the impact of imposition of such liability. Standards should doubtless be established applicable to the multifarious types of employment and the various circumstances of discharge. *If the rule of nonliability for termination of at-will employment is to be tempered, it should be accomplished through a principled statutory scheme, adopted after opportunity for public ventilation, rather than in consequence of judicial resolution of the partisan arguments of individual adversarial litigants.*[64]

Although *Murphy* apparently put to rest attempts to modify the employment-at-will doctrine through the tort of abusive discharge, the recent appellate division opinion in *Bergamini v. The Manhattan and Bronx Surface Transit Operating Authority*[65] reinforces the notion that "a public employee ... [has] greater rights than a private employee because of the nature of the employment."[66] The first department panel in *Bergamini* distinguished its case from *Murphy*. Recognizing that *Murphy* "leaves no room for doubt as to the controlling rule in this state," Judge Sandler continued, noting that:

---

[62]*Id.* at 301, 448 N.E.2d at 89, 461 N.Y.S.2d at 235.

[63]Jacobs, *Abusive Discharge in New York: Some Confusing Signals From the Courts,* 1984 N.Y. St. B. J. 29, 30 (Feb. 1984) [hereinafter cited as Jacobs, *Abusive Discharge in New York*].

[64]*Id.* at 302-03, 448 N.E.2d at 89-90, 461 N.Y.S.2d at 235-36 (emphasis added).

[65]62 N.Y.2d 897, 467 N.E.2d 521, 478 N.Y.S.2d 857 (1984).

[66]*See* Jacobs, *Abusive Discharge in New York, supra* note 63, at 31.

arguably the considerations which led the Court of Appeals in *Murphy* to prefer the legislative route to change in this area are less compelling with regard to exempt, permanent, public employees who have been employed for a number of years under circumstances in which there is a reasonable expectation, indeed, "mutually explicit understandings that the employment will not be terminated except for cause."[67]

Although the appellate division did not disregard *Murphy*, "it did intimate that there is room for a public employment exception to the at-will rule in New York."[68]

Despite the Murphy court's explicit ruling against the tort of wrongful discharge and its implied obligation of good faith and fair dealing, the judiciary did not have the opportunity to address the contract-based exceptions to the employment-at-will doctrine. Indeed, it is along this legal avenue that exceptions to the at-will rule in New York must advance. This road, however, as indicated in the following discussion, does not look very promising.

CONTRACT EXCEPTIONS

Just as the New York courts have resisted permitting public policy tort exceptions to the employment-at-will doctrine, they have been equally hesitant in their treatment of contract-based exceptions. Attempts by discharged employees to assert breach of contract claims are often barred by the state's statute of frauds,[69] which requires contracts not capable of performance within one year to be in writing.[70] And, as a further impediment, New York courts have been generally unreceptive to recognizing language in company handbooks or personnel manuals as creating enforceable contract rights.[71]

---

[67]*Id.* (quoted in Jacobs, *Abusive Discharge in New York, supra* note 63, at 32.

[68]Jacobs, *Abusive Discharge in New York, supra* note 63, at 32.

[69]*See, e.g.,* Edwards v. Citibank, N.A., 100 Misc.2d 59, 60, 418 N.Y.S.2d 269, 270 (Sup. Ct. 1979); Savodnik v. Korvettes, Inc., 488 F.2d 822, 824 (1980). For an excellent discussion of the New York courts' treatment of the statute of frauds and wrongful discharge, see, Comment, *Is New York Still at Will?, supra* note 2, at 254-57.

[70]N.Y. GEN. OBLIG. LAW §. 5-701 (a) (1) (McKinney 1978 & Supp. 1987).

[71]*See* Comment, *Is New York Still At Will?, supra* note 2, at 257 note 90, *citing* Edwards v. Citibank, N.A., 100 Misc.2d 59, 418 N.Y.S.2d 269 (Sup. Ct. 1979); Chin v. American Tel. & Tel. Co., 96 Misc.2d 1070, 410 N.Y.S.2d 737 (Sup. Ct. 1978).

Statute of Frauds

It is usually the case that an employee who is hired for an indefinite period has no written contract.[72] Discharged employees bringing an action for wrongful discharge, therefore, attempt to show the existence of an oral contract for permanent employment.[73] Such claims arising from oral contracts, however, are barred frequently by New York's statute of frauds, which provides in pertinent part that:

> a. Every agreement, promise or undertaking is void, unless it or some note or memorandum thereof be in writing, and subscribed by the party to be charged therewith, or by his lawful agent, if such agreement, promise or undertaking:
> 1. By its terms is not to be performed within one year from the making thereof or the performance of which is not to be completed before the end of a lifetime.[74]

"The purpose of this provision," as Professor Corbin suggests, "is to avoid leaving to memory the terms of a contract which is longer than a year."[75] Generally, the New York courts, on both the state and federal levels, have interpreted the statute's bar narrowly, giving effect to oral contracts "where there is *any* possibility of performance within one year even though the likelihood of such performance is remote."[76]

For nearly a century, the rule in New York has been that employment agreements in which either party may terminate the relationship within one year are hirings at will, capable of performance within the one-year limit and thus not barred by the statute of frauds.[77] Under such legal construction, termination is viewed by the

---

[72]*See* Comment, *Is New York Still At Will?*, *supra* note 2, at 254.

[73]*Id.*

[74]N.Y. Gen. Oblig. Law § 5-701 (a) (1) (McKinney 1978 & Supp. 1987) (quoted in Comment, *Is New York Still At Will?*, *supra* note 2, at 255 note 73).

[75]Comment, *Is New York Still At Will?*, *supra* note 2, at 255, *citing* 2 A. Corbin, Corbin on Contracts, Section 444, at 534 (1950). "Where actions on contracts are long delayed, injustice is likely to be done because of bad memory and because witnesses have died or moved away, so that mistakes will be made and perjury is more likely to be successful. And in the case of a contract whose performance is to cover a long period of time, actions are likely to be long delayed." *Id.*

[76]Comment, *Is New York Still At Will?*, *supra* note 2, at 255 & note 75, *citing* Weisse v. Engelhard Minerals & Chem. Corp., 571 F.2d 117, 119 (2d Cir. 1978); North Shore Bottling Co. v. Schmidt & Sons, 22 N.Y.2d 171, 175-76, 239 N.E.2d 189, 191, 292 N.Y.S.2d 86, 89-90 (1968).

[77]*See* Blake v. Voight, 134 N.Y. 69, 31 N.E. 256 (1892) (cited in Comment, *Is New York Still At Will*, *supra* note 2, at 256.

courts as performance of the contract, rather than its destruction; that is, "[t]ermination does not defeat the contract, but simply advances the period of fulfillment."[78]

Problems of interpretation do arise, however, when the option to terminate the contract is unilateral. The New York courts have been divided on the question of whether a unilateral termination option creates a contract capable of performance within one year. In one instance the courts held that the unilateral provision is indistinguishable from the bilateral situation;[79] in another, that the unilateral provision creates a distinctly different employment contract that

> should not be extended to make enforceable an oral agreement for permanent employment, where the right to cancel or terminate is limited unilaterally to plaintiff. For in such cases defendant's liability endures indefinitely, subject only to the uncontrolled voluntary act of the party who seeks to hold defendant. Under such circumstances it is illusory, from the point of view of defendant, to consider the contract terminable or performable within one year.[80]

In many ways the courts' narrow interpretation of the statute of frauds frustrates the very purpose of the rule.[81] "If the parties contemplate that the employment agreement will last indefinitely ... it is likely that an action for breach will be brought years after the agreement is made when memories are no longer fresh."[82] Indeed, this was the very problem the statute of frauds sought to prevent.[83]

Personnel Manuals

New York courts have consistently rejected claims by discharged employees that personnel manuals, employee handbooks, or employment applications create an implied contract of employment that is

---

[78]Comment, *Is New York Still At Will?*, supra note 2, at 256 note 80, *citing Blake*, 134 N.Y. at 72, 73 N.E. at 256, 257.

[79]*See* Raymond Spector Co. v. Servtan Co., 60 N.Y.S.2d 212, 213 (Sup. Ct. 1945), *aff'd*, 270 A.D. 993, 63 N.Y.S.2d 213 (App. Div. 1st 1946) (cited in Comment, *Is New York Still At Will?*, supra note 2, at 256).

[80]*See* Harris v. Home Indemnity Co., 6 A.D.2d 861, 861, 175 N.Y.S.2d 603, 604 (App. Div. 1958) (quoted in Comment, *Is New York Still At Will?*, supra note 2, at 256). *See also* Supplee v. Hallon, 14 Misc.2d 658, 179 N.Y.S.2d 725 (Sup. Ct. 1958) (plaintiff, who had an oral agreement for lifetime employment with a unilateral option to cancel within one year, did not remove the bar of the Statute of Frauds because of the one-sided nature of the agreement) (cited in Comment, *Is New York Still At Will?*, supra note 2, at 256 note 83).

[81]*See* Comment, *Is New York Still at Will?*, supra note 2, at 256-57 note 84.
[82]*Id.*
[83]*Id.*

legally binding and enforceable against the employer.[84] Despite the trend in many jurisdictions to recognize enforceable contract rights arising out of corporate documents,[85] the judiciary in New York has agreed for the most part that such documents are nothing more than "broad internal policy guidelines."[86] Manuals, according to the courts' rationale, are insufficient as actionable contracts of employment since these documents rarely contain all the necessary terms of employment, such as the duties of the position, the length of employment, and compensation.[87]

In 1982, however, the New York Court of Appeals, in *Weiner v. McGraw-Hill*,[88] handed down a decision in stark contrast to the state's historical judicial stance against contract-based exceptions to the employment-at-will doctrine. The *Weiner* court held that "on an appropriate evidentiary showing, a limitation on the employer's right to terminate an employment of indefinite duration might be implied from an express provision in the employer's handbook or personnel policies and procedures."[89] *Weiner* was particularly alarming because the court could have easily dismissed the plaintiff's claim based on the employment-at-will doctrine long recognized in New York, but instead "attempted to protect an otherwise remediless employee ... by finding contractual protection based upon the employer's manual."[90]

Prior to the decision in *Weiner*, New York courts generally disallowed contract exceptions to the employment-at-will rule on the rationale that employee manuals do not contain the terms and conditions of employment sufficient to constitute a legally enforceable contract. In the *Chin* case discussed earlier, the plaintiff alleged that

---

[84]*See, e.g.*, O'Connor v. Eastman Kodak Company, 65 N.Y.2d 724, 481 N.E.2d 549, 492 N.Y.S.2d 9 (1985); Wexler v. Newsweek, Inc., 109 A.D.2d 714, 487 N.Y.S.2d 330 (App. Div. 1985); Tyson v. Hess, 109 A.D.2d 1068, 487 N.Y.S.2d 206 (App. Div. 1985); Rizzo v. Int'l Brotherhood of Teamsters, Local 237, 109 A.D.2d 639, 486 N.Y.S.2d 220 (App. Div. 1985); Hager v. Union Carbide Corp., 106 A.D.2d 348, 483 N.Y.S.2d 261 (App. Div. 1984); Pedone v. Avco Financial Services of New York, Inc., 102 A.D.2d 885, 476 N.Y.S.2d 933 (App. Div. 1984); O'Donnell v. Westchester Community Service Council, Inc., 96 A.D.2d 885, 466 N.Y.S.2d 41 (App. Div. 1983).

[85]*See, e.g.*, Cleary v. American Airlines, Inc., 111 Cal. App. 3d 443, 168 Cal. Rptr. 722 (2d Dist. 1980); Touissaint v. Blue Cross & Blue Shield of Michigan, 408 Mich. 579, 292 N.W.2d 880 (1980) (cited in Comment, *Is New York Still At Will?*, *supra* note 2, at 258 note 91).

[86]Edwards v. Citibank, N.A., 100 Misc.2d 59, 60, 418 N.Y.S.2d 292, 270 (Sup. Ct. 1979) (cited in Comment, *Is New York Still At Will?*, *supra* note 2, at 258).

[87]Chin v. American Tel. & Tel. Co., 96 Misc.2d 1070, 1073, 410 N.Y.S.2d 737, 739 (Sup. Ct. 1978) (cited in Comment, *Is New York Still At Will?*, *supra* note 2, at 259).

[88]57 N.Y.2d 458, 443 N.E.2d 441, 457 N.Y.S.2d 193 (1982).

[89]Jacobs, *Abusive Discharge in New York*, *supra* note 63, at 31.

[90]*Id.*

AT&T's "Code of Conduct" established the only grounds on which he could be discharged.[91] "Although the code of conduct governed some conditions of employment, the court concluded that it was defective as an enforceable employment agreement because it did not contain all the necessary terms" of the employment relationship.[92] In addition, the court held, the document was not signed by the defendant company, a condition necessary to binding a party to a contract.[93]

Similarly, in *Edwards* the state supreme court relied on *Chin* to dismiss the plaintiff's claim that Citibank's company handbook and manual constituted a contractual agreement that limited the bank's right to terminate to just cause only. Since plaintiff retained the right to terminate the relationship at any time, the court found Edwards' contract claim unenforceable since there was no mutuality of obligation.[94] And, in the same vein as *Chin*, the manuals did not constitute a written contract because they did "not exclusively and completely define the terms and conditions of employment, its duration or the rate of compensation, i.e., all the essential elements of a contract of employment."[95]

The apparent anomaly presented by the *Weiner* decision may best be explained by the peculiar fact situation, a factor which the court itself emphasized.[96] Weiner left his job at Prentice-Hall in 1969 to join McGraw-Hill, seeking job security and advancement.[97] During discussions prior to his being hired, Weiner received oral assurances from McGraw-Hill supervisors that since it was the firm's policy to discharge for cause only, his position was secure as long as his job performance was satisfactory.[98] When Weiner applied for the job he signed an application form, which several representatives of McGraw-Hill also signed, stating that he agreed to be bound by the terms of the employment handbook.[99] The handbook stated clearly

---

[91]*Chin*, 96 Misc.2d at 1072, 410 N.Y.S.2d at 739 (cited in Comment, *Is New York Still At Will?*, *supra* note 2, at 259).

[92]Comment, *Is New York Still At Will?*, *supra* note 2, at 259, citing *Chin*, 96 Misc.2d at 1073, 410 N.Y.S.2d at 739.

[93]*Id.* & note 96, *citing* N.Y. GEN. OBLIG. LAW § 5-701 (a) (McKinney Supp. 1982).

[94]*Edwards*, 100 Misc.2d at 60, 418 N.Y.S.2d at 270 (cited in Comment, *Is New York Still At Will?*, *supra* note 2, at 259).

[95]*Id.* (quoted in Comment, *Is New York Still At Will?*, *supra* note 2, at 259).

[96]*Weiner*, 57 N.Y.2d at 460, 443 N.E.2d at 442, 457 N.Y.S.2d at 194.

[97]*Id.*

[98]*Id.*

[99]*Id.* at 460-61, 443 N.E.2d at 442, 457 N.Y.S.2d at 194.

that employees could be discharged for just cause only.[100] For eight years, Weiner performed his job with no problems, then, in 1977, he was discharged for "lack of application."[101] Weiner alleged that his termination was in retaliation for a dispute he had had with his supervisor.[102]

In addition to his breach of contract claim, Weiner alleged in his complaint tort claims against McGraw-Hill for intentional interference with a contract and wrongful inducement of breach of contract. The New York Supreme Court, Special Term dismissed these latter claims, but upheld Weiner's breach of contract action.[103] The appellate division reversed the supreme court's denial of the defendant's motion to dismiss, holding that *Edwards* and *Marinzulich* were controlling and specifically stood for the rule that manuals are not employment contracts.[104] Finally, the court of appeals reversed the appellate division, concluding that the record contained "sufficient evidence of a contract and a breach to sustain a cause of action"[105] and ordered a retrial.

In reaching this conclusion, the court of appeals had to overcome several obstacles of New York precedent. First, the defendant's claim that the entire action was barred by the state statute of frauds was summarily dismissed by the court without any discussion concerning whether the employment was one that could be performed within one year. Rather, the court in a conclusory manner simply stated that "the agreement between Weiner and McGraw-Hill ... is not one which 'by its terms' could not be performed within one year, and, therefore, is not one which is barred."[106] Second, the court readily dismissed the defendant's claim that the contract would be lacking

---

[100]*Id.* "[The handbook provided in relevant part] that '[t]he company will resort to dismissal for just and sufficient cause only, and only after all practical steps towards rehabilitation and salvage of the employee have been taken and failed. However, if the welfare of the company indicates that dismissal is necessary, then that decision is arrived at and is carried out forthrightly.' Handbook, Section 8.20, p.[8]." *Id.*

[101]*Id.* at 461, 443 N.E.2d at 442-43, 457 N.Y.S.2d at 194-95.

[102]*Id.* at 461, 443 N.E.2d at 443, 457 N.Y.S.2d at 195.

[103]*See* Comment, *Is New York Still at Will?, supra* note 2, at 261 "Supreme court, at special term, interpreted the [intentional interference] action as an allegation of a *prima facie* tort. Since an essential element, a purely malicious motive, had not been pleaded adequately and because there was no economic justification for the firing, the cause of action was dismissed. The [wrongful inducement] action, also interpreted as one in tort, was dismissed for insufficiency because it was against Weiner's supervisor, an officer of McGraw-Hill, and such a claim was not available against the officers of a party to a contract." (citations omitted).

[104]83 A.D.2d 810, 442 N.Y.S.2d 11 (App. Div. 1981) (cited in Comment, *Is New York Still At Will?, supra* note 2, at 262).

[105]*Weiner*, 57 N.Y.2d at 465, 443 N.E.2d at 445, 457 N.Y.S.2d at 197.

[106]*Id.* at 463, 443 N.E.2d at 444, 457 N.Y.S.2d at 196.

in mutuality and, therefore, would be unenforceable if the plaintiff was free to terminate the employment and the company was not, as the court had held in *Edwards*. Mutuality, the court reasoned, is not always essential for the formation of a binding contract.[107] Consideration, the court felt, was the essential element in the formation of any contract, and consideration does not have to benefit the promisor directly, as long as the promisee suffers some detriment.[108] To support this contention that detrimental reliance can supply adequate consideration, the court quoted Corbin extensively:

> [I]f the employer made a promise, either express or implied, not only to pay for the service but also that the employment should continue for a period of time that is either definite or capable of being determined, that employment is not terminable by him "at will" after the employee has begun or rendered some of the requested service or has given any other consideration. ... This is true even though the employee has made no return promise and has retained the power and legal privilege of terminating the employment "at will." The employer's promise is supported by the service that has been begun or rendered or by the other executed consideration.[109]

Applying the Corbin test to the specific facts of the case, the court concluded that Weiner's consideration was adequate to constitute a binding contract, since

> [f]irst, plaintiff was induced to leave Prentice-Hall with the assurance that McGraw-Hill would not discharge him without cause. Second, this assurance was incorporated into the employment application. Third, plaintiff rejected other offers of employment in reliance on the assurance. Fourth, appellant alleged that, on several occasions when he had recommended that certain of his subordinates be dismissed, he was instructed by his supervisors to proceed in strict compliance with the handbook and policy manuals because employees could be discharged only for just cause. He also claims that he was told that, if he did not proceed in accordance with the strict procedures set forth in the handbook, McGraw-Hill would be liable for legal action.[110]

In sum, the court held that Weiner had provided adequate consideration in the form of detrimental reliance in order to make binding McGraw-Hill's promise to discharge only for just cause. Furthermore, the company was equitably estopped by its own words and actions from asserting that the employment was at will.

---

[107]*Id.* at 464, 443 N.E.2d at 444, 457 N.Y.S.2d at 196.

[108]*Id.* at 464, 443 N.E.2d at 444, 457 N.Y.S.2d at 197.

[109]*Id.* at 465, 443 N.E.2d at 445, 457 N.Y.S.2d at 197 (quoting 1A A. CORBIN, CORBIN ON CONTRACTS § 152, at 14 (1963)) (also cited in Comment, *Is New York Still At Will?*, *supra* note 2, at 265).

[110]*Id.* at 465-66, 443 N.E.2d at 445, 457 N.Y.S.2d at 197.

Ordering a retrial, the court of appeals warned the trial court that the at-will rule as adopted by the state in *Martin* in 1895 was not a rule of law, but only a *rebuttable presumption*.[111] So, the Court of Appeals instructed the lower court that:

> The trier of facts will have to consider the "course of conduct" of the parties, "including their writings" and their antecedent negotiations. Moreover ... it is not McGraw-Hill's subjective intent nor "any single act, phrase or other expression," but "the totality of all of these, given the attendant circumstances, the situation of the parties, and the objectives they were striving to attain," which will control.[112]

It is not surprising that the *Weiner* holding created apprehension and confusion throughout New York as to the status of the employment-at-will doctrine. Later cases, discussed below, have revealed that the *Weiner* holding is narrow. Moreover, *Weiner* does not abandon the at-will rule in New York. Management is still free to discharge an at-will employee without just cause. As one commentator notes, *Weiner* holds that "only when an employer, by his own statements and actions, goes as far as McGraw-Hill apparently did in assuring an employee that his employment is not at-will, will it be estopped from later asserting that it was."[113]

Indeed, the fears spawned by *Weiner* have not been realized. No significant contract exception to the employment-at-will doctrine has materialized, and New York courts have consistently rejected plaintiffs' breach of contract claims.[114] Notably, the *Weiner* decision was recently limited to its facts by *Wexler v. Newsweek, Inc.*[115] In *Wexler,* the plaintiff had worked for Newsweek for more than nineteen years as a publicity director when he was dismissed allegedly because of "budget considerations."[116] Plaintiff Wexler alleged that the stated policy in the employer's manual, providing that an employee satisfactorily performing his job could be terminated "only under extreme circumstances" constituted an employment contract, and, since no such extreme circumstances existed at the time of his dismissal, Newsweek breached the contract.[117]

---

[111]*Id.* at 466, 443 N.E.2d at 446, 457 N.Y.S.2d at 198.

[112]*Id.* at 466-67, 443 N.E.2d at 446, 457 N.Y.S.2d at 198.

[113]Comment, *Is New York Still at Will?, supra* note 2, at 273.

[114]*See, e.g.,* Tyson v. Hess, 109 A.D.2d 1068, 487 N.Y.S.2d 206 (App. Div. 1985); Rizzo v. Int'l Brotherhood of Teamsters, Local 237, 109 A.D.2d 639, 486 N.Y.S.2d 220 (App. Div. 1985); Hager v. Union Carbide Corp., 106 A.D.2d 348, 483 N.Y.S.2d 261 (App. Div. 1984); Pedone v. Avco Financial Services of New York, Inc., 102 A.D.2d 885, 476 N.Y.S.2d 933 (App. Div. 1984).

[115]487 N.Y.S.2d 330 (App. Div. 1985).

[116]*Id.* at 331.

[117]*Id.*

The *Wexler* court disagreed with the plaintiff's claim, distinguishing *Weiner* as follows:

> [I]n the case now before us, plaintiff's employment was at will, a relationship in which the law accords the employer an unfettered right to terminate the employment at any time. In the context of such an employment it would be incongruous to say that an inference may be drawn that the employer impliedly agreed to a provision which would be destructive of his right of termination. The parties may by express agreement limit or restrict the employer's right of discharge, but to imply such a limitation from the existence of an unrestricted right would be internally inconsistent.[118]

New York courts have apparently followed the limited applicability of *Weiner* as enunciated in *Wexler.* Most recently, for example, in *O'Connor v. Eastman Kodak Company,*[119] the court of appeals rejected the plaintiff's allegation that Kodak's popular perception as a "womb-to-tomb" employer and its "Performance Appraisal System" requiring periodic evaluation of each employee formed a contractual promise of permanent employment. Rather, the court concluded, it merely stated that defendant Kodak would strive to maintain a stable environment and to evaluate performance fairly.[120] In addition, recent cases under New York law have held that the employee must show that he relied upon the handbook in order to possibly sustain a breach of implied contract claim.[121]

In short, the post-*Weiner* decisions illustrate that the New York courts have returned to their traditional view regarding the inability of personnel manuals to limit the employer's right to terminate at-will employees. In other words, personnel manuals, policies, employment applications, and other corporate documents will be viewed by the courts merely as broad internal policy guidelines, unless the company, through its words and actions, leads the employee so far as to assure him that his employment is other than at-will. Although there is no "bright line" test to determine where the employer crosses the boundary out of employment-at-will, it is not likely that a court applying New York law will hold that corporate policy documents standing alone create contractual obligations.

---

[118]*Id.* at 332.

[119]65 N.Y.2d 724, 481 N.E.2d 549, 492 N.Y.S.2d 9 (1985).

[120]*Id.*

[121]*See, e.g.,* Greaney v. Prudential-Bache Securities, Inc., N.Y.L.J. 14 (Sup. Ct. Feb. 4, 1985) (court dismissed plaintiff's claim that he relied upon handbook promise in accepting job since he did not receive copy of manual until after commencing employment); Luisi v. JWT Group, Inc., 128 Misc.2d 291, 488 N.Y.S.2d 554 (Sup. Ct. 1985); Wenham v. The Right Reverend Paul Moore, Jr., N.Y.L.J. 7 (Sup. Ct. April 15, 1985).

CONCLUSION

New York has been the most reluctant of the state jurisdictions examined up to this point to derogate the at-will employment doctrine. As recently as 1982 in *Murphy,* the state's highest court held that it is New York's long-settled rule that where employment is for an indefinite term, it is presumed to be a hiring at will which may be freely terminated by either party at any time and for any reason or even for no reason. In that same decision the court declined to recognize the tort of abusive discharge in violation of public policy, concluding that such a fundamental shift in the state's employment law is best left to the legislature. New York courts have been similarly unwilling to recognize an employee's implied contractual rights arising from personnel handbooks or policy manuals and have generally applied the state's statute of frauds to bar such claims.

A review of the progressive derogation of the at-will employment doctrine in New York, Pennsylvania, Michigan and California illustrates the complexity of this area of employment law. Each state has chosen to recognize, or has refused to recognize, various tort- or contract-based exceptions to the common law at-will rule. To be sure, these permutations of the law produce a great deal of confusion. Therefore, it is necessary at this point to gain perspective of the larger problem by stepping back from the state-level development and considering the broad economic and social consequences likely to result from a weakened employment-at-will doctrine.

CHAPTER VIII

Impact of a Weakened Employment-At-Will Rule

Despite the vast amount of literature on the employment-at-will rule, few commentators have focused on the economic consequences stemming from a modification of the at-will doctrine.[1] The absence of such analysis is not surprising when one considers the complexity of the issue and the far-reaching economic consequences stemming from any alteration of termination rights. Nonetheless, it is certain that as employers' power to discharge employees is circumscribed either through judicial or legislative action, there will be a realignment throughout the entire economy, affecting employers, employees, unions, and consumers. To better comprehend the impact of such a shift, the discussion below attempts to identify the areas of the economy which a weakened employment-at-will rule will be likely to affect and offer data from analogous situations where the at-will rule has been significantly diluted or a just cause requirement imposed. In this regard, this chapter will first examine the economic consequences arising from an alteration of at-will employment, then detail the impact felt on the corporate level, and conclude with an appraisal of the change's impact on the structure of collective bargaining.

---

[1]Among the commentators who have examined the economic consequences, *see* Harrison, *The "New" Terminable-at-Will Employment Contract: An Interest and Cost Incidence Analysis*, 69 Iowa L. Rev. 327 (1984)[hereinafter cited as Harrison, *Cost Incidence Analysis*]; Note, *Protecting At Will Employees Against Wrongful Discharge: The Duty to Terminate Only in Good Faith*, 93 Harv. L. Rev. 1816, 1828-36 (1980); Brake, *Limiting the Right to Terminate at Will—Have the Courts Forgotten the Employer?*, 35 Vand. L. Rev. 201, 204-05 (1982)[hereinafter cited as Brake, *Have the Courts Forgotten?*]; Sheffler, *Terminable At-Will Employment in Michigan: A Survey of Business Opinions and Current Employment Practices*, (MBA Thesis, Central Michigan University 1985) [hereinafter cited as Sheffler, *At-Will in Michigan*].

ECONOMIC CONSIDERATIONS

Cost Considerations

Many of the commentators who advocate a modification of employment-at-will propose that discharge cases be adjudicated by the courts, administrative agencies, or arbitrators. To meet the costs of this adjudication, these authors make several suggestions, ranging from the payment of a $50-$100 fee[2] to the "sharing of fees and expenses by the parties."[3]

Professor Jack Stieber has provided some rough estimates of the number of potential wrongful discharge cases per year which help to calculate the magnitude of the costs associated with such proposals.[4] Starting with the statistic that "the annual discharge rate in manufacturing industries is approximately 4.6 percent,"[5] Stieber estimates "that approximately 2.3 million private-sector employees not covered by collective bargaining agreements were discharged in 1977."[6] Of these, he calculated that about one million were not probationary employees, who are usually excluded from job protection proposals.[7]

Nathan Lipson and J. Douglas Korney have carried forward Stieber's estimates and postulated that if only one-half of those one million potential plaintiffs invoked a right to review their discharge, then "[t]he result would be a case-load more than ten times the NLRB's [National Labor Relations Board's] 47,115 case intake in fiscal year 1982."[8] Moreover, if one considers the decrease in union membership since the time Steiber's estimates were first made and

---

[2]*See* Howlett, *Due Process for Non-Unionized Employees: A Practical Proposal* (proceedings of the 32nd Annual Meeting, Industrial Relations Research Association, ed. Barbara Dennis) (1980) at 164 (cited in Lipson & Korney, *A Case Against Statutory Review of Private Sector Discharge Cases*, 1983 MICH. B. J. 764, 768 & note 28 (Sept. 1983) [hereinafter cited as Lipson & Korney, *Against Statutory Review*].

[3]*See* Michigan House Bill No.5892, introduced June 17, 1982 by representatives Bullard and Emerson (cited in Lipson & Korney, *Against Statutory Review, supra* note 2, at 768 & note 29).

[4]*See* Stieber, *The Case for Protection of Unorganized Employees Against Unjust Discharge*, (proceedings of the 32nd annual meeting, Industrial Relations Research Association, ed. Barbara Dennis) (1980) (cited in Lipson & Korney, *Against Statutory Review, supra* note 2, at 768 & note 31).

[5]Lipson & Korney, *Against Statutory Review, supra* note 2, at 768.

[6]*Id.*

[7]*Id.*

[8]*Id.* As Lipson and Korney observe: "About 110 administrative law judges issued 1,105 decisions in fiscal 1982. The total NLRB budget for fiscal year 1983 [was] $124,045,000." *Id.* (citations omitted).

the increased propensity among employees to pursue wrongful discharge litigation, it is likely that the magnitude of the potential caseload would be even more staggering.

Turning to the costs associated with processing such reviews, Lipson and Korney provide the following useful statistics: first, "[t]he average arbitrator's charge in cases handled by the Federal Mediation and Conciliation Service in 1981 was $1,132.31"; second, "[t]he arbitrator's average per diem that year was $300"; and lastly, "[t]he average number of days charged per case was 3.32."[9] Factoring in these averages, the authors conclude that the cost of arbitrating Steiber's estimated 500,000 cases annually would be approximately $566 million in 1982 dollars.[10] Adjusting for a much heavier caseload, the increase in arbitrators' fees, and inflation, one would expect this cost estimate to be much greater today.

Arbitration costs, however, represent only a fraction of the total costs involved in handling the review process.[11] As Lipson and Korney point out, each side in an arbitration usually prepares and presents witnesses and exhibits.[12] In addition, there is the time spent preparing for hearings,[13] and "post-hearing briefs are common."[14] With these attendant costs added in, the average cost of each arbitration case would be in the "thousands of dollars," making the total cost to society "into the billions."[15] Moreover, the authors note, a discharged employee would most likely not have the resources to finance such a legal venture.[16] Accordingly, "to make the right [to a discharge review] more than illusory, the employee's share would arguably have to be financed by the state, which would mean new taxes."[17]

---

[9]*Id., citing* Federal Mediation and Conciliation Service, 34th Annual Report, Fiscal Year 1981.

[10]Lipson & Korney, *Against Statutory Review, supra* note 2, at 768.

[11]*Id.*

[12]*Id.*

[13]*Id.*

[14]*Id.*

[15]*Id.* at 768-69.

[16]*Id.* at 769. It should be noted, however, that frequently wrongful discharge cases are handled on a contingency fee basis.

[17]*Id.*

Impact on Supply and Demand in the Labor Market

In a useful study, Professor Jeffrey Harrison has employed basic microeconomic analysis to suggest the effect that altering the employment-at-will rule would have on the labor market.[18] Figure VIII-1 below diagrams the labor market under competitive conditions.[19] The horizontal axis corresponds to units of labor employed; wages are plotted along the vertical axis. The curve labelled S represents the supply of labor in the market. Its upward slope "indicates that as wages increase, the quantity of labor available to be hired increases."[20] The D curve represents the demand for labor in the market. The demand curve's slope shows that "as wages decrease, the quantity of labor demanded will increase."[21] The intersection of the supply and demand curves corresponds to the wage rate and employment level when the labor market is in equilibrium.

Harrison demonstrates that judicial or legislative actions which alter the terminable-at-will nature of employment will produce effects on both the supply and demand sides of the market.[22] As illustrated in Figure VIII-2,[23] assume that D_1 represents the demand for labor prior to any modification of the at-will rule. As changes in the at-will rule increase job security, the cost of labor to the employer will rise. "This cost is a combination of the employer's subjective preference for employees that can be discharged at will and the expected quantifiable costs, such as those associated with less flexibility and increased litigation expenses."[24] This cost to the employer is represented on Figure VIII-2 by the vertical distance between D_1 and D_2. As the cost of the labor input rises, the demand for labor will contract. This decrease in demand is shown in Figure VIII-2 by the downward shift of the D_1 curve to D_2.

---

[18]*See* Harrison, *Cost Incidence Analysis, supra* note 1. The author is greatly indebted to Professor Harrison for his microeconomic analysis. All references in this chapter to the microeconomic analysis come from Harrison's study.

[19]*See id.* at 332, Figure I.

[20]*Id.* & note 38:

> A distinction must be drawn between supply and the quantity supplied. Supply refers to the entire supply curve. It is a schedule of prices and quantities. The quantity supplied is the amount on a supply curve that is associated with a particular price or wage. *See* P. SAMUELSON, ECONOMICS, 62-63 (10th ed. 1976).

Id.

[21]*Id.* at 333 note 45.

[22]*See id.* at 335-38.

[23]*Id.* at 335, Figure III.

[24]*Id.* at 335.

FIGURE VIII-1*
*Supply and Demand in the Labor Market
Under Competitive Conditions*

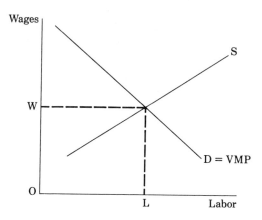

FIGURE VIII-2*
*Change in Supply and Demand for Labor Resulting from
a Weakened Employment-at-Will Rule*

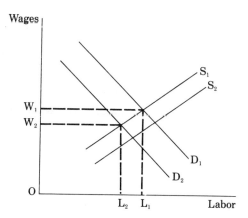

The impact of this shift in demand is a lower wage level and a lesser quantity of labor employed. As Figure VIII-2 illustrates, the intersection of the original supply curve, S_1, and the new demand curve, D_2, is at wage W_2 and employment level L_2. Both W_2 and L_2 are lower than the original wage, W_1, and employment level, L_1.

Harrison observes that changes in the at-will rule will likely have an effect on the supply side of the labor market as well.[25] Some sellers of labor are likely to value the increase in job security and be "willing to offer the same quantities of labor as before [but] at [a] lower wage."[26] In short, there would be an increase in the supply of labor, as represented by the outward shift of the S curve from S_1 to S_2. "The decrease in the amount of wages required by workers at specific quantities of labor is a measure of the value attributed to job security and is reflected in the vertical distance between the supply curves at any employment level."[27]

It is clear from Harrison's simple microeconomic analysis that shifts in either the demand or the supply curve will produce lower wages.[28] The acceptance of lower wages is the cost employees pay for the increased job security which arises from altering employment-at-will.[29] The new level of employment, however, is more difficult to predict. Its final level depends on the relative strength of the shifts in supply and demand.[30]

Harrison also points out that shifts in the supply and demand of labor have an impact on allocative efficiency in the economy.[31] As mentioned earlier, the vertical distance between the demand curves represents the value (cost) that employers attribute to lost discharge rights. Correspondingly, the vertical shift in the supply curves measures the value in increased job security perceived by the employees.[32] According to economic theorists, when the vertical distance of the demand shift is less than the vertical drop in supply, there has

---

[25]*Id.* at 336.
[26]*Id.*
[27]*Id.* & note 58: "In effect it now takes a lower wage to attract each unit of labor because workers regard increased job security as a type of compensation." *Id., citing* C. FERGUSON S. MARICE, ECONOMIC ANALYSIS: THEORY AND APPLICATION, 450-52 (3d ed. 1978).
[28]Harrison, *A Cost Incidence Analysis, supra* note 1, at 336.
[29]*Id.*
[30]*Id.*
[31]*See id.* at 337.
[32]*Id.*

been a shift to a more efficient economic state.[33] Conversely, if the vertical shift in demand exceeds the supply shift, the change is inefficient.[34]

Although a complete discussion of Professor Harrison's economic analysis is beyond the scope of this chapter, it should be noted that Harrison concludes that the actual impact of a change in termination "rights" will be determined by the following five factors: (1) "the relative magnitudes of the shifts in the supply and demand for labor in response to the change" in employment-at-will; (2) "the relative elasticities of supply and demand in the labor market," which correspond to the responsiveness of buyers and sellers of labor to changes in wages; (3) "the existence of a minimum wage in the labor market"; (4) "the character of the labor market"; and (5) the impact on output.[35]

Not surprisingly, the complex interaction of these five factors makes it difficult to predict the actual impact of an altered employment-at-will rule on the economy. It is clear to Harrison, however, that "the costs of a general increase in job security" resulting from either judicial or legislative action "may be felt more by employees in a labor market characterized by a relatively inelastic supply and elastic demand."[36] In other words,"an increase in job security, for any reason, is likely to be paid for disproportionately by workers with low skills and few alternative employment opportunities."[37] This impact is particularly troublesome to Harrison since "it is not the employees themselves who are consenting to this exchange of wages and employment opportunities for job security . . . . Thus, the less affluent may pay what amounts to a regressive tax in order to finance the promotion of public interest."[38] Such a regressive tax, at the least, arguably stands in sharp contrast to our society's historical acceptance of a progressive or proportionate tax system as the equitable means of generating revenues for the production of public goods.[39]

---

[33]*Id.*

[34]*Id.* & note 64, *citing* R. POSNER, THE ECONOMICS OF JUSTICE, 91-92 (1981); Coleman, *Efficiency, Exchange and Auction: Philosophical Aspects of the Economic Approach to Law,* 68 CALIF. L. REV. 221, 237-49 (1980); Hicks, *The Foundations of Welfare Economics,* 49 ECON. J. 696, 707-09 (1939); Kaldor, *Welfare Propositions of Economics and Interpersonal Comparison of Utility,* 49 ECON. J. 549, 550-51 (1939).

[35]Harrison, *A Cost Incidence Analysis, supra* note 1, at 359-60.

[36]*Id.* at 360.

[37]*Id.*

[38]*Id.*

[39]*See* Harrison, *The Price of the Public Policy Modification of the Terminable-at-Will Rule,* 34 LAB. L. J. 581, 584 (1983).

IMPACT ON THE CORPORATE LEVEL

Many commentators argue that a unilateral "obligation not to terminate an employee without just cause should be imposed on the
employer, apparently assuming that this expense can be borne easily by the companies or consumers."[40] "Recent concessions in union
contracts in the auto[mobile] industry [,however,] make it clear that
labor costs cannot be spread to the consumer indefinitely."[41] "For
courts simply to impose protections against terminations in all
employment contracts without requiring economic sacrifices by the
employees would create an imbalance against the employers which
would have grave effects on industry."[42]

By far the most deleterious effect such protection could create is a
rise in indirect labor costs for employers forced to protect themselves from lawsuits and arbitration proceedings. The negative
impact of increased indirect labor costs to employers has been
stressed by many commentators.[43] A study in Michigan noted that
the implications of the costs associated with a weakened
employment-at-will rule are staggering.[44] "The impact of legal proceedings, court costs and damages could represent a genuine obstacle to the small firm."[45] Considering that small firms usually have
only limited operational funds available and that approximately 93
percent of U.S. business is classified as small, the litigation of discharged at-will employees might have a substantial impact on the
business community as a whole.[46]

In Pennsylvania, a recent study published by the Business Council
of Pennsylvania, echoed the same theme.[47] In describing the Commonwealth's competitive position relative to seventeen other states
studied, the report notes that "indirect labor costs ... are significantly higher in Pennsylvania than other states and constitute a
major obstacle to business expansion and growth in Pennsylva-

---

[40]Note, *The Development of Exceptions to At-Will Employment: A Review of Case
Law from Management's Viewpoint*, 51 CINN. L. REV. 616, 632 (1982) [hereinafter
cited as Note, *Management's Viewpoint*].

[41]*Id., citing* Wall Street Journal, April 12, 1982, at 4, col.2; March 1, 1982, at 3,
col. 1.

[42]Note, *Management's Viewpoint, supra* note 30, at 632.

[43]*See, e.g.,* Sheffler, *At-Will in Michigan, supra* note 1, at 8; Business Council of
Pennsylvania, *1985 Update: The Competitive Position of Pennsylvania Businesses,* at
34 (1985) [hereinafter cited as Pennsylvania Business Council, *Competitive Position*].

[44]Sheffler, *At-Will in Michigan, supra* note 1, at 8.

[45]*Id.*

[46]*Id.* (citations omitted).

[47]Pennsylvania Business Council, *Competitive Position, supra* note 43, at 34.

nia."[48] The report continues, "[w]hen other indirect costs and taxes are added into the picture, the cost-of-doing business in Pennsylvania is a significant disincentive to new firm formation."[49] It is clear that the indirect labor costs associated with a weakened at-will rule would stall real economic growth and dull Pennsylvania's competitive advantage.[50] Moreover, employers faced with the potentially great indirect costs of labor arising from at-will litigation, may be discouraged from locating in a state which has significantly abrogated the at-will doctrine.

In order to gauge the potential impact of an alteration of employment-at-will, it may be helpful at this point to examine countries where increased job security has been statutorily enacted. In the last decade, while the United States has created approximately twenty million jobs, Western Europe has lost some two million.[51] Of course there are many possible explanations for this significant gap, but one which many labor economists point to is the presence in Europe of strict governmental regulation of the workplace. In Great Britain, for example, the government established an industrial tribunal system whose provisions are similar to the unjust dismissal bills presently before several states' legislatures. Under the British system, individuals who believe they have been unfairly dismissed are entitled to take their employer to a tribunal for a ruling, and possibly compensation.

In Britain's faltering economy, industrial tribunals have become one of the country's few areas of actual growth.[52] In 1982 alone, more than 40,000 applications for tribunal hearings were received by the Central Office of Industrial Tribunals for England and Wales, with unfair dismissals comprising the vast bulk of complaints.[53] Employers, on the one hand, complain that the system deters them from dismissing inefficient workers and discourages badly needed productivity gains.[54] On the other hand, labor unions are not pleased with the system's inefficiencies and evidentiary procedure.[55] Apparently, few Britons are satisfied with the tribunal system.

---

[48]*Id.* at 8.
[49]*Id.* at 9.
[50]*Id.* at 34.
[51]New York Times, June 17, 1984, Section 3, at 1.
[52]New York Times, May 11, 1982, Section D, at 1.
[53]*Id.* at Section D, p.9.
[54]*Id.*
[55]*Id.*

One segment of the British economy that has benefitted from the tribunal system is the insurance market which sells protection against tribunal hearings to companies.[56] Such firms handle a company's defense and pay any awards. An employee determined to have been unfairly dismissed may be awarded up to $32,000.[57] Typically, premiums average $20 per employee annually, which for a large employer is a sizeable expense.[58] But it appears the real expense in the whole system is the nuisance value inherent in such proceedings.[59] Experts in the United Kingdom estimate that the cost to a company for defending itself at a one-day hearing, in time and legal fees, can reach $2000.[60]

France, too, has been experiencing difficulty with its highly regulated workplace and is considering a new proposal known as ENCA (*Emplois Nouveaux a Contraintes Allegées*, that is, New Jobs With Eased Constraints).[61] French experts believe that abolishing the present restriction which imposes an obligation on the employer to obtain prior governmental approval before dismissing an employee as a result of redundancy would create some 367,000 jobs.[62]

"In 1975, Portugal adopted a comprehensive law regulating virtually every aspect of labor-management relations."[63] Under the present Portugese system nearly all dismissals must be reviewed by the labor courts. As the *Wall Street Journal* reported:

> [E]mployers have found dismissals for cause difficult to prove in the courts. Workers who prevail may be reinstated with full back pay—often several years' worth—and often become sources of agitation after returning to work. Employers say that they would rather put up with absenteeism and low productivity than undergo the time and expense of the labor courts.[64]

Professor Drucker sums up the negative aspects of the countries' experiences by noting that the governments' provision of quasi-property rights in jobs carries a real danger of rigidity and immobility.[65] Pointing to the Belgian system of redundancy payments, he

---

[56]*Id.*

[57]*Id.* In fact, the awards tend to be modest. In 1980, the average compensation was $1075. *Id.*

[58]*Id.*

[59]*Id.*

[60]*Id.*

[61]127 European Industrial Relations Review, 57, 57-58 (Aug. 1984).

[62]*Id.*

[63]Lipson & Korney, *Against Statutory Review, supra* note 2, at 769.

[64]Wall Street Journal, April 20, 1983 (quoted in Lipson & Korney, *Against Statutory Review, supra* note 2, at 769).

[65]*See* Forbes & Jones, *A Comparative, Attitudinal, and Analytic Study of Dismissal of At-Will Employees Without Cause*, 37 LAB. L. J. 157, 164-65.

concludes that while the system "may prevent employers from laying off people ... it also keeps them from hiring workers they might need."[66] "Thus, [the system] creates more unemployment than it prevents or arranges."[67]

Within the United States, it is clear that one of the most immediate effects of introducing exceptions to the employment-at-will doctrine is the increase in both the threat and expense of litigation. As courts at both the state and federal levels continue to recognize a wide range of causes of action for discharged employees, "the array of facts that will constitute a *prima facie* case [of unjust dismissal] and, therefore put an employee's claim before a jury," also expands.[68] Therefore,"[i]f an employee can raise questions of fact sufficient to avoid summary judgment or a directed verdict, his chance of success before the jury is excellent."[69] Professor Blades has noted the "propensity of jurors to sympathize with employees":[70]

> There is the danger that the average jury will identify with, and therefore believe, the employee. This possibility could give rise to vexatious lawsuits by disgruntled employees fabricating plausible tales of employer coercion. If the potential for vexatious lawsuits by discharged employees is too great, employers will be inhibited in exercising their best judgment as to which employees should or should not be retained... [t]he employer's prerogative to make independent, good faith judgments about employees is important to our free enterprise system.[71]

Vexatious lawsuits from discharged employees have apparently been encouraged. One attorney notes, "[t]here is a great willingness on the part of employees to sue their employers, and now the courts, especially the juries, are amenable to giving large awards."[72] Some cautious employers often will settle out of court even those claims that may border on being frivolous rather than risk an adverse finding by a jury, particularly in jurisdictions that recognize actions in tort thereby subjecting the employer to possible punitive damages.[73]

---

[66]*Id.* at 165.

[67]*Id.*

[68]Brake, *Have the Courts Forgotten?, supra* note 1, at 223.

[69]*Id.*

[70]*Id.*

[71]Blades, *Employment-At-Will vs. Individual Freedom: On Limiting the Abusive Exercise of Employer Power,* 67 COLUM. L. REV. 1404, 1428 note 9 (1967) (quoted in Brake, *Have the Courts Forgotten?, supra* note 1, at 223 note 114).

[72]Halbert, *Pittsburgh's Employment Law Firm: Gallo & Weiner,* 6 PA. L. J. (Feb. 14, 1983) at 11.

[73]*See id.*

It is well established that wrongful discharge litigation can prove extremely costly to the employer. Many commentators have noted that the possibility of a discharged employee recovering punitive damages could make the costs to the employer devastating.[74] For example, Justice Underwood of the Illinois Supreme Court in his dissenting opinion in *Kelsay v. Motorola* warned that: "[h]enceforth, no matter how indolent, insubordinate, or obnoxious an employee may be ... [the] employer may thereafter terminate him only at the risk of being compelled to defend a suit for unlimited punitive damages."[75]

According to a survey by a San Francisco law firm, jury verdicts in wrongful discharge cases in California in 1986 averaged $424,527 in general and punitive damages.[76] Out of the fifty-one jury verdicts during 1986 in wrongful discharge cases, discharged employees prevailed in 78 percent of the cases.[77] Those verdicts totaled $16,981,101 in general and punitive damages.[78] As one of the surveyors noted, these statistics are "quite sobering for all employers."[79] In another study conducted by a special committee of the State Bar of California focusing on wrongful discharge cases between 1980 and 1982, it was reported that in 53 percent of the cases in which discharged employees prevailed, punitive damages were awarded.[80] Damage awards of $100,000 or more were reported in more than 76 percent of the cases and damages of $600,000 or more were reported in approximately 35 percent of the cases.[81] Based on these statistics, the committee concluded that "the prospect of large and uncertain

---

[74]*See* Note, *Management's Viewpoint, supra* note 40, at 632-33.

[75]744 Ill. 2d 172, 192, 384 N.E.2d 353, 362 (1978) (Underwood, J., dissenting) (quoted in Note, *Management's Viewpoint, supra* note 40, at 633 & note 109, *citing* Palmateer v. Int'l Harvester Co., 85 Ill.2d 124, 135, 421 N.E.2d 876, 881 (1981) (Ryan, J., dissenting); Rozier v. St. Mary's Hospital, 88 Ill.App.3d 994, 111 N.E.2d 50 (1980)]. "An Indiana appellate court has expressed reservations about permitting a cause of action for a discharge that breaches a non-codified public policy, because punitive damages permitted therefor also are measured by the same indefinite source." Note, *Management's Viewpoint, supra* note 40, at 633 & note 10, *citing* Martin v. Platt, 386 N.E.2d 1026, 1028 (Ind. Ct. App. 1979).

[76]*See* Bureau of National Affairs (BNA), 35 DAILY LAB. REP., at A-4 (Feb. 24, 1987). It should be noted that this average is skewed somewhat by two awards that exceeded $1 million each. But, even if those awards are not counted, the average was still $251,010. *Id.*

[77]*Id.*

[78]*Id.*

[79]*Id.*

[80]*To Strike A New Balance,* (Report of the Ad-Hoc Committee on Termination at Will and Wrongful Discharge, Employment Law Section of the State Bar of California) (Feb. 8, 1984).

[81]*Id.*

damage awards has both introduced an element of destabilization in the employer-employee relationship and also promoted considerable litigation in its wake."[82]

Another impact on the corporate level arising from exceptions to the employment-at-will doctrine centers on the disruptive effect such changes will have on the internal decision-making policies of most organizations.[83] This directly undermines the premise, traditionally recognized by most courts, that management's employment decisions are constrained by economic considerations:

> a company, no matter how large, can afford only so many uneconomic decisions, and it is well to remember that the marketplace contains a system of rewards and penalties independent of those prescribed by law. To the extent that appellant's discharge was uneconomic, [it] has been penalized by the loss of a valuable employee.[84]

Finding themselves uncertain about what courts might find sufficient to constitute policy mandates or implied promises, employers might very well be placed in a situation where they will be "inhibited from critically evaluating their employees because of the constant threat of litigation."[85]

As one scholar suggests, this situation is particularly troublesome when managerial or salaried employees are the subject of review.[86] In contrast to the hourly wage earner, "whose performance generally can be measured by an objective standard, upper echelon employees are judged to a much greater degree by more intangible qualities such as imagination, initiative, drive, and personality":[87]

> The employer's evaluation of higher ranking employees is usually a highly personalized, intuitive judgment, and, as such, is more difficult to translate into concrete reasons which someone else—a juryman—can readily understand and appreciate.... Compromise of the employer's power to make such judgments about professional, managerial and other high ranking employees ... is especially undesirable.[88]

---

[82]*Id.*

[83]*See* Note, *Management's Viewpoint, supra* note 40, at 631.

[84]Yaindl v. Ingersoll-Rand Co., 422 A.2d 611, 621 (Pa. Super. Ct. 1981) (quoted in Note, *Management's Viewpoint, supra* note 40, at 632 note 104).

[85]Brake, *Have the Courts Forgotten?, supra* note 1, at 229.

[86]*See* Blades, *Employment-At-Will vs. Individual Freedom: On Limiting the Abusive Exercise of Employer Power,* 67 COLUM. L. REV. 1404, 1428-29 [hereinafter cited as Blades, *Limiting Abusive Discharge*].

[87]Brake, *Have the Courts Forgotten?, supra* note 1, at 229.

[88]Blades, *Limiting Abusive Discharge, supra* note 86, at 1428-29 (quoted in Note, *Have the Courts Forgotten?, supra* note 1, at 229-30).

Moreover, any constraints in decisions concerning discharge are likely to be carried over to other personnel decisions, including choices about pay increases, decreases, promotions, and demotions.[89] This impact on management's ability to make personnel decisions could prove particularly damaging to small businesses. "Because smaller companies employ fewer workers, and because their survival is often linked to a few key individuals, these companies will especially be hurt if their ability to evaluate their workforce critically is impaired" by judicial or legislative intervention.[90]

IMPACT ON THE STRUCTURE OF COLLECTIVE BARGAINING

In addition to the direct impact an eroded employment-at-will doctrine would have on employers and employees, it appears that the current trend of judicial intervention into discharge decisions would also have far-reaching effects on the entire structure of collective bargaining. Although critics of the employment-at-will rule justify judicial intervention as a necessary move in order to protect workers' rights, these authors in many cases fail to address what may be serious and fundamental consequences of their advocations. As the judiciary steps in as the chief protector of employees' interests, many argue that the attractiveness of union membership decreases. In effect, the courts will usurp the role previously held by the unions.

A weakened employment-at-will doctrine might decrease union organization activities by influencing employees' perceptions of the marginal advantage of a union contract. First, as one management attorney suggests, "[s]ome employees may get the idea that tort actions for wrongful discharge render unions superfluous," since in a traditional union grievance for wrongful discharge, backpay and reinstatement are the only available remedies.[91] The plaintiff in a tort action who prevails on damages for emotional distress may come out farther ahead monetarily than he would if he were covered by a union contract.[92] Secondly, the promise of "[j]ob security is the principle benefit of unionization to employees"[93] if the workers per-

---

[89]J. BARBASH, J. FEERICK & J. KAUFF, UNJUST DISMISSAL AND AT WILL EMPLOYMENT at 16-17 (1982).

[90]Brake, *Have the Courts Forgotten?, supra* note 1, at 230.

[91]BNA, *The Employment-At-Will Issue: A BNA Special Report,* DAILY LAB. REP., No.224, at 20-21 (Nov. 19, 1982) (interview with Ralph Baxter).

[92]*Id.* at 21.

[93]*Id.*

ceive that "the courts [and not the unions] are guaranteeing job security," the apparent value to employees of joining a union will decrease.[94] Increased judicial intervention could blur one of the major distinctions between union and nonunion companies: the opportunity to have grievances decided by a neutral outsider. Ordinarily, nonunion companies do not use grievance procedures culminating in a decision by a neutral third party. Obtaining such arbitration is frequently one of the chief incentives for workers to organize. Evidence indicates that neutralizing this selling point would defuse organizing campaigns.[95]

Pennsylvania, for example, ranks high in comparison to other states in the level of union membership among nonagricultural workers in the private sector, with 23.6 percent of the private-sector employees in the union ranks.[96] This figure, however, represents a sharp decline in Pennsylvania's private-sector unionization, which stood as 32.3 percent as recently as 1975.[97] This decline, although the product of many forces affecting the Pennsylvania economy, coincides with the courts' erosion of the employment-at-will doctrine. Indeed, as nonunion employees increasingly enjoy the protection negotiated by and paid for by union employees, the advantages of organization become less compelling.

A more detailed study conducted by George R. Neumann and Ellen R. Rissman at Northwestern University supplies empirical evidence that unionization rates across the country fall in response to the judiciary's recognition of exceptions to the employment-at-will doctrine.[98] This article examines trends in union membership during the twentieth century. The authors advance the hypothesis that the "provision of certain social welfare benefits by government substitutes for the private provision by the unions, thereby reducing the attractiveness of union membership."[99] The authors examine the implications of their hypothesis through the use of time-series data on aggregate union membership from 1904-1980 and pooled state data from 1964-1980. These later data are used to examine the effect

---

[94]*Id.*

[95]*See* Neumann & Rissman, *Where Have All the Union Members Gone?* 2 J. LAB. ECON. 175, 190 (1984) [hereinafter cited as Neumann & Rissman, *Union Members*].

[96]TROY & SHEFLIN, UNION SOURCEBOOK, at 7-8 (1st ed. 1985).

[97]*Id.*

[98]Neumann & Rissman, *Union Members, supra* note 95.

[99]*See id.* at 175.

of the erosion of the at-will doctrine. "Both the time-series and cross-section evidence suggest that government supply of 'union-like' services reduces union membership."[100]

Neumann and Rissman's findings, which are presented in Table VIII-1 below, "speak plainly to the issue of substitution of government services for union services."[101] The evidence illustrates the declines in union membership, particularly in those states that have adopted what the authors view as the strongest deviation from the traditional concept of employment-at-will, the implied contract exception.[102] The recognition of just cause for discipline and discharge "and the availability of third party review of personnel action ... strikes at the heart of services provided by unions."[103] Naturally, there are many other factors that may better explain the decline in union membership than the weakening of the at-will rule, such as the change from heavy industry to a service economy, exhorbitant union wage scales, and foreign competition.

In light of the fact that union membership as a percentage of the total workforce has been declining since 1945, the effects outlined above predict that employers will face even weaker unions at the bargaining table. As suggested earlier, however, the union-management bargaining table will no longer be the place of dispute resolution. Rather, the determination of employees' interests will take place in the courtroom. The problem, according to Professor Madison, is that the ultimate exercise of discretion regarding whether to approve employee discharges will be shifted from employers to the courts, with no more concrete legal standards to guide the courts than have constrained employers in the past.[104] Therefore, in the effective absence of a union-management relationship, one must consider which party is better suited to evaluate the

---

[100]*Id.*

[101]*Id.* at 190. Neumann and Rissman's statistical evidence suggests that the public policy exception to the employment-at-will doctrine has not had a significant impact on unionization rates. As they note, "[p]ublic policy exceptions to established common law, a topic not often dealt with in collective bargaining contracts, primarily because of its relevance to white-collar workers who historically have not been unionized, seem to have insubstantial effects on unionization rates." *Id.*

[102]*Id.*

[103]*Id.* at 188. Incidentally, as Neumann and Rissman observe, the recorded position of the AFL-CIO resembles statements made by existing firms when new entrants to the market arrive: "[t]he AFL-CIO does not believe that it is a 'possibility' that workers can have 'just cause' protection with respect to employment 'without unions,'" according to Rudy Oswald, chief economist for the AFL-CIO. *Id.* & note 14. " 'If such legislation existed,' he continued, 'hardly would it put unions out of business.' " *Id.*

[104]Madison, *The Employee's Emerging Right to Sue for Arbitrary or Unfair Discharge,"* 6 EMPL. REL. L. J. 422 (1980/81).

TABLE VIII-1

Cross-Section Regressions of State Unionization Rates, 1964–80

	1	2	3	4	5
Constant	23.1260	23.1250	23.3540	23.2120	23.4840
	(1.4973)	(1.4969)	(1.4615)	(1.4744)	(1.4644)
% Mfg.	.0725	.0725	.0739	.0741	.0746
	(.0280)	(.0280)	(.0273)	(.0276)	(.0273)
Unemp.	.8128	.8126	.8043	.8023	.7357
	(.2294)	(.2281)	(.2182)	(.2202)	(.2247)
Time	−.4089	−.4089	−.3849	−.3923	−.3772
	(.0924)	(.0925)	(.0904)	(.0912)	(.0905)
RTWS	−9.8356	−9.8312	−9.8617	−9.6987	−9.7145
	(.8008)	(.7955)	(.7744)	(.7822)	(.7825)
D_1	−.1470	—	—	—	1.6054
	(1.2380)				(1.2641)
$D_1 T$	—	−.0912	—	—	—
		(.1460)			
D_2	—	—	−6.3215	—	−6.8566
			(1.3817)		(1.4436)
$D_2 T$	—	—	—	−1.0260	—
				(.2908)	
R^2	.4176	.4176	.4438	.4335	.4458
SEE	7.1084	7.1084	6.9467	7.0109	6.9419

Source: Neumann & Rissman, *Where Have All the Union Members Gone?*, 2 JOURNAL OF LABOR ECONOMICS, 175, 188 (1984).

Table VIII-1 "contains ordinary least squares (OLS) estimates for the pooled observations on the 50 states for the nine observations available per state. In columns 1 and 2 we present results concerning whether a public policy exception to the employment-at-will doctrine has any effect on unionization rates. Although the coefficients on D_1 and $D_1 T$ are negative in columns 1 and 2, neither is large relative to its standard error, and both would be properly judged as insignificant.

Columns 3 and 4, dealing with the effect of implicit contract exceptions to the employment-at-will doctrine, tell quite a different story. There both D_2 and $D_2 T$ have significant negative coefficients, indicating that unionization rates fall in response to this particular form of exception to the employment-at-will doctrine. As it turns out, the specification of the effect of employment-at-will exceptions seems to be better captured by the indicator variable D_2 than by the trend $D_2 T$, a result that might be expected given that the implicit contract exceptions are of such recent vintage." *Id.* at 189-90.

decision to terminate an employee.[105] On the one hand, the judge or arbitrator is likely to be unfamiliar with the nature of the employment relationship and is responsible only to the state to judiciously administer the laws and render an equitable decision.[106] The employer, on the other hand, is constrained by market forces.[107] An employer who continually discharges good workers without cause would soon have a company unable to produce its product competitively and to attract and to retain employees.[108] As a matter of economic efficiency, then, it would be unwise to transfer the final decision of whether a worker will be continued to be employed away from the employer, who is committed to the continued viability of his enterprise, to an outside party, who is not.[109]

CONCLUSION

Although it is difficult to predict with accuracy the consequences resulting from a weakened employment-at-will doctrine, many commentators have suggested broad areas of the economy that would be likely to be affected by any change in this aspect of employment law. First, it may be argued that any alteration of the at-will rule by the imposition of a just cause standard would impose a significant cost on society and further burden an already overloaded judiciary system. Second, it is likely that alteration of the at-will rule will decrease the average wage level and quantity of labor employed, resulting in what one expert calls a "regressive tax" on those workers least able to bear such a burden. The impact of a weakened at-will doctrine will also be felt by employers as their ability to manage their workforce effectively is circumscribed by the threat of litigation. Finally, as Neumann and Rissman suggest, union membership has fallen in recent years as a result of the courts' usurpation of the unions' traditional role of protecting employees from arbitrary discharge.

Of course, one can hardly challenge or disagree with the desirability of taking certain steps to instill a sense of "equity" or to decrease "unfairness" in the workplace. Unfortunately, these are very subjective factors to begin with and a failure to appraise the process by which judicial standards of equity and unfairness are developed realistically or to evaluate critically the consequences of

---

[105] *Id.*
[106] *Id.*
[107] *Id.*
[108] *Id.*
[109] *Id.*

such development could result in a fundamental disservice to those persons whom proponents of at-will litigation are ostensibly seeking to help.

Despite the various negative impacts of a weakened at-will employment doctrine presaged by these commentators, employers today must cope with the present trend among the courts to further erode the at-will rule. The next chapter will discuss several preventive measures which many corporations have adopted to avoid liability for wrongful discharge.

CHAPTER IX

Preventive Measures: Avoiding Liability for Wrongful Discharge

As the previous chapters have illustrated, courts in both the state and federal systems have developed wrongful discharge theories largely as "justifications for penalties imposed on employer conduct perceived to be arbitrary and capricious."[1] It is not surprising then that employers are adopting preventive measures which "are efforts to install 'corporate due process' into personnel practices."[2] Central to such due process is the requirement that all procedures relating to the employment relationship be applied uniformly and consistently. In short, fairness is the best policy for avoiding liability for wrongful discharge.[3]

As a first step in any preventive strategy, a company should scrutinize its present personnel practices with an attorney knowledgeable in current wrongful discharge law, examining all junctures of the employment, from the recruitment and hiring procedures, through any communications made to the employee during the course of employment, to any termination procedures.[4] If after conducting such a review it is concluded "that new and current employees are hired on a 'just cause' basis, the employer must make a policy decision as to whether it wishes to have such a contractual arrangement with its employees."[5] Of course, the employer is more con-

---

[1]Cathcart & Kruse, *The New American Law of Wrongful Terminations*, INTERNATIONAL BUSINESS LAWYER, Feb. 1984, at 75 [hereinafter cited as Cathcart & Kruse, *Law of Wrongful Terminations*].

[2]*Id.* at 75.

[3]Several companies have adopted policies which have proved successful in avoiding wrongful discharge lawsuits. For example, Federal Express has a system where the company pledges to promptly and fairly investigate and adjudicate any employee grievance. The Bank of America has another system where complaints or concerns are quickly investigated by a neutral employee at a fairly high level. If the employee is still unsatisfied, appeals are provided in both companies' plans. The Polaroid Corporation also has a very structured in-house grievance procedure that it feels has dramatically cut down on the number of lawsuits filed against it.

[4]*See* Green, *An Ounce of Prevention: Avoiding Litigation By Lawfully Terminating Employees*, at 29 (unpublished paper presented at meeting of the American Financial Services Association, May 13-14, 1986)[hereinafter cited as Green, *Prevention*].

[5]*Id.*

strained in his termination decisions where a "just cause" standard is present. Among the requirements imposed on an employer subject to a "just cause" standard are that:

> [1] The employee is forewarned by the company of the possible disciplinary consequences of his or her action[;]
> [2] The company's requirements of the employee are reasonable in relation to the efficient and orderly operation of the company's business and the employee's capabilities[;]
> [3] The supervisor, before discharging the employee, makes a reasonable effort to discover whether or not the employee's performance was unsatisfactory. Hearsay or opinions are not permitted, and the employee has a chance to tell his or her side of the story[;]
> [4] The investigation by the company is conducted in a fair and objective manner. The company keeps an open mind[;]
> [5] The investigation produces sufficient evidence of proof of guilt[;]
> [6] The company treats this employee the same way it had treated others under similar circumstances[;]
> [7] The discipline fits the crime, considering the employee's past record and any possible mitigating circumstances.[6]

Although maintenance of a "just cause" standard will decrease an employer's liability, most employers find such a system either too restrictive or, what may more frequently be the case, too easily distorted to become a vehicle for litigation or other challenges by employees who have been terminated for just cause. For purposes of this chapter, the discussion will focus on the preventive steps an employer may take while maintaining the at-will employment relationship even though the employer may endeavor to terminate an individual's employment for just cause or the equivalent.

"If an employer concludes after his review that it has an at-will contractual relationship with its employees," one commentator advises that "the employer should take affirmative steps to ensure the continuance of the employees' at-will status."[7] This chapter will examine preventive measures that have been suggested by attorneys and adopted by human resource managers in an effort to avoid an employer's liability in a wrongful discharge lawsuit. The preventive measures target the chronological stages of the employment relationship. This ordering serves to highlight the expansive reach of wrongful discharge theories. Of course, wrongful discharge is not limited solely to the termination decision.

---

[6]Stevens, *Firing Without Fear,* MANAGEMENT WORLD, March 1984, at 13 [hereinafter cited as Stevens, *Firing*]; *See also* Nye, *Fire At Will—Careful, Now, Careful,* ACROSS THE BOARD, Nov. 1982, at 40 [hereinafter cited as Nye, *Fire At Will*].
[7]Green, *Prevention, supra* note 4, at 29.

It is important to note at the outset that the measures discussed herein are not meant in any way to provide the employer with absolute protection from legal liability. Rather, they represent steps which a company may take so that when its termination decision is reviewed by the court, a judge or jury will be less likely to hold that the termination decision fell within the boundaries of what has been judicially recognized as "wrongful." Furthermore, the suggested measures contained in this chapter are not exhaustive of the preventive steps possible. Particularly in view of the state-by-state differences and rapidly evolving laws which proliferate in this area, it is highly recommended by this author that any employer contemplating modification of its personnel practices consult a knowledgeable attorney before instituting any changes.

RECRUITMENT

With the growing trend among jurisdictions to imply contractual status to the employment relationship, many advisors recommend that employers be careful not to lead the prospective employee to believe at any point during the stages of recruitment that his employment "is grounded in an employment contract."[8]

Advertisements

For instance, advertisements for available positions should not contain any reference or implication that the employment is permanent.[9] In particular, advertisements should avoid using such terms as "guaranteed employment," "permanent employment," or "tenure." Similarly, job advertisements should avoid any "reference to a fixed duration of employment."[10] In addition, any job description should catalog "all the tasks the employee will be expected to perform."[11] "A worker dismissed for an inability to perform a task not listed in the job description" will have ammunition with which "to file a wrongful discharge claim."[12]

---

[8]Bureau of National Affairs (BNA), *At-Will Terminations, BNA Policy and Practice Series, Personnel Management at 207:582* [hereinafter cited as BNA, *Personnel Management*].

[9]Green, *Prevention, supra* note 4, at 30.

[10]*Id.*

[11]BNA, *Personnel Management, supra* note 8, at 207:582.

[12]*Id.*

Interviews

Although seemingly innocent, language used in a hiring interview can often give rise later in a wrongful discharge suit to a question of fact for the jury as to whether there was an agreement between the parties for a contract of employment terminable only for cause.[13] In *Toussaint v. Blue Cross and Blue Shield,*[14] for example, the interviewer's statement to the employee that "as long as [you] do your job ... [you will] be with the company," created a question for the jury.[15] Similarly, in *Forman v. BRI Corp.,* the interviewer's description of the job as one in which the plaintiff could "stay and grow" created a question for the jury.[16] The danger inherent in such instances is that juries tend to be more sympathetic to individual plaintiffs than to large corporate defendants. Therefore, a noted employment law attorney cautions, "interviewers must be trained to avoid making representations regarding duration of employment, as such statements may later be used as evidence that an employee was hired on a just cause basis for a specific duration."[17]

Offer Letters

Just as in the advertising and interviewing steps, the employer should avoid all language in the offer of employment letter which might suggest a contractual term of employment.[18] For example, "such phrases as 'long and successful career' should be deleted."[19]

Disclaimers

It is strongly suggested by many authorities that employers include disclaimers on all literature received by an employee (including employment applications, handbooks and policy manuals) clearly stating that the employment is terminable at the will of the

---

[13]*See* Green, *Prevention, supra* note 4, at 30.
[14]408 Mich. 579, 292 N.W.2d 880 (1980).
[15]*Id.* at 583, 292 N.W.2d at 884 (cited in Green, *Prevention, supra* note 4, at 30).
[16]532 F. Supp. 49 (E.D. Pa. 1982) (cited in Green, *Prevention, supra* note 4, at 30).
[17]Green, *Prevention, supra* note 4, at 30.
[18]*See* id.
[19]*Id.*

employer.[20] Although the use of such disclaimers may chill employee morale, many corporations have found the protection afforded by such disclaimers against potential liability for wrongful discharge to be worth the cost. Indeed, the majority of courts at both the state and federal systems have upheld the effectiveness of at-will disclaimers to negate a plaintiff-employee's claim that a "just cause" standard applied to the employment relationship.[21] In drafting disclaimers, it is recommended that the disclaimer provide that *only* a specific, named individual, such as the company's president, has the authority to enter into any contract of employment and that any such contract must always be in writing.[22]

Recently, the Ninth Circuit Court of Appeals, in *Gianaculus v. Trans World Airlines, Inc.*,[23] upheld the force of an at-will disclaimer. In that case, three former management-level employees had signed an employment application which contained the following disclaimer: "[i]f given employment, I hereby agree that such employment may be terminated by the company at any time without advance notice and without liability to me for wages or salary."[24] The plaintiffs contended that a policy manual, which limited the company's right to terminate its at-will employees, preempted the at-will disclaimer and created an implied "just cause" standard for discharge.[25] The Ninth Circuit, however, rejected this argument, holding that the policy manual could not be viewed as "a manifestation of the intent of the parties."[26] Rather, the court quoted an earlier California appellate court decision and concluded that "[t]here cannot be a valid express contract and an implied contract each embracing the same subject and requiring different results."[27] Several other

[20]*Id.* For other authors who recommend the use of at-will disclaimers, see, e.g., Bakalay & Grossman, *How to Avoid Wrongful Discharge Suits*, MANAGEMENT REVIEW, Aug. 1984, at 41-46 [hereinafter cited as Bakalay & Grossman, *How to Avoid Suits*]; BNA, *Personnel Management, supra* note 8; Cathcart & Kruse, *Law of Wrongful Termination, supra* note 1; Copus & Lindsay, *Successfully Defending the Discriminatory/Wrongful Discharge Case*, 10 EMPL. REL. L. J. 456 [hereinafter cited as Copus & Lindsay, *Successfully Defending*]; Nye, *Fire At Will, supra* note 6; Panken, *How to Keep Firing from Backfiring*, NEW ENGLAND BUSINESS, Sept. 17, 1984, at 105-107; Stevens, *Firing, supra* note 6.
[21]*See, e.g.*, cases cited in chapter II, *supra* at 23 note 54.
[22]*See* Reid v. Sears, Roebuck & Co., 1 IER Cases 451 (6th Cir. 1986) (such a disclaimer upheld).
[23]761 F.2d 1391 (9th Cir. 1985) (cited in Green, *Prevention, supra* note 4, at 30).
[24]*Id.* at 1391.
[25]*Id.*
[26]*Id.* at 1393.
[27]*Id., quoting* Shapiro v. Wells Fargo Realty Advisors, 152 Cal. App. 3d 467, 482, 199 Cal. Rptr. 613, 622 (1984).

cases in the federal system,[28] as well as in the state system,[29] have similarly upheld the use of at-will disclaimers to defeat wrongful discharge claims.

One commentator points out an important footnote to the use of at-will disclaimers: even with the presence of an effective disclaimer, the consistency of the employer's other actions and literature is critical. For instance, if the disclaimer conflicts with language in other employment literature, or is directly contrary to any oral assurances made to an employee, then a question of fact arises for the jury's deliberation.[30]

Termination Contracts, One-Year Contracts

As an alternative to the use of at-will disclaimers, one authority recommends the use of termination contracts in hiring agreements, particularly for upper-level managerial personnel and executives.[31] A termination contract is similar to a release (discussed later in this chapter under "Termination"), but is signed at the beginning of employment.[32] In short, a termination contract provides that the employer pay the employee a stipulated amount to forego all claims against the employer in the event the employee is terminated.[33] As one author observes, the termination contract gives the parties greater flexibility: "the parties know in advance that the employee is hired at will, and that he can be dismissed at any time, and that his obligations are essentially to perform a generally understood task

---

[28]*See* Green, *Prevention, supra* note 4, at 31-32, *citing* Leahy v. Federal Express Corp., 609 F. Supp. 668 (E.D.N.Y. 1985) (employment application disclaimer upheld); Schaeffer v. Sperry Corp., 119 L.R.R.M. 2688 (C.D. Cal. 1984) (disclaimer negates plaintiff's implied contract claim); Batchelor v. Sears, Roebuck & Co., 547 F. Supp. 1480 (E.D. Mich. 1983) (disclaimer is part of the contract between the parties); Crain v. Burroughs Corp., 560 F. Supp. 849 (C.D. Cal. 1983); Summers v. Sears, Roebuck & Co., 549 F. Supp. 1157 (E.D. Mich. 1982) (disclaimer language contained in employment application precludes plaintiff's legitimate expectation of a "just cause" determination); Novosel v. Sears, Roebuck & Co., 495 F. Supp. 344 (E.D. Mich. 1980).

[29]*See* Green, *Prevention, supra* note 4, at 31-32, *citing* Woolley v. Hoffman-La Roche, Inc., 119 L.R.R.M. 2380, 2387 (Sup. Ct. N.J. 1985); Shelby v. Zayre Corp., 474 So.2d 1069, 120 L.R.R.M. 2224 (Ala. 1985); Wagenseller v. Scottsdale Memorial Hospital, 119 L.R.R.M. 3166, 3175 (Ariz. 1985); Leikvold v. Valley View Community Hospital, 688 P.2d 170, 116 L.R.R.M. 2193 (Ariz. 1984).

[30]*See* Green, *Prevention, supra* note 4, at 32, *citing* Tirano v. Sears, Roebuck & Co., 99 App. Div. 2d 675, 472 N.Y.S.2d 49 (App. Div. 1984); Shipani v. Ford Motor Co., 102 Mich. App. 606, 302 N.W.2d 307 (1981).

[31]*See* BNA, *Personnel Management, supra* note 8, at 207:582, *quoting* Stanley H. Lieberstein, *Who Owns What Is In Your Head? (1979).*

[32]*Id.*

[33]*Id.*

but with no specific goals."[34] The use of termination contracts, however, has not been litigated. It is important to note that such contracts might possibly be deemed contracts of adhesion, and, in general, courts have been reluctant to enforce any release of future, unknown claims.

Another alternative to at-will disclaimers is the use of one-year contracts.[35] Under this option, employers enter into a written contract with at-will employees for a specified period of time, generally one year.[36] Then, if an employer wishes to discharge the employee, it need only "fail to renew the contract" when it expires.[37] Obviously the downside of the one-year contract is that it is a contract; and, as such, "[i]f the employer wished to terminate the employee before the year was up, it would have to have good cause to do so."[38] Otherwise, the employee would have a viable cause of action for breach of the contract.

COURSE OF EMPLOYMENT

Courts deciding wrongful discharge cases will frequently recognize an implied contractual relationship between the employer and the employee arising from either written or oral representations made during the course of employment. In most cases, a plaintiff argues that the employer, either through its handbooks, discipline procedure or oral assurances, effectively "promised" that it would discharge employees only for "just cause". It is critical, therefore, for employers to take affirmative steps during the course of employment to ensure the at will status of its employees.

Handbooks and Manuals

Employee handbooks and manuals have proved to be the greatest source of implied contractual rights in wrongful discharge litigation. Naturally, an employer should direct special attention to every aspect of such literature.

Dissemination. One of the first issues to be decided is which employees are covered by the handbook's provisions.[39] To solve this problem, it is recommended that a "handbook should expressly indi-

---

[34]*Id.*

[35]For a discussion of one-year contracts, see Bakalay & Grossman, *How To Avoid Suits, supra* note 20, at 46.

[36]*Id.*

[37]*Id.*

[38]*Id.*

[39]Green, *Prevention, supra* note 4, at 33.

cate the classifications of employees intended to be covered by the provisions of the handbook."[40] For those employees who are covered by the handbook, the employer should "allow employees to read the handbook on company time," have the employees sign an acknowledgment that they have received and read the handbook (including any at-will disclaimers), and "place the [signed] acknowledgment in each employee's personnel file."[41] Such written acknowledgment will help negate any subsequent claim by a discharged employee that he believed a "just cause" standard applied to the job.

Language. Loose or ambiguous handbook language can create damaging effects to an employer when a discharged employee claims that he interpreted the language as a promise by the employer of an employment contract subject to a "just cause" standard. Moreover, a fundamental rule of contract interpretation provides that any ambiguous language contained in a contract will be construed against the drafter of such language.[42] Any words or phrases, then, that might possibly give rise to contractual obligations on the part of the employer, even by omission or negative implication, should be modified or removed.[43]

One study provides the following useful illustration:

> [S]uppose the handbook has a section entitled "Probationary Period," which says something like this: "The first 90 days of employment are a probationary period. During this period an employee may be terminated at any time." The provision, which is a very common one, seems harmless enough. Yet, an employee could well argue that there is an implication in it that after the probationary period is over, an employee may not be terminated at any time. Therefore, once an employee successfully completes the probationary period, he can be terminated only for good cause.[44]

Similarly, "if a list of grounds for discharge is included in the personnel manual, a statement should be added that the list is intended only by way of example, and in no way constitutes the sole grounds for dismissal."[45]

---

[40]*Id.*

[41]*Id.*

[42]*See* 4 S. WILLISTON, WILLISTON ON CONTRACTS § 621 (3d ed. 1961): "Since one who speaks or writes, can by exactness of expression more easily prevent mistakes in meaning, than one with whom he is dealing, doubts arising from ambiguity of language are resolved in favor of the latter ..." *Id* (citations omitted).

[43]Green, *Prevention, supra* note 4, at 33.

[44]Bakalay & Grossman, *How to Avoid Suits, supra* note 20, at 44. *See also* Walker v. Northern San Diego Hospital District, 135 Cal. App. 3d 896, 185 Cal. Rptr. 617 (4th Dist. 1982) (cited in Green, *Prevention, supra* note 4, at 34).

[45]Green, *Prevention, supra* note 4, at 34.

Procedures. As discussed in chapter II concerning the legal theories underlying a wrongful discharge claim, it is alleged in some cases that the employer, by instituting set procedures for termination, is contractually bound by such terms. Plaintiffs have successfully alleged that any termination which deviates from these procedures constitutes a breach of contract or a breach of the implied covenant of good faith and fair dealing.[46]

Confronted with this dilemma, one alternative is for employers not to expressly indicate that all termination procedures and progressive discipline provisions are mandatory.[47] Rather, handbooks should state "that such procedures are set forth 'merely as guidelines' and that 'each case will be decided on an individual basis.'"[48] Note, however, that "[a]lthough a handbook provision expressly indicates that the procedures are not mandatory, it is critical ... that to the extent a progressive discipline procedure is used, it should be applied uniformly and fairly" in order to avoid liability on discrimination grounds.[49] In brief, "[s]imilarly situated employees should be treated in a similar fashion."[50]

Despite the inherent dangers of termination and progressive discipline procedures, many employers find that they provide a useful internal mechanism for resolving employee complaints. Such a system may require that "an oral warning [be given] to the employee for the first offense, a written warning for the second, suspension for the third, and termination for the fourth."[51] Of course, employers should reserve the right to dismiss an employee immediately for extreme infractions.[52]

The use of a progressive discipline-termination procedure provides many advantages to the employer. Most important, such a procedure will provide documentation of the employment, which is critical evidence when an employer is seeking to argue that it did not wrong-

---

[46]*See id.,* citing Weiner v. McGraw-Hill, Inc., 57 N.Y.2d 458, 443 N.E.2d 44, 457 N.Y.S.2d 1983 (1982) (set procedures for termination in an employer's personnel manual contractually obligate the employer to refrain from discharging the employee for less than "just cause"); Cleary v. American Airlines, Inc., 111 Cal. App. 3d 443, 168 Cal. Rptr. 722 (2d Dist. 1980) (employer's deviation from set termination procedure constitutes a breach of the implied covenant of good faith and fair dealing); Small v. Springs Industries, Inc., S.C. Sup. Ct. No. 22737 (June 8, 1987) (employer's deviation from termination procedure in handbook constituted a breach of contract).
[47]*See* Green, *Prevention, supra* note 4, at 34.
[48]*Id.*
[49]*Id.* at 35.
[50]*Id.*
[51]*See* Bakalay & Grossman, *How To Avoid Suits, supra* note 20, at 45.
[52]*Id.*

fully discharge its employee.[53] A progressive discipline procedure also "requires the manager involved to articulate the cause for discipline at each stage."[54] Additionally, "[t]he employee will be given a chance to correct any minor problem, or to rebut false accusations, before any final action is taken."[55] This procedure decreases the likelihood of an arbitrary or capricious termination decision.[56]

There are several disadvantages associated with the use of a grievance-arbitration system. It is likely that such a procedure would lead to possible decreases in the flexibility of the workforce, as management decisions are scrutinized constantly. Moreover, as management's decisions are placed under a magnifying glass and, on occasion, overturned, morale among upper-level management will likely decrease. Lastly, a grievance-arbitration procedure could result in long-run cost increases if the majority of employees were to use such a grievance system.

Some employers have gone beyond internal progressive discipline-termination procedures and have instituted grievance and third party arbitration systems similar to those found in union contracts. Among the benefits of a grievance-arbitration procedure, one commentator lists: (1) "channel[ing] complaints within the company and thereby avoiding costly and potentially embarrassing litigation"; (2) "enhanc[ing] worker morale and productivity"; (3) having "an arbitrator hear the case, rather than a jury"; and (4) decreasing the number of wrongful discharge lawsuits, since "courts generally hold that a party who has agreed to arbitrate a dispute is required to do so and may not sue in court."[57]

Changing the Status of Current Employees

One of the thorniest issues confronted by employers taking steps to minimize or avoid exposure to wrongful discharge lawsuits is whether a court will recognize as effective an employer's change in policy instituted *during* an employee's tenure to defeat a worker's claim that might have been viable at the time he was initially hired.[58] In these cases, plaintiffs often argue that the policy modification effectively created a new contract between the employer and the employee and that additional consideration by the employer was

---

[53]*Id.*
[54]*Id.* at 45-46.
[55]*Id.* at 46.
[56]*Id.*
[57]*Id.*
[58]*See* Green, *Prevention, supra* note 4, at 35.

required at that time in order for the employer to receive the right to discharge at will. Another frequently used argument is that the new at-will language constitutes an adhesion contract and is therefore invalid.

Many state and federal courts, however, have rejected such arguments when advanced by plaintiffs and have held that the new policy changes creating an at-will relationship are effective.[59] In one case, *Pine River State Bank v. Mettille,*[60] for example, the Minnesota Supreme Court held that the at-will language which the company had inserted into its employee handbook was a unilateral contract, and since the offer was extended to the employee via the handbook, the employee's continuing to work constituted constructive acceptance of the new offer.[61]

It should be stressed that other courts have been hesitant to permit the insertion of at-will language to preclude automatically a current employee's breach of contract claim.[62] For this reason, one attorney suggests that an employer wishing to institute at-will status to an employment relationship *after* the employee has been hired should enter into a post-hire agreement with the employee.[63] A "Post-Hire Memorandum of Understanding" would expressly set out the at-will nature of the employment and state "that no representations to the contrary are effective."[64]

Performance Evaluations

A problem frequently cited by employers litigating wrongful discharge suits is the lack of candor and accuracy in performance evaluations.[65] Too often an employer who is attempting to argue that an employee was discharged for poor performance is confronted with performance evaluations which all report the employee's performance as either "good" or "satisfactory."[66] More frequently, the disparity between the documentation and the actual quality of the

---

[59]*Id., citing* Shapiro v. Wells Fargo Realty Advisors, 152 Cal. App. 3d 467, 199 Cal. Rptr. 618 (2d Dist. 1984); Ledl v. Quik Pik Food Stores, Inc., 133 Mich. App. 583, 349 N.W.2d 529 (1984).

[60]333 N.W.2d 622 (Minn. 1983) (cited in Green, *Prevention, supra* note 4, at 35).

[61]*See* Green, *Prevention, supra* note 4, at 35.

[62]*Id., citing* Reid v. Sears, Roebuck & Co., 588 F. Supp. 558 (E.D. Mich. 1984); Taylor v. General Motors Corp., 588 F. Supp. 562 (E.D. Mich. 1984).

[63]*See* Green, *Prevention, supra* note 4, at 37.

[64]*Id.*

[65]*See, e.g.,* Bakalay & Grossman, *How To Avoid Suits, supra* note 20, at 45; Johnston & Taylor, *Employee Handbooks: A Selective Survey of Emerging Developments,* 11 EMPL. REL. L. J. 225.

[66]*See* Bakalay & Grossman, *How To Avoid Suits, supra* note 20, at 45.

employee's work stems from the evaluating supervisor's desire to keep peace within the workplace by not offending anyone. Unfortunately, such avoidance only leads to the maintenance of unproductive workers and potentially costly liability for the employer in a subsequent wrongful discharge lawsuit.

One commentator advises employers to "evaluate their evaluations."[67] In particular, David Copus and Ronald Lindsay make the following recommendations: (1) "Supervisors should be provided with an evaluation form that requires them to list not only employees' strengths but also their weaknesses"; (2) "Supervisors should also be provided with the criteria for evaluating employees as well as be made to understand the importance of candid evaluations"; (3) "An upper-level supervisor ought to review an evaluation before it is given to an employee in order to determine whether the evaluation is sufficiently candid"; and (4) "[E]valuations should be made whenever appropriate, not simply on a periodic basis ... these documents should be shown to the employee before being put into his or her personnel file."[68] By following these guidelines, employers should be able to avoid the danger of being overly lenient in performance evaluations.

TERMINATION

In light of the current uncertainty of the employment-at-will doctrine, employers should regard the termination decision as an important event "that could trigger substantial employer liability."[69] Any measures taken by the employer at this juncture of the employment relationship must be carefully reviewed. The following recommendations may help to alert employers to various "red flags" that arise during the termination decision-making process.

Termination Reviews

Several employment law experts recommend that employers appoint one member of management who is familiar with wrongful discharge issues to be responsible for reviewing all discharge decisions prior to actual termination.[70] These "termination czars"[71]

---

[67]*Id.*

[68]Copus & Lindsay, *Successfully Defending, supra* note 20, at 458-59.

[69]BNA, *Personnel Management, supra* note 8, at 207:583-84.

[70]*See, e.g.,* BNA, *Personnel Management, supra* note 8, at 207:583-84; Copus & Lindsay, *Successfully Defending, supra* note 20, at 458.

[71]Copus & Lindsay, *Successfully Defending, supra* note 20, at 457.

would review all relevant documents, including the employee's personnel file, the supervisor's reports, and reports by the same supervisor of other employees for comparison purposes.[72]

In particular, the review should address the following issues prior to actual termination:

> (1) the employee's seniority, minority group status, age and sex; (2) the reasons for discharge which would be stated if a dispute or litigation arises; (3) whether the decision makers proposing termination can identify specific tasks, projects or responsibilities that were not properly carried out; (4) whether the reasons stated for discharge adequately match the applicable standard; (5) the credibility of the evidence establishing the event or events triggering the discharge; (6) the presence or absence of evidence of progressive discipline, involving successive warnings, was attempted; (7) any explanations or defenses presented by the employee in response to the claim of deficient job performance or misconduct; and, (8) all evidence showing that the employer has or has not followed its own contractual, policy or employee procedures regarding discipline and discharge.[73]

By centralizing the termination decision in one individual the employer is able to produce a "star witness" who is familiar with all the facts of the case and who could clearly articulate the employer's reasons for termination at trial.[74] Moreover, as one article notes, there is the added advantage that "a jury will be less inclined to view the case as a struggle between one individual and a large, impersonal corporation;" rather, the dispute will represent a test of the "termination czar's" fairness and credibility.[75]

Exit Interviews and Employee Releases

In addition to the termination review procedures outlined above, an employer should conduct an exit interview with the terminated employee in which the worker is informed of the specific and documented reasons for the termination decision.[76] Use of such "exit interviews can ... correct misperceptions about the termination and uncover and defuse a potentially litigious situation."[77] As a further step, subject to cost considerations, an employer may wish to offer the discharged employee outplacement assistance and counsel-

---

[72]Cathcart & Kruse, *Law of Wrongful Termination, supra* note 1, at 77.
[73]*Id.*
[74]Copus & Lindsay, *Successfully Defending, supra* note 20, at 458.
[75]*Id.*
[76]*See* BNA, *Personnel Management, supra* note 8, at 207:583.
[77]*Id.*

ing.[78] An employer is likely to decrease the possibility that an
employee will bring a wrongful discharge lawsuit by providing these
services.

It is particularly important that exit interviewers prepare a candid and accurate answer to the question "why me?" Although this
point may appear to be self-evident, employers and their attorneys
are often confronted with situations where the persons explaining
the reasons for a particular termination have provided the wrong
reasons for the termination, or have expressed personal disagreement with the termination decision, or have blamed the decision on
persons other than those who actually made it. In subsequent litigation, any discrepancy between information conveyed in the exit
interview and information relied upon by the employer may surface
and either impair the company's credibility or buttress the employee's claims that he or she was treated unfairly or dishonestly. Company representatives should also be carefully instructed to avoid
casual references to age, race, youth, or any reputation that the
employee might have as a "troublemaker." Company representatives
conducting exit interviews should also be aware of the need to over-
document all aspects of the decision, as well as all statements made
by the employee or by the company representatives during the exit
interview itself.[79]

Finally, it is important that at least two company representatives
participate in every termination interview to ensure that two company witnesses will able to corroborate one another if there is disa-
greeement in litigation as to what was said during the interview. It
is frequently the case that the person conducting the interview on
behalf of the employer might himself or herself be included in a
workforce reduction or be terminated for some other reason, which
will make the former company representative uncooperative or
unavailable at trial. If only one company manager or representative
conducts an exit interview, the company may be virtually defense-
less in litigation initiated by the terminated employee if the company
representative himself is subsequently terminated or becomes disen-
chanted with the company. Having at least two company representatives participating in the exit interview makes this a significantly
less likely outcome.

Securing the employee's voluntary resignation with his signing of
an agreement to release all legal claims against the employer is
another preventive measure which will aid the employer in avoiding

---

[78]*Id.*
[79]Letter from Philip A. Miscimarra, Esq. to Andrew D. Hill (May 29, 1987).

wrongful discharge liability. The employer should offer the employee severance pay above what is normally given when reaching a release agreement with an employee, so that adequate consideration is given for the employee's granting the release.[80] If prospective employers should inquire about the employee's departure, the previous employer, as a matter of policy, should only confirm the employee's hire and termination dates and positions held while at the company without giving any reasons for the employee's departure. An artificially favorable reference to a prospective employer causes a number of concerns, including the potential for possible misrepresentation liability as to prospective employers who may be deceived into hiring unqualified applicants.[81] Again, part of the agreement may include the employer's offer of outplacement assistance.[82] This is particularly the case with the termination of upper-level, managerial employees.

In drafting any release an employer should be aware of the legal requirements that the employee enter into the agreement "knowingly and intelligently" in order for the agreement to be valid and binding.[83] Of course, determination of whether these conditions were present will be decided by the facts of each particular case. Some of the legal pitfalls leading to the invalidation of a release include "failure of consideration, duress, inapplicability to a particular cause of action, lack of understanding and full agreement at the time of the signing, mistake or fraudulent inducement."[84]

In addition, employers should be prepared with the proper responses to questions which frequently arise when an employee is asked to sign a release. First, the consequence for not signing a release is that the termination decision stands, all accrued benefits will still be paid, but additional amounts in severance pay will be unavailable. Second, the employer should assure the employee, if asked, that he is free to take the release to an attorney for review. If that occurs, the company should be prepared to renegotiate certain language changes as appropriate. Lastly, the employee should be told that whether or not he chooses to sign the release, his decision will not affect the type of information provided to prospective employers. Employees generally should not be threatened with a

---

[80]*See* Bakalay & Grossman, *How To Avoid Suits, supra* note 20, at 46.

[81]Letter from Philip A. Miscimarra, Esq. to Andrew D. Hill (May 29, 1987).

[82]*See* Bakalay & Grossman, *How To Avoid Suits, supra* note 20, at 46.

[83]Green, *Prevention, supra* note 4, at 37, *citing* Ackerman v. Diamond Shamrock Corp., 670 F.2d 66 (6th Cir. 1982); EEOC v. Bethlehem Steel Corp., 583 F. Supp. 1357 (W.D. Pa. 1984).

[84]Green, *Prevention, supra* note 4, at 37.

negative reference if they refuse to sign a release, because such threats may give rise to defamation liability as well as violations of various anti-blacklisting statutes.[85]

An example of the general language and provisions of a release are as follows:

> As a material inducement to the Company to enter into this General Release, Employee hereby irrevocably and unconditionally releases, acquits and forever discharges the Company and each of the Company's owners, stockholders, predecessors, successors, assigns, agents, directors, officers, employees, representatives, attorneys, divisions, subsidiaries, affiliates (and agents, directors, officers, employees, representatives and attorneys of such parent companies, divisions, subsidiaries and affiliates), and all other persons acting by, through, under or in concert with any of them (collectively "Releasees"), or any of them, from any and all charges, complaints, claims, liabilities, obligations, promises, agreements, controversies, damages, actions, causes of action, suits, rights, demands, costs, losses, debts and expenses (including attorneys' fees and costs actually incurred) of any nature whatsoever, known or unknown, suspected or unsuspected, including but not limited to, rights under federal, state or local laws prohibiting age or other forms of discrimination, claims growing out of any legal restrictions on the Company's right to terminate its employees ("Claim" or "Claims"), which Employee now has, owns or holds, or claims to have, own or hold, or which Employee at any time heretofore had, owned or held, or which Employee at any time hereinafter may have, own or hold, or claim to have, own or hold against each or any of the Releasees.[86]

It should be noted, however, that technical-sounding releases, such as the one above, might have the negative result of educating employees on potential causes of action, or at least scare certain individuals to the point that they retain attorneys to review whether they have potential claims against the employer. There is a great deal of tension between making a release extremely detailed (which would be of greater protection in litigation but which employees are less likely to sign at least without the assistance of an attorney) or less detailed (which would be of more questionable value in litigation but which is more likely to be signed by terminated employees without question).[87] For the purpose of contrast, Figure IX-1 is a "plain English" release which one attorney has found useful:

---

[85]Letter from Philip A. Miscimarra, Esq. to Andrew D. Hill (May 29, 1987).

[86]Green, *Prevention, supra* note 4, at 37-38.

[87]Letter from Philip A. Miscimarra, Esq. to Andrew D. Hill (May 29, 1987).

FIGURE IX-1
Acknowledgment of Separation Pay and Release

I, _____, have received from

_____ the net amount

(after standard deductions) of _____

dollars ($_____)—consisting of _____ dollars

($_____) in severance pay and _____ dollars

($_____) in vacation pay. In exchange for this

payment, I release _____

as well as their directors, managers, staff members, program

coordinators, supervisors, and other agents from any claims or causes

of action that are connected in any way with my employment or the

termination of my employment by _____.

I have read this release and understand it. I also accept the

payment described above as a final and complete settlement of all

claims and causes of action that I have or may have against _____

_____.

Signed this _____ day of _____ 19 _____.

_____

_____
Witness

_____
Witness

CONCLUSION

This chapter has attempted to provide employers with useful suggestions gathered from employment law experts and human resource managers to decrease the likelihood of employees' bringing wrongful discharge lawsuits and to avoid liability for the employer when confronted with such claims. As the discussion illustrates, steps must be taken at all junctures of the employment relationship which will instill a sense of "corporate due process" into the personnel practices, while at the same time defeat any implied contractual arrangement which might be alleged to exist between the employer and the employee. To this end, employers must clearly communicate to employees during recruitment that their employment is at-will and can be terminated at any time by the employer. During the course of employment, handbooks and personnel manuals must provide a fair and unambiguous standard for employee discipline and termination. Finally, at the termination of employment, the discharge decision should be carefully reviewed by a member of the management familiar with the issues of wrongful discharge. At this point the employer may seek from the employee a release from all legal claims for additional consideration.

Arthur Rutkowski, an employment law attorney, has developed a quick test (presented in Figure IX-2) which employers can use to determine the legality of discharging an at-will employee. Although originally drafted to apply to hospital workers, this checklist provides a useful overview of the points discussed in this chapter.

Figure IX-2
A Quick Test to Assess the Legality of Firing an At-Will Employee

The checklist that follows may be used to determine whether the discharge of an at-will hospital employee would be lawful. It applies to the discharge of both nonunion and union employees. A key to the answers appears at the end of the checklist.

1. Will the employee be discharged for any of the following reasons?
   (a) race
   (b) religion
   (c) sex
   (d) age (over 40)
   (e) national origin
   (f) children or childbirth
   (g) pregnancy
   (h) handicap

2. Will the employee be discharged for acting in concert with other employees to
   (a) organize collectively?
   (b) push for a raise or shorter hours?
   (c) ask for changes in other working conditions?
   (d) support another employee in his/her protesting?

3. Will the discharge violate any type of contract?
   (a) Does the hospital's employee handbook provide that warnings must be given before an employee may be discharged or that an employee may be discharged only "for cause"?
   (b) Does the hospital have written employee policies that promise "fair treatment"?
   (c) Is there a written, signed employment contract?

4. Will the discharge constitute a tort?
   (a) Has the hospital committed the tort of *outrage,* by being abusive during the discharge through either high-handed interrogation methods or flagrant misrepresentations to the employee as to the reason for discharge?
   (b) Has the hospital been *negligent* by failing to follow its own policies, which failure resulted in the employee's discharge?

5. Will the employee be discharged for any of the following acts or omissions?
   (a) refusing to do an illegal act
   (b) filing a worker's compensation claim
   (c) reporting violations of EEO, OSHA, or ERISA regulations
   (d) "whistle-blowing" on the hospital's possible violations of laws

6. Will the employee be discharged for refusing to do a job he or she considers unsafe (giving rise to a possible OSHA violation)?
   (a) Would doing the job *reasonably* place the employee in imminent danger?
   (b) Has the job been performed safely numerous times in the past? If so, why does the employee now consider it unsafe? Has there been an accident on the job shortly before the refusal so that the employee has reason for concern?

7. Will the hospital deny a hearing (with witnesses present) to provide the employee an opportunity to admit or deny the reasons for discharge?

8. Has the hospital failed to give the employee an oral or written warning to correct the conduct?

9. Has the hospital let other employees get away with what the employee is to be discharged for?

10. Did the hospital promise the employee, at the time of hire or subsequently, that "the job will be yours for as long as you want it? Was the employee promised an "annual salary"?

11. Will the employee be discharged for a physical condition (for example, high blood pressure, diabetes, or a back condition) in violation of a state statute prohibiting discrimination on the basis of handicap? Has the hospital tried to make reasonable accommodations for the employee to work at some other, less strenuous job.

12. Is there no written evidence (for example, prior reprimands) of a conduct leading to the employee's discharge?

13. Did the employee give up a job and/or home in another city to work at the hospital? Were promises made to induce the employee to do so?

14. Will the hospital call the discharge one motivated by a need for reduction in work force when in fact the reason is unsatisfactory work performance?

15. If the hospital plans to hold an investigatory interview prior to the discharge, will the employee be denied a union or coworker representative, despite his or her request?

Key: Each of these questions states the facts of a state or federal case litigating an employer's right to discharge an at-will employee. In each case, the employer answered "yes"—and lost. Still, the answer to any particular question does not necessarily determine whether the discharge contemplated would be lawful. It is the *process* of asking and answering these questions—with the help of counsel—that can alert a hospital to potential liability and thereby help to avoid liability.—*Arthur D. Rutkowski, J.D., partner, Bowers, Harrison, Kent & Miller, Evansville, IN. Copyright 1984 by Arthur D. Rutkowski. All rights reserved. (Reprinted with permission).*

CHAPTER X

Conclusion

As this study has shown, the courts have created a vast tangle of exceptions and exemptions to the traditional common law employment-at-will rule which vary according to the jurisdiction and focus of each individual case. Despite the confusion this trend has spawned, it must be remembered that the flood of wrongful termination cases reflects a broader social problem which the judiciary has been left to resolve. This problem, as a California federal district court observed, "is what to do about the large numbers of executives and high-level employees, now in their fifties and older, who 'paid their dues' by working their way up corporate ladders which can no longer support their collective weight."[1]

The wrongful discharge cases are simply instances in the evolution of this larger societal problem where the courts are being asked to determine on a case-by-case basis which of these employees "have a 'right' to their jobs, and which do not."[2] To be sure, this is a difficult question to answer at any time. Unfortunately, the present fundamental changes in the American economy only intensify the difficulty of any such "rights" determination. Technological advancements, a rise in foreign competition, "and countless other reasons", render corporate employers no longer "able to provide the ... 'promise'" of job security which was once held out to today's higher level employees when they first joined the corporate ranks.[3] In addition, this decade will see a 42 percent jump in the number of employees aged 35-44, as a result of the post-World War II baby boom.[4] It is at this age that many employees enter middle management.[5] It is likely that most of these employees' expectations will be disappointed. According to a Bureau of Labor Statistics survey, job

---

[1]Cox v. Resilient Flooring Div. of Congoleum Corp., 638 F. Supp. 726, 735 (C.D. Cal. 1986).

[2]*Id.*

[3]*Id.*

[4]D. Nye, *Fire at Will—Careful, Now, Careful,* 37 ACROSS THE BOARD (Nov. 1982), at 39 [hereinafter cited as Nye, *Fire at Will*].

[5]*Id.*

openings for managers and administrators in the 1980s will increase only 19.1 percent, less than half the rate of increase in the prime age group.[6]

In grappling with this difficult problem, the courts have been moving in the direction that most long-term employees are entitled to have a jury determine whether they are entitled to keep their jobs. This view, as many have noted, ignores economic reality.[7] "To suggest that juries will be able to decide fairly which executives should stay and which should go is to impute to them knowledge and wisdom about wider issues as to which the trial process cannot adequately advise them."[8]

"The legitimate interests of the employer in guiding the policies and destiny of his operation cannot not be ignored,"[9] notes one judge. An organization must have the right to terminate incompetent personnel.[10] It must also have the right to reduce its workforce in hard times, if that is necessary for economic survival.[11] Present employment practices, however, suggest that management is not adequately dealing with the larger social problem either. Issues of job security and wrongful discharge are not limited to nonunion or managerial employees. Employees covered by collective bargaining agreements are pursuing actions in state courts for wrongful discharge based on public policy agruments "which exist independent of privately negotiated contract right or duties."[12] These actions assume that states have an interest in protecting certain implied contract rights to job security necessary to ensure social stability."[13] On the other hand, judicial intervention at the state level could well mean a decline in interest of employees in unions and the end of uniformity in labor relations policies for companies which operate in more than one state. Obviously, this would benefit neither companies nor unions, and probably not the public. As one author has noted, "[b]oth employers and unions may have to respond to protect their established relationships and to keep their employee/members out of state court. No one, it seems, can afford to stay neutral. Even

---

[6]*Id., citing* Bureau of Labor Statistics Survey.

[7]*See Cox,* 638 F. Supp. at 735.

[8]*Id.*

[9]Palmateer v. Int'l Harvester Co., 421 N.E.2d 876, 884 (Ill. 1981) (Ryan, J., dissenting).

[10]Horton, *Dear New Hire: We Reserve the Right to Fire You,* 2 MANAGEMENT REVIEW (Aug. 1984), at 2 [hereinafter cited as Horton, *Dear New Hire*].

[11]*Id.* at 3.

[12]G. Brooks, *Preemption of Federal Labor Law by the Employment at Will Doctrine,* 38 LAB. L. J. (June 1987) at 344.

[13]*Id.* at 345.

the NLRB has a reason to be concerned: if bargaining unit employees can gain relief and expansive financial settlements, the Board could become superfluous.[14] Much of the courts' "intrusion has been invited," one manager notes, "by poor management practices with regard to human resources."[15]

A study appearing in the 1980 issue of *Business* magazine made it clear that managerial discontent is growing.[16] That study, conducted by a public opinion pollster, showed that while clerical and hourly employees' attitudes toward work had improved significantly since the mid-1970s, those of managerial employees had declined in a proportionate degree during the same time period. In that study, managers cited the following areas of malcontent: (1) the corporation's communications among its employees; (2) the corporation's willingness to listen to employee's problems and complaints and to act to ameliorate the problems; (3) the employees' rights as individuals to treatment with respect by the corporation; and (4) job security and advancement opportunity.[17] When this managerial discontent is coupled with the threatening changes in the economy, it is not surprising that these managers are in court arguing that they are in fact entitled to more consideration from their companies.

Today's corporate managers have an opportunity to address the broader social problem underlying the at-will controversy before governmental intrusion is mandated by society. Thomas Horton, President and CEO of American Management Association best summarizes the task before managers:

> If the specter of legislation disturbs us, then our senior managers must ensure that our companies behave in a responsible fashion so that we will be able to retain control over termination. Each of us, as employers, should think carefully about what we expect of employees and what our policies with respect to them should be. We have to face the fact that our attitudes and behavior help determine employees' values as well as influence legal outcomes.[18]

---

[14]*Id.* at 347.

[15]*Id.* at 2.

[16]Nye, *Fire at Will, supra* note 4, at 39, *citing* survey conducted by Opinion Research Corporation appearing in "Early Warning Signals—Growing Discontent Among Managers," Business (1980).

[17]*Id.*

[18]Horton, *Dear New Hire, supra* note 10, at 3.

Appendix A

A State-by-State Survey of Employment-At-Will

Appendix A*

A State-by-State Survey of Employment-At-Will

ALABAMA

A. *Implied Contracts*
   1. Handbooks. Alabama courts have rejected the view that personnel handbooks can provide implied contractual rights so as to alter the status of an at-will employment. *See, e.g.,* McCluskey v. Unicare Health Facility, Inc., 484 So.2d 398 (Ala. 1986); Cunningham v. Etowah Quality of Life Council, 484 So.2d 1075 (Ala. 1986); White v. Chelsea Industries, Inc., 425 So.2d 1090 (Ala. 1983). *But see* United Steelworkers of America, AFL-CIO v. University of Alabama, 599 F.2d 56 (5th Cir. 1979) (federal circuit court held that Alabama law may recognize handbooks as a potential source of contractual obligations).
   2. Oral Promises. Oral promises alone are not sufficient to modify an at-will employment. *See* Wilson v. Vulcan Rivet and Bolt Corp., 439 So.2d 65 (Ala. 1983). There must be independent consideration from the employee. *See* Murphree v. Alabama Farm Bureau Insurance Co., 449 So.2d 1218 (Ala. 1984).
   3. Promissory Estoppel. If the employee has relocated or given up a former job in reliance on the employer's promise, the employer may be estopped from discharging the employee at will. *See, e.g., Murphree, supra;* Scott v. Lane, 409 So.2d 791 (Ala. 1982).

---

*The sources of the research contained in this Appendix were K. McCulloch, Termination of Employment (Prentice-Hall 1986), D. Cathcart & M. Dichter, eds., Employment-At-Will: A 1986 State-By-State Survey (National Employment Law Institute 1987), supplemented with more recent cases. These publications provide an excellent review of the most current case law in each jurisdiction. This author recommends that readers consult either publication to get a more detailed discussion of the status of the employment-at-will doctrine in any particular jurisdiction before taking any action.

4. Disclaimers. Explicit disclaimers contained in employer's literature can operate to defeat an oral promise. *See* Shelby v. Zayre Corp., 474 So.2d 1069 (Ala. 1985) (discharged employee who signed employment application which explicitly reserved employer's right to terminate at-will could not reasonably rely on contrary representations by assistant manager).

B. *Public Policy Exceptions*

Alabama courts have declined to recognize any public policy exceptions to the at-will rule. *See, e.g.,* Hinrichs v. Tranquilaire Hospital, 352 So.2d 1130 (Ala. 1977); Meeks v. Opp Cotton Mills, Inc., 459 So.2d 814 (Ala. 1984) (plaintiff's claim that he was discharged for filing worker's compensation claim rejected). The Alabama Supreme Court even refused to create a public policy exception where plaintiff was discharged allegedly for serving on a jury. *See* Bender Ship Repair Inc. v. Stevens, 379 So.2d 594 (Ala. 1980). The *Bender* decision, however, was subsequently overruled by legislation. *See* ALA. CODE § 12-16-8.1 (Supp. 1983).

ALASKA

A. *Implied Contracts*

1. Handbooks. A public employee whose contract provides that he may only be terminated after being given a specified amount of notice has a legitimate expectation of continued employment under due process clause of the U.S. and Alaska Constitutions. *See* Breeden v. City of Nome, 628 P.2d 924 (Alas. 1981).
2. Oral Promises. Oral promises of employment "until retirement" or "so long as performance is satisfactory" have been held to be contractually binding upon the employer and to create a just cause requirement for discharge. *See* Eales v. Tohana Valley Medical-Surgical Group, Inc., 663 P.2d 958 (Alas. 1983).
3. Promissory Estoppel. If the employer promises long-term work and a definite amount of work, it may be estopped from discharging at will. *See* Glover v. Sager, 667 P.2d 1198 (Alas. 1983).
4. Implied Covenant of Good Faith and Fair Dealing. The covenant has been recognized where the employer is discharging the employee in order to avoid paying him profits due. *See* Mitford v. de Lasala, 666 P.2d 1000 (Alas. 1983).

B. *Public Policy Exceptions*

Alaska has not specifically recognized any public policy exceptions to the at-will rule. But in one case, the Alaska Supreme Court reversed a lower court's dismissal of plaintiff's claim that he was discharged in violation of public policy for informing his superior that other employees were drinking and abusing drugs on the job. *See* Knight v. American Guard & Alert, Inc., 714 P.2d 788 (Alas. 1986).

ARIZONA

A. *Implied Contracts*

1. Handbooks. The Arizona Supreme Court has held that the employment-at-will rule is "at best a rule of construction" and "not a limit on the parties' freedom to contract." *See* Leikvold v. Valley View Community Hospital, 688 P.2d 170 (Ariz. 1984). Accordingly, "an employer's representations in a personnel manual can become terms of the employment contract and can limit an employer's ability to discharge his or her employees." *Id.* at 172. The court cautioned, however, that "we do not mean to imply that *all* personnel manuals will become part of employment contracts. *Id.* at 174 (emphasis added).

2. Disclaimers. Explicit disclaimers expressing the at-will nature of the employment can be effective to defeat an implied contract claim. *See Leikvold, supra.* But, such disclaimers will not "absolutely insulate an employer from liability. If contrary written or oral assurances are given to the employee at the hiring interview or during employment, such promises may constitute implied contracts." *Id.* at 178.

3. Oral Promises. Oral promises can supplement the written contract for employment. *See, e.g., Leikvold, supra;* Suciu v. AMFAC Distributing Corp., 675 P.2d 1333 (Ariz. Ct. App. 1983).

4. Implied Covenant of Good Faith and Fair Dealing. Arizona Supreme Court has held that employment contracts, including employment-at-will situations, include implied covenants of good faith and fair dealing. This covenant, however, does not create an affirmative duty for the employer to discharge for cause only. *See* Wagenseller v. Scottsdale Memorial Hospital, 710 P.2d 1025, 1028, 1040 (Ariz. 1985).

5. Notice. If a written contract is subject to termination only upon notice, notice must precede termination. *See* Davis v.

Tucson Ariz. Boys Choir Society, 137 Ariz. 228, 664 P.2d
1005 (App. 1983); Thermo-Kinetic Corp. v. Allen, 16 Ariz.
App. 341, 493 P.2d 508 (1972).

B. *Public Policy Exceptions*

Arizona has recognized a potentially expansive public policy
exception to the at-will rule, providing an employee with a cause
of action in tort under this theory if the discharge was for a
cause "morally wrong," regardless of whether there was a criminal law violation. *See Wagenseller, supra,* at 1035. "It would be a
violation of public policy to compel the employee to do an act
ordinarily proscribed by the law." *Id.*

ARKANSAS

A. *Implied Contract*

   1. Handbooks. The Arkansas Supreme Court recently affirmed
      its position that handbook provisions cannot provide implied
      contractual rights to an employee. *See* Bryant v. Southern
      Screw Machine Products Co., Inc., 707 S.W.2d 321 (Ark.
      1986).
   2. Oral Promises. Statute of frauds can defeat an oral promise to
      modify an at-will employment. *See* Harris v. Arkansas Book
      Co., 700 S.W.2d 41 (Ark. S. Ct. 1985).
   3. Promissory Estoppel. Employer may be estopped from dis-
      charging employee at will where employee detrimentally
      relied on employer's promise by relocating and giving up
      former job. *See* Scholtes v. Signal Delivery Service, Inc., 548
      F.Supp. 487 (W.D. Ark. 1982).

B. *Public Policy Exceptions*

Arkansas does recognize a public policy exception to the at-will
rule where an employee is discharged for refusing to give in to
her employer's sexual demands. *See* Lucas v. Brown & Root,
Inc., 736 F.2d 1202 (8th Cir. 1984). *See also* M.B.M. Co. v.
Counce, 596 S.W.2d 681 (Ark. 1980) (court indicated that it
might recognize a public policy exception under proper circumstances, although declined to recognize one in the instant case).

CALIFORNIA *See* chapter IV, *supra,* at 55-75.

COLORADO

A. *Implied Contracts*
    1. General. Historically, Colorado courts have adhered to the general rule that a contract of indefinite duration which establishes an annual salary but in the absence of specific consideration is terminable at will by either party without liability for breach. *See* Justice v. Stanley Aviation Corp., 530 P.2d 984 (Colo. 1974).
    2. Handbooks. Handbook provisions may be contractually binding upon the employer if: (a) issued to employees at the time of hiring; and, (b) employees relied on handbook provisions. *See* Wing v. JMB Property Management Corp., 714 P.2d 916 (Colo. App. 1985); Salimi v. Farmers Ins. Group, 684 P.2d 264 (Colo. App. 1984); Lampley v. Celebrity Homes, Inc., 594 P.2d 605 (Colo. App. 1979). *But see* Garcia v. Aetna Finance Co., 752 F.2d 488 (10th Cir. 1984) (applying Colo. law) (manual providing for annual performance review and yearly salary does not create employment for definite term).

B. *Public Policy Exceptions*
    Colorado implicitly recognized a public policy exception to the at-will rule, where a federal court allowed a discharged employee to proceed with his wrongful discharge claim, alleging that he was discharged for refusing to participate in his employer's exclusive dealing contracts which were violative of state and federal antitrust laws. *See* Winther v. DEC Int'l, Inc., 625 F. Supp. 100 (D. Colo. 1985). *See also* Rawson v. Sears, Roebuck & Co., 530 F. Supp. 776 (D. Colo. 1982), *later proceeding,* 554 F. Supp. 327 (D. Colo. 1983) (cause of action for wrongful discharge recognized whenever termination violates an employee's statutory right or duty).

CONNECTICUT

A. *Implied Contracts*
    1. Handbooks. The Connecticut Supreme Court has not yet expressly decided whether handbook provisions can create implied contracts. In the *dicta* of one case, however, it did hold that an implied promise to discharge for cause only was contained in a handbook. *See* Magnan v. Anaconda Industries, Inc., 479 A.2d 781 (Conn. 1984). Other courts in the state have held that handbooks and manuals may be the basis of

implied contracts of employment. *See, e.g.,* Lincoln v. Sterling Drug, Inc., 622 F. Supp. 66 (D. Conn. 1985) (terms of employment manual will be considered terms of employment contract); Burns v. Preston Trucking Co., Inc., 621 F. Supp. 366 (D. Conn. 1985); Murray v. Bridgeport Hospital, 480 A.2d 610 (Conn. Super. Ct. 1984) (provisions regarding performance evaluations bound employer to conduct such evaluations).

2. Implied Covenant of Good Faith and Fair Dealing. The Connecticut Supreme Court has held that a cause of action for breach of the implied covenant of good faith and fair dealing cannot be maintained solely on discharge without cause. *See Magnan, supra.* But a lower Connecticut court has held that it would recognize a cause of action based on breach of the implied covenant where an employer discharges its employee in order to deprive him or her of earned compensation. *See* Cook v. Alexander & Alexander of Connecticut, 488 A.2d 1295 (Conn. Super. 1985)

3. Promissory Estoppel. The state supreme court has held that an employee's detrimental reliance upon employer's representations can require employer to discharge for cause only. *See Magnan, supra;* Sheets v. Teddy's Frosted Foods, Inc., 427 A.2d 385 (Conn. 1980).

B. *Public Policy Exceptions*

The Connecticut Supreme Court has recognized public policy exceptions to the employment-at-will doctrine in the following cases: *Sheets, supra* (employee dismissed for reporting employer's violation of state statute regulating labeling of food products); *Magnan, supra* (limited *Sheets* to those discharges which involve "important violations of public policy." *Id.* at 475) Lower courts in the state have been more expansive in their recognition of a cause of action for violation of public policy as indicated by the following cases: Schmidt v. Yardney Electric Corp., 492 A.2d 512 (Conn. App. 1985) (employee discharged for reporting company's fraudulent insurance claim); *Cook, supra* (employee discharged to avoid paying him bonus and vested benefits).

DELAWARE

A. *Implied Contracts*

1. Handbooks. Delaware courts have held that personnel handbooks are unilateral expressions of a company's policies and

procedures and do not alter an otherwise at-will employment. *See, e.g.,* Heidick v. Kent General Hospital, Inc., 446 A.2d 1095 (Del. 1982); Avallone v. Wilmington Medical Center, 553 F. Supp. 931 (D. Del. 1982).

B. *Public Policy Exceptions*
The Delaware courts have not yet addressed public policy exceptions to the at-will rule. A federal court applying Delaware law, however, has recognized a limited public policy exception to the at-will rule where an employee is discharged for refusing to participate in an employer's illegal and unethical conduct. *See* Hansroe v. American Industrial Technologies, Inc., 586 F. Supp. 113 (W.D. Pa. 1984) (applying Delaware law).

DISTRICT OF COLUMBIA

A. *Implied Contracts*
  1. Handbooks. Several D.C. courts have recognized that provisions of a personnel handbook can create the terms of an implied contract of employment. *See, e.g.,* Washington Welfare Association v. Wheeler, 496 A.2d 613 (D.C. App. 1985); National Rifle Association v. Ailes, 428 A.2d 816 (D.C. App. 1981); Washington Welfare Association, Inc. v. Poindexter, 479 A.2d 313 (D.C. App. 1984). In one case, however, a court rejected an employee's implied contract claim where it was proved that he was not aware of the handbook until after the discharge. *See* Snyder v. Washington Hospital Center, No. 83-1790 (D.D.C. 1984). *See also* Sullivan v. Heritage Foundation, 399 A.2d 856 (D.C. 1979) (mutual promises between employer and employee to employ and serve at an agreed salary do not alter at-will status). Courts in the District of Columbia have found handbook disclaimers to be effective to defeat implied contract claims raised by an employee. *See* McCauley v. Thygerson, 732 F.2d 978 (D.C. Cir. 1984).
  2. Oral Promises. Courts have held that the statute of frauds may be used to bar any oral promises which seek to modify the at-will employment. *See* Hodge v. Evans Financial Corp., No. 84-5224 (D.C. Cir. 1985); Prouty v. National Railroad Passenger Corp., 572 F. Supp. 200 (D.C. Cir. 1983).

B. *Public Policy Exceptions*
In one case, the D.C. Court of Appeals expressly rejected a public policy exception to the at-will rule. *See* Ivy v. Army Times

Publishing Co., 428 A.2d 831 (D.C. Ct. App. 1981). Several district court opinions, however, suggest that a public policy exception may exist. *See, e.g.,* Chichester v. Associated Dry Goods, Inc., C.A. No. 83-0021, slip op. (D.D.C. Oct. 13, 1983); Kitzmiller v. Washington Post, Inc., 115 L.R.R.M. 3015 (D.D.C. 1984); Newman v. Legal Services Corp., 628 F. Supp. 535 (D.D.C. 1986).

FLORIDA

A. *Implied Contracts*
   1. Handbooks. Most Florida courts have rejected implied contract claims based on personnel handbooks or policies. *See, e.g.,* Caster v. Hennessey, 727 F.2d 1075 (11th Cir. 1984); La Roca v. Xerox Corp., 587 F. Supp. 1002 (S.D. Fla. 1984); DeFelice v. Moss Manufacturing, Inc., 461 So.2d 209 (Fla. App. 1984); Mayo v. Highland Park Hospital Corp., 460 So.2d 571 (Fla. App. 1984). *But see* Falls v. Lawnwood Medical Center, 427 So.2d 361 (Fla. App. 1983).
   2. Oral Promises. Promises of "permanent employment" will not alter the at-will status. *See, e.g.,* Hamlen v. Fairchild Industries, Inc., 413 So.2d 800 (Fla. App. 1982); Russell & Axon Consulting Engineers v. Handshoe, 176 So.2d 909 (Fla. App. 1965), *cert. denied,* 188 So.2d 317 (1966).
   3. Promissory Estoppel. Florida courts have held that an employer may be estopped from discharging at will. *See* Chantelier v. Robertson, 118 So.2d 241 (Fla. Ct. App. 1960) (employee transferred his manufacturing business to his employer in exchange for promise of lifetime employment). *But see* Servamerica, Inc. v. Rolfe, 318 So.2d 178 (Fla. App. 1975) (employer not estopped from discharging his employee where employee left his former job in reliance on employer's promise of promotion); Hope v. National Airlines, Inc., 99 So.2d 244 (1957), *cert. denied,* 102 So.2d 728 (1958) (employee's promise to work through strike in reliance upon employer's promise of permanent employment not sufficient consideration to estop employer from discharging at will).

B. *Public Policy Exceptions*
   A public policy exception has been recognized, but only where there is a law specifically prohibiting the employer's action. *See* Smith v. Piezo Technology & Professional Administrators, 427 So.2d 182 (Fla. 1983) (public policy exception recognized where

employer violated statute for discharging employee in retaliation for filing a worker's compensation claim); Dean v. Publix Supermarkets, Inc., 438 So.2d 1 (Fla. 1983).

GEORGIA

A. *Implied Contracts*

1. Handbooks. Georgia courts have rejected the implied contract exception to the employment-at-will rule based on personnel handbooks or policies. *See, e.g.,* Miles v. Bibb Co., 339 S.E.2d 316 (Ga. App. 1985); Anderberg v. Georgia Electric Membership Corp., 332 S.E.2d 326 (Ga. App. 1985); Nelson v. M & M Products Co., 308 S.E.2d 607 (Ga. App. 1983).

2. Oral Promises. Georgia courts have recognized the statute of frauds as a bar to an employee's attempt to use an oral promise to modify an at-will relationship. *See* White v. I.T. & T., 718 F.2d 994 (11th Cir. 1983), *cert. denied,* 104 S.Ct. 914, *reh'g denied,* 104 S.Ct. 267 (1984). *See also* Cannon v. Geneva Wheel & Stamping Corp., 322 S.E.2d 69 (Ga. App. 1984); Land v. Delta Air Lines, Inc., 203 S.E.2d 316 (Ga. App. 1973).

3. Promissory Estoppel. A Georgia court has found in one instance that an employer's oral assurances of severance pay in exchange for an employee's remaining on the job until the division where he had been working was sold did estop the employer's discharge at will. *See* Amax, Inc. v. Fletcher, 305 S.E.2d 601 (Ga. App. 1983). *But see* Loy's Office Supplies, Inc., v. Steelcase, Inc., 331 So.2d 75 (Ga. App. 1985) (promissory estoppel claim rejected).

B. *Public Policy Exceptions*

The Georgia Supreme Court and lower state courts have refused to recognize any public policy exceptions to the employment-at-will doctrine. *See, e.g.,* Quinn v. Cardiovascular Physicians, P.C., 326 S.E.2d 460 (Ga. 1985); Georgia Power Co. v. Busbin, 250 S.E.2d 442 (Ga. 1978); Evans v. Bibb Co., 178 Ga. App. 139, _____ S.E.2d _____ (1986) (no exception recognized where employee discharged allegedly for pursuing rights under Georgia Worker's Compensation Act).

HAWAII

A. *Implied Contracts*
   1. Handbooks. The Hawaii Supreme Court has recognized in one case that handbook provisions may create implied contract terms. *See* Kinoshita v. Canadian Pacific Airlines, Ltd., 724 P.2d 110 (Hawaii 1986).
   2. Oral Promises. One Hawaii court has held that an employer's oral assurances alone do not alter an employee's otherwise at-will status. *See* Stancil v. Mergenthaler Linotype Co., 589 F. Supp. 78 (D. Hawaii 1984).
   3. Promissory Estoppel. A Hawaii court has held that an employer is estopped from discharging at will where the employee quit his former job and made plans to move in reliance on employer's promise. *See* Ravelo v. County of Hawaii, 658 P.2d 883 (Hawaii 1983).
   4. Implied Covenant of Good Faith and Fair Dealing. The Hawaii Supreme Court has specifically rejected an implied covenant claim. *See* Parnar v. Americana Hotels, Inc., 652 P.2d 625 (Hawaii 1983).

B. *Public Policy Exceptions*
   Hawaii has recognized a narrow public policy exception to the at-will rule where an employee was discharged to prevent her from testifying regarding her employer's possible violations of federal antitrust laws. *See Parnar, supra.*

IDAHO

A. *Implied Contracts*
   1. Handbooks. The Idaho Supreme Court has held that an employee handbook can be contractually binding on the employer with respect to termination procedures, retirement benefits, and vacation pay. *See, e.g.,* Harkness v. City of Burley, 715 P.2d 1283 (Idaho 1986); Watson v. Idaho Falls Consolidated Hospitals, Inc., 111 720 P.2d 632 (Idaho 1986); Jackson v. Minidoka Irrigation District, 563 P.2d 54 (Idaho 1977); Johnson v. Allied Stores Corp., 673 P.2d 640 (Idaho 1984). *But see* Spero v. Lockwood, Inc., 721 P.2d 174 (Idaho 1986) (handbook does not create terms of implied contract where employee never read or relied on manual); Service Employees Int'l Union, Local 6 v. Idaho Dept. of Health and Welfare, 683

P.2d 404 (Idaho 1984) (state agency's policy manual merely an internal guideline, not an enforceable contract).

B. *Public Policy Exceptions*

The Idaho Supreme Court has suggested that it will recognize a public policy exception where the employee is discharged for such reasons as refusing to commit perjury or for serving on a jury. *See Jackson, supra* (employee failed to show employer's reasons for discharge violated public policy). *See also* Staggie v. Idaho Falls Consolidated Hospitals, Inc., 715 P.2d 1019 (Idaho App. 1986) (bad faith discharge does not constitute a violation of public policy); *Watson, supra* (discharge because of union membership might fall within public policy exception).

ILLINOIS

A. *Implied Contracts*

1. Handbooks. The Illinois Supreme Court has held that handbook provisions may give rise to enforceable contract rights if the handbook language contains a promise clear enough that an employee would reasonably believe an offer has been made, the employee is aware of the offer, and accepts it. *See, e.g.,* Duldulao v. St. Mary of Nazareth Hospital Center, 115 Ill.2d 482 (Ill. 1987); Puvil v. Smart Buy, Inc., 607 F. Supp. 440 (N.D. Ill. 1985). Other courts have limited the implied contract exception to instances where the handbook modifies an existing contract and the parties have given sufficient additional consideration or where a separate document expressly incorporates the handbook provisions into the employment contract. *See, e.g.,* Johnson v. Friggie, International, Inc., 477 N.E.2d 795 (Ill. App. 1985); Kaiser v. Dixon, 468 N.E.2d 822 (Ill. App. 1984).

2. Oral Promises. An employer's oral promises may alter the at-will employment. *See* Brudnicki v. General Electric Co., 535 F. Supp. 84 (N.D. Ill. 1982). *But see* Payne v. AHFI/ Netherlands, B.V., 522 F. Supp. 18 (N.D. Ill. 1980) (statute of frauds bar recognized).

3. Promissory Estoppel. An employer may be estopped from discharging an employee at will where the employee has given sufficient consideration. *See* Martin v. Federal Life Ins. Co., 490 N.E.2d 998 (Ill. App. 1982) (employee gave up another job offer).

4. Implied Covenant of Good Faith and Fair Dealing. An employer has been held to have breached the implied covenant where he discharged an employee in order to avoid paying earned bonuses and commissions. *See* Kulins v. Malco, a Microdot Co., Inc., 459 N.E.2d 1038 (Ill. App. 1984); Gordon v. Matthew Bender & Co., 562 F. Supp. 1286 (N.D. Ill. 1983); Manuel v. Int'l Harvester Co., 502 F. Supp. 45 (N.D. Ill. 1980).

B. *Public Policy Exceptions*
The Illinois courts have recognized public policy exceptions to the at-will rule in a variety of circumstances. *See, e.g.,* Wheeler v. Caterpillar Tractor Co., 485 N.E.2d 372 (Ill. 1985) (employee discharged for refusing to work under conditions violative of federal standards); Kelsay v. Motorola, Inc., 384 N.E.2d 353 (Ill. 1978) (employee discharged for filing a worker's compensation claim); Palmateer v. Int'l Harvester Co., 421 N.E.2d 876 (Ill. 1981) (employee discharged for giving police information on coworker's possible criminal activity); Bartley v. University Asphalt Co., Inc., 472 N.E.2d 499 (Ill. App. Ct. 1984) (employee discharged for cooperating with FBI investigation). It is important to note that under Illinois law, public policy claims are available even to employees covered by collective bargaining agreements. *See* Midgett v. Sackett-Chicago, Inc., 473 N.E.2d 1280 (Ill. 1984), *cert. denied,* No.85-217 (U.S. 1985); Gonzalez v. Prestress Engineering Corp., 473 N.E.2d 1280 (Ill. S. Ct. 1984), *cert. denied,* 105 U.S. 3513 (1985).

INDIANA

A. *Implied Contracts*
1. Handbooks. Indiana courts have held that employee handbooks and personnel provisions do not give rise to implied contractual rights. *See, e.g.,* Shaw v. S.S. Kresge Co., 328 N.E.2d 775 (Ind. 1975); Mead Johnson & Co. v. Oppenheimer, 458 N.E.2d 668 (Ind. App. 1984); McQueeney v. Glenn, 400 N.E.2d 806 (Ind. App. 1980), *cert. denied,* 449 U.S. 1125 (1981).
2. Oral Promises. Unless the employee has given additional consideration beyond the services rendered, oral promises made by the employer will not alter the at-will relationship. *See, e.g.,* Ryan v. J.C. Penney Co., 627 F.2d 836 (7th Cir. 1980); Hamblen v. Danners, Inc., 478 N.E.2d 926 (Ind. App. 1985).

B. *Public Policy Exceptions*
Indiana courts have recognized a public policy exception to the at-will rule; however there must be a statutory violation involved. *See, e.g.,* Frampton v. Central Indiana Gas Co., 297 N.E.2d 425 (Ind. 1973) (employee discharged for filing worker's compensation claim); *Mead, supra;* Perry v. Hartz Mountain Corp., 537 F. Supp. 1387 (S.D. Ind. 1982) (employee discharged for refusing to participate in antitrust violation). Note that a federal court interpreting Indiana law has held that a tort cause of action for wrongful discharge based on a public policy violation is not available to employees covered by a collective bargaining agreement. *See* Vantine v. Elkhart Brass Manufacturing Co., Inc., 119 L.R.R.M. 2465 (7th Cir. 1985).

IOWA

A. *Implied Contracts*
Iowa has not yet recognized an implied contract exception to the at-will rule.

B. *Public Policy Exceptions*
Iowa has not specifically recognized a public policy exception to the at-will rule; however, in one case, the Iowa Supreme Court did suggest its willingness to recognize an exception when presented with appropriate facts. *See, e.g.,* Northrup v. Farmland Industries, 372 N.W.2d 193 (Iowa 1985) (court refused to recognize public policy exception where employee claimed he was discharged allegedly for participation in alcoholism treatment program); Abrisz v. Pulley Freight Lines, Inc., 270 N.W.2d 454 (Iowa S. Ct. 1978).

KANSAS

A. *Implied Contracts*
  1. Handbooks. One Kansas court rejected an implied contract claim based on an employer's handbook, holding that the handbook was merely a unilateral expression of the employer's policies and procedures. *See* Johnson v. National Beef Packing Co., 551 P.2d 779 (Kan. 1976). *See also* Rouse v. People's Natural Gas Co., 605 F. Supp. 230 (D. Kan. 1985) (employee manual is only unilateral expression). *But see* Fletcher v. Wesley Medical Center, 585 F. Supp. 1260 (D. Kan. 1984) (manual might create contractual obligations). Dis-

claimers in handbooks, however, may be effective to defeat an employee's contract claim. *Id.*

2. Oral Promises. Oral assurances made by the employer may be considered when determining whether an implied contract existed. *See* Allegri v. Providence-St. Margaret Health Center, 684 P.2d 1031 (Kan. App. 1984).

3. Implied Covenant of Good Faith and Fair Dealing. A federal district court in New York, applying Kansas law, refused to recognize an implied covenant exception. *See* Hunter v. H. D. Lee Co., Inc., 563 F. Supp. 1006 (N.D.N.Y. 1983) (applying Kansas law).

B. *Public Policy Exceptions*

A public policy exception to the at-will rule has been recognized by a Kansas court where an employee was discharged for filing a worker's compensation claim. *See* Murphy v. City of Topeka-Shawnee County Dept. of Labor Services, 630 P.2d 186 (Kan. App. 1981). An exception has also been recognized where an employee is discharged for testifying against his employer in a state unemployment compensation hearing. *See* Kistler v. Life Care Centers of America, Inc., 620 F. Supp. 1268 (D. Kan. 1985). It is important to note that a federal district court in Kansas has allowed an employee to proceed on a public policy claim where the claim alleged race bias, despite the availability of remedies under Title VII and state antidiscrimination laws. *See* Wynn v. Boeing Military Airplane Co., 595 F. Supp. 727 (D. Kan. 1984).

KENTUCKY

A. *Implied Contracts*

1. Oral Promises. The Kentucky Supreme Court has held that an employer's oral promise to discharge only for cause in accordance with the personnel manual was held to be enforceable against the employer. *See* Shah v. American Synthetic Rubber Corp., 655 S.W.2d 489 (Ky. 1983).

B. *Public Policy Exceptions*

Kentucky has recognized a public policy exception to the at-will rule where the discharge violates "a constitutionally protected right or a right implicit in a statute." *See* Firestone Textile Co. v. Meadows, 666 S.W.2d 730 (Ky. 1983) (public policy exception recognized where employee discharged allegedly for filing worker's compensation claim); Pari-Mutuel Clerks Union v. Jockey Club, 551 S.W.2d 801 (Ky. 1977); A public policy exception has also been recognized where an employee was discharged for reporting illegal conduct to his employer and civil authorities. *See* Brown v. Physicians Mutual Ins. Co., 679 S.W.2d 836 (Ky. App. 1984). *But see* Grzyb v. Evans, 700 S.W.2d 399 (Ky. 1985) (Kentucky Supreme Court criticized *Brown* and reiterated that public policy exception to at-will rule is narrow).

LOUISIANA

A. *Implied Contracts*
1. Handbooks. Handbooks do not give rise to enforceable implied contract claims under Louisiana law. *See, e.g.,* Thibodeaux v. Southwest Louisiana Hospital Association, 488 So.2d 743 (La. App. 1986); Thebner v. Xerox Corp., 480 So.2d 454 (La. App. 1985), *cert. denied,* 484 So.2d 139 (La. 1986); Williams v. Delta Haven, Inc., 416 So.2d 637 (La. App. 1982). Moreover, one Louisiana appellate court has upheld an employer's use of an at-will disclaimer to defeat an employee's implied contract claim. *See Thebner, supra.*
2. Oral Promises. An employer's promise of permanent or lifetime employment does not create a fixed duration of employment, and the employee retains his at-will status. *See* Baynard v. Guardian Life Ins. Co., 399 So.2d 1200 (La. App. 1981).
3. Promissory Estoppel. One Louisiana court rejected a plaintiff's promissory estoppel claim where he alleged that he had moved with his family from another state in reliance on employer's promise of employment. *See* Griffith v. Sollay Foundation Drilling, Inc., 373 So.2d 979 (La. App. 1979).

B. *Public Policy Exceptions*
Louisiana has rejected all attempts to create a public policy exception to the at-will rule. *See* , e.g., Gil v. Metal Service Corp., 412 So.2d 706 (La. App. 1982), *cert. denied,* 414 So.2d 397 (La. 1982) (no public policy exception recognized where employee discharged for refusing to commit an an illegal act). *See also* Frichter v. National Life and Accident Insurance Co., 620 F. Supp. 922 (E.D. La. 1985), *aff'd without opinion,* 790 F.2d 891 (5th Cir. 1986); Schultheiss v. Mobil Oil Exploration & Producing Southeast, Inc., 592 F. Supp. 628 (W.D. La. 1984).

MAINE

A. *Implied Contracts*

1. Handbooks. Under Maine law, a handbook may give rise to an implied contract claim. *See, e.g.,* Larabee v. Penobscot Frozen Foods, Inc., 486 A.2d 97 (Me. 1984); Wyman v. Osteopathic Hospital of Maine, Inc., 493 A.2d 330 (Me. 1985); Greene v. Union Mutual Life Ins. Co., 623 F. Supp. 295 (D. Me. 1985).

2. Oral Promises. An employer's oral assurances may give rise to an implied contract of employment for a definite term. *See* Terrio v. Milinocket Community Hospital, 379 A.2d 135 (Me. 1977) (implied contract found where employer told employee that she was secure in her job for the rest of her life); *Larabee, supra;* Buchanan v. Martin Marietta Corp., 494 A.2d 677 (Me. 1985). *But see* Broussard v. CACI, Inc., 780 F.2d 162 (1st Cir. 1986) (employer's statements about potential for lifetime employment held not to be implied contract).

3. Implied Covenant of Good Faith and Fair Dealing. The Maine Supreme Court has refused in one case to recognize a claim for breach of the implied covenant in an employment situation. *See Larabee, supra. See also* Poirier v. Sears, Roebuck & Co., No. CV 80-231 (Me. Super. Ct. 1983).

B. *Public Policy Exceptions*

Although Maine has not yet recognized a public policy exception to the at-will rule, the state's highest court has suggested that it will recognize an exception when an appropriate case is presented. *See* , e.g., *Larabee, supra;* MacDonald v. Eastern Fine Paper, Inc., 485 A.2d 228 (Me. 1984).

MARYLAND

A. *Implied Contracts*

1. Handbooks. Maryland does recognize implied contract claims arising from an employee handbook or personnel manual. *See, e.g.,* Staggs v. Blue Cross of Maryland, Inc., 486 A.2d 798 (Md. Sp. App. 1985); Dahl v. Brunswick Corp., 356 A.2d 221 (Md. App. 1976).

2. Oral Promises. An employer's oral assurances, absent sufficient consideration by the employee, cannot be used to stop an employer from discharging an otherwise at-will employee. *See, e.g.,* Page v. Carolina Coach Co., 667 F.2d 1156 (4th Cir.

1982); Paice v. Maryland Racing Commission, 539 F. Supp. 458 (D. Md. 1982).
3. Implied Covenant of Good Faith and Fair Dealing. A federal district court applying Maryland law has held that the implied covenant is not recognized in every employment contract. *See* Vasques v. National Geographic Society, No.J 81-3008 (D. Md. 1982).

B. *Public Policy Exceptions*
Maryland does recognize a public policy exception to the at-will rule, but it appears that the mandate of public policy must be specified in a statute. *See* Adler v. American Standard Corp., 432 A.2d 464 (Md. App. 1981). *See also* Teays v. Supreme Concrete Block, Inc., 441 A.2d 1109 (Md. Sp. App. 1982). Exceptions based on violations of public policy have been recognized for a discharge in violation of the state's polygraph law [*see* Moniodis v. Cook, 494 A.2d 212 (Md. Sp. App. 1985)], and for retaliatory discharge for filing a worker's compensation claim [*see* Roberts v. Citicorp Diners Club, Inc., 597 F. Supp. 311 (D. Md. 1984)]. For public employees, one Maryland court has held that the at-will rule is inapplicable "if the decision to terminate the public employment was made because of the employee's exercise of constitutionally protected first amendment rights." *See* DeBleecker v. Montgomery County, 438 A.2d 1348, 1353 (Md. App. 1982).

MASSACHUSETTS

A. *Implied Contracts*
1. Handbooks. Massachusetts courts generally recognize an implied contract claim arising from an employee handbook. *See, e.g.,* Hass v. Picker International, 122 L.R.R.M. 2367 (D. Mass. 1986); Garrity v. Valley View Nursing Home, Inc., 406 N.E.2d 423 (Mass. App. 1980); Pavadore v. School Committee of Canton, 473 N.E.2d 205 (Mass. App. 1985). *But see* Bouzianis v. U.S. Air, Inc., No. 84-3798-K (D. Mass. Sept. 30, 1985) (handbooks are merely directives for internal corporate management).
2. Oral Assurances. An employer may be bound by oral representations made to its employees for employment of a definite duration. *See Hass, supra.*
3. Implied Covenant of Good Faith and Fair Dealing. Massachusetts does recognize the implied covenant but apparently has

limited its recognition to those cases where the employee can prove that the employer received a financial windfall by discharging the employee. *See* Fortune v. National Cash Register Co., 364 N.E.2d 1261 (Mass. 1977); McCone v. New England Tel. & Tel. Co., 471 N.E.2d 47 (Mass. 1984); Phillips v. Youth Developmment Program, Inc., 459 N.E.2d 453 (Mass. 1983); Maddaloni v. Western Massachusetts Bus Lines, Inc., 438 N.E.2d 351 (Mass. 1982); Gram v. Liberty Mutual Ins. Co., 429 N.E.2d 21 (Mass. 1981).

B. *Public Policy Exceptions*

Massachusetts has recognized a public policy exception to the at-will doctrine. *See* Siles v. Travenol Laboratories, Inc., 433 N.E.2d 103 (Mass. App. 1982), *app. denied,* 440 N.E.2d 1176 (Mass. 1982) (employee discharged allegedly in order for employer to avoid payment of sales commissions); Stepanischen v. Merchants Dispatch Transportation Corp., 722 F.2d 922 (1st Cir. 1983) (employee covered by Railway Labor Act discharged allegedly for anti-union animus).

MICHIGAN   *See* chapter V, *supra,* at 77-99.

MINNESOTA

A. *Implied Contracts*

1. Handbooks. The Minnesota Supreme Court has held that an employer's handbook which provides detailed disciplinary procedures becomes part of the employment contract. *See, e.g.,* Lewis v. The Equitable Life Assurance Society, No. C8-84-1065, slip op. (Minn. July 3, 1986); Pine River State Bank v. Mettille, 333 N.W.2d 622 (Minn. 1983). *But see* Hunt v. IBM Mid-America Employees Union, 384 N.W.2d 853 (Minn. 1986) (handbook held not part of employment contract since it contained neither detailed disciplinary procedures nor specific examples of offenses warranting termination).

2. Oral Promises. Minnesota has held in one case that an employer's oral assurances are barred by the parol evidence rule and cannot modify an otherwise at-will arrangement. *See* Montgomery v. American Hoist and Derrick Co., 350 N.W.2d 405 (Minn. App. 1984). *But see* Elkund v. Vincent Brass & Aluminum Co., 351 N.W.2d 371 (Minn. App. 1984) (discharged employee's breach of oral contract recognized).

3. Promissory Estoppel. A Minnesota court has held that an employer is estopped from discharging its at-will employee where the employee gave up a former job in reliance on the employer's promise of employment. *See* Grouse v. Group Health Plan, Inc., 306 N.W.2d 114 (Minn. 1981). *But see* Dumas v. Kessler & Maguire Funeral Home, Inc., 380 N.E.2d 544 (Minn. App. 1986) (promissory estoppel does not create employer liability whenever at-will employee discharged).
4. Implied Covenant of Good Faith and Fair Dealing. The Minnesota Supreme Court has refused to recognize the implied covenant in an at-will employment contract. *See Hunt, supra. But see Elkund, supra* (breach of implied covenant claim recognized).

B. *Public Policy Exceptions*
Minnesota has not yet recognized any public policy exceptions to the at-will rule.

MISSISSIPPI

A. *Implied Contracts*
The general rule in Mississippi is that an implied contract claim will be recognized only where there is clear evidence of such a contract and the implied contract is supported by consideration in addition to the services rendered by the at-will employee. *See* Sartin v. Columbus Utilities Commission, 421 F. Supp. 393 (N.D. Miss. 1976), *aff'd without opinion,* 573 F.2d 84 (5th Cir. 1978). *See also* Shaw v. Burchfield, 481 So.2d 247 (Miss. 1985) (court refused to recognize implied contract claim to abrogate employment-at-will doctrine, but noted harsh result of doctrine's application).

B. *Public Policy Exceptions*
Mississippi has declined to recognize a public policy exception to the at-will rule, even where the employee was allegedly discharged in retaliation for filing a worker's compensation claim. *See, e.g.,* Kelly v. Mississippi Valley Gas Co., 397 So.2d 874 (Miss. 1981); Green v. Amerada Hess Corp., 612 F.2d 212 (5th Cir. 1980), *cert. denied,* 449 U.S. 952 (1980). In another case, a federal circuit court refused to recognize a public policy exception where an employee was discharged allegedly for filing a petition for bankruptcy. *See* McLellan v. Mississippi Power and Light Co., 545 F.2d 919 (5th Cir. 1977).

MISSOURI

A. Implied Contracts

1. Handbooks. Missouri has held that an implied contract claim may arise from an employer's personnel handbook, despite the fact that the parties did not mutually agree to terms. *See, e.g.,* Arie v. Intertherm, Inc., 648 S.W.2d 142 (Mo. App. 1983); Wilson v. Mobay Chemical Corp., No. 84-0137-CV-W-6 (W.D. Mo. May 31, 1984); Enyeart v. Shelter Mutual Ins. Co., 693 S.W.2d 120 (Mo. App. 1985); Gavan v. Madison Memorial Hospital, 700 S.W.2d 124 (Mo. App. 1985).

2. Oral Promises. A federal district court applying Missouri law has held that an employer's oral promises and the employee's reliance on such promises can alter the at-will status of an employee. *See* Stoetzel v. Continental Textile Corp., No. 84-1613 (8th Cir. 1985). *But see* Anselmo v. Manufacturers Ins. Co., 595 F. Supp. 541 (W.D. Mo. 1984) (statute of frauds defense upheld).

3. Promissory Estoppel. The Missouri Supreme Court has held that an employer is estopped from discharging an at-will employee without cause where there has been a promise of permanent employment given in return for a transfer of property. *See* Lopp v. Peerless Serum Co., 382 S.W.2d 620 (Mo. 1964).

4. Implied Covenant of Good Faith and Fair Dealing. Missouri has declined to recognize the implied covenant in every employment contract. *See* Kempe v. Prince Gardner, Inc., 569 F. Supp. 779 (E.D. Mo. 1983). *See also* Walker v. Modern Realty of Missouri, Inc., 675 F.2d 1002 (8th Cir. 1982) (court refused to recognize implied covenant in an at-will situation).

B. *Public Policy Exceptions*

Missouri has recognized a public policy exception to the at-will rule where an employee was discharged discriminatorily for filing a worker's compensation claim. *See* Henderson v. St. Louis Housing Authority, 605 S.W.2d 800 (Mo. App. 1978). An exception has also been recognized where an employee was discharged for threatening to report employer's violation of federal safety regulations. *See* Boyle v. Eyewear, Inc., 700 S.W.2d 859 (Mo. App. 1985).

MONTANA

A. *Implied Contracts*
1. Handbooks. The Montana Supreme Court has held that a handbook given to an at-will employee after he was employed did not constitute an implied contract because the provisions of the handbook were not bargained for. *See* e.g. Gates v. Life of Montana Ins. Co. (I), 638 P.2d 1063 (Mont. 1982).
2. Implied Covenant of Good Faith and Fair Dealing. The Montana Supreme Court has held that the implied covenant of good faith and fair dealing may arise from an employer's personnel handbook. *See, e.g., Gates (I), supra;* Gates v. Life of Montana Insurance Co. (II), 668 P.2d 213 (Mont. 1983); Dare v. Montana Petroleum Marketing Co., 687 P.2d 1015 (Mont. 1984). The implied covenant has been extended to cover even probationary employees. *See* Crenshaw v. Bozeman Deaconess Hospital, 693 P.2d 487 (Mont. 1984).

B. *Public Policy Exceptions*
Montana is unusual in that it has codified its public policy exception into state law. *See* Mont. Code Ann. (1985) § 39-2-505 (employer's willful or permanent breach of its obligation to its employee will constitute grounds for a public policy exception). The Montana Supreme Court has said that it will recognize a public policy claim where an employee is discharged for refusing to commit perjury, asserting a worker's compensation claim, or refusing to have sexual relations. *See* Keneally v. Orgain, 606 P.2d 127 (Mont. 1980). *See also* Nye v. Dept. of Livestock, 639 P.2d 498 (Mont. 1982) (state's administrative rules may provide source of public policy).

NEBRASKA

A. *Implied Contracts*
1. Handbooks. Nebraska has recognized an employee's implied contract claim arising from an employer's personnel handbook. *See, e.g.,* Morris v. Lutheran Medical Center, 340 N.W.2d 388 (Neb. 1983); Sanders v. May Broadcasting Co., 336 N.W.2d 92 (Neb. 1983); Serafin v. City of Lexington, Nebraska, 547 F. Supp. 1118 (D. Neb. 1982). The Nebraska Supreme Court has upheld the use of handbook provisions which stated the employee's at-will status. *See* Feola v. Valmont Industries, Inc., 304 N.W.2d 377 (Neb. 1981).

B. *Public Policy Exceptions*
Nebraska has not yet recognized any public policy exceptions to the at-will rule. *See* Mueller v. Union Pacific Railroad, 371 N.W.2d 732 (Neb. 1985).

NEVADA

A. *Implied Contracts*
1. Handbooks. Nevada has recognized an implied contract claim arising from an employer's personnel handbook. *See* Southwest Gas Corp. v. Ahmad, 668 P.2d 261 (Nev. 1983); Mannikko v. Harrah's Reno, Inc., 630 F. Supp. 191 (D. Nev. 1986). *See also* United Brotherhood of Carpenters & Joiners v. Drake, 714 P.2d 177 (Nev. 1986). In one case, the Nevada Supreme Court refused to enforce directly an at-will disclaimer contained in an employment application because there remained a question of material fact as to whether this constituted the parties' mutual understanding. *See* Stone v. Mission Bay Mortgage Co., 672 P.2d 629 (Nev. 1983). In addition, the *Stone* court also held that handbook provisions could create contractual obligations even to probationary employees. *Id.*
2. Oral Promises. The Nevada Supreme Court has held that an employer's oral promises may create implied contractual obligations. *See, e.g.,* Tropicana Hotel Corp. v. Speer, 692 P.2d 499 (Nev. 1985); *Stone, supra;* Southwest Gas Corp. v. Ahmad, 668 P.2d 261 (Nev. 1983).
3. Implied Covenant of Good Faith and Fair Dealing. Nevada will recognize the implied covenant in limited circumstances. *See, e.g.,* Wolber v. Service Corp. Int'l, 612 F. Supp. 235 (D. Nev. 1985); Savage v. Holiday Inn Corp., Inc., 603 F. Supp. 311 (D. Nev. 1985) (covenant will be implied in contractual relationships which involve a "special element of reliance." *Id.* at 315).

B. *Public Policy Exceptions*
The Nevada Supreme Court has recognized a public policy exception where the employee has been discharged for filing a worker's compensation claim. *See* Hansen v. Harrah's, 675 P.2d 394 (Nev. 1984). Nevada courts have also recognized a public policy exception to the at-will rule for discharge on the basis of age or sex discrimination despite the availability of a federal remedy. *See, e.g., Wolber, supra; Savage, supra.*

NEW HAMPSHIRE

A. Implied Contracts

A federal district court in New Hampshire has recognized an implied contract exception to the at-will rule based on an employee's longevity of service and relocation of entire family. *See* Foley v. Community Oil Co., 64 F.R.D. 561 (D. N.H. 1974).

B. *Public Policy Exceptions*

The New Hampshire Supreme Court has recognized a broad public policy exception to the at-will rule, whenever the discharge was motivated primarily by the employer's bad faith, malice, or retaliation. *See, e.g.,* Cloutier v. Great Atlantic & Pacific Tea Co., 436 A.2d 1140 (N.H. 1981); Howard v. Dorr Woolen Co., 414 A.2d 1273 (N.H. 1980); Monge v. Beebe Rubber Co., 316 A.2d 549 (N.H. 1974). *See also* O'Brien v. Papa Gino's, 780 F.2d 1067 (1st Cir. 1986). In addition, a federal district court in New Hampshire has held that a retaliatory discharge for an employee's exercise of rights under the state constitution is a *per se* public policy violation. *See* Fulford v. Burndy, 120 L.R.R.M. 3539 (D. N.H. 1985).

NEW JERSEY

A. *Implied Contracts*

1. Handbooks. The New Jersey Supreme Court has recognized that an employer's promise of job security contained in a handbook widely distributed to employees can form the basis of a discharged employee's breach of implied contract claim. *See* Woolley v. Hoffman-LaRoche, Inc., 491 A.2d 1257 (N.J. 1985). *See also* Guidice v. Drew Chemical Corp., 509 A.2d 200 (N.J. Super. Ct., App. Div. 1986); Ware v. Prudential Ins. Co., No. L-39171-83 (N.J. Super. Ct., Camden Cnty June 24, 1985). *But see* McQuitty v. General Dynamics Corp., 499 A.2d 526 (N.J. Super. 1985) (court refused to recognize plaintiff's claim of implied job security following contract's expiration). The state supreme court has indicated, however, that disclaimers would be effective to defeat any such implied contract claims. *See Woolley, supra.*

2. Implied Covenant of Good Faith and Fair Dealing. A federal district court applying New Jersey law has held that the implied covenant does not extend to employment contracts

under New Jersey law. *See* Smith v. Hartford Ins. Co., No. 85-2323, slip op. (E.D. Pa. 1985) (applying New Jersey law).

B. Public Policy Exceptions

New Jersey has recognized a wrongful discharge cause of action for a violation of public policy. *See, e.g.,* Pierce v. Ortho Pharmaceutical Corp., 417 A.2d 505 (N.J. 1980) (although public policy exception recognized, plaintiff's facts held insufficient to maintain cause of action); Lalley v. Copygraphics, 428 A.2d 1317 (N.J. 1981) (exception recognized where employee discharged for filing a worker's compensation claim); Herring v. Prince Macaroni of New Jersey, Inc., 799 F.2d 120 (3d Cir. 1986) (worker's compensation claim). It is important to note that New Jersey has refused to recognize a public policy exception where the employees were not being asked to break the law but objected to the employer's directives on personal beliefs or professional ethics. *See Ortho, supra* (employees rightfully discharged for opposing research of controversial drug because of personal beliefs); *see also* Warthen v. Toms River Community Memorial Hospital, 488 A.2d 229 (N.J. 1985) (nurse rightfully discharged for refusing to perform procedure on terminally ill patient based on professional code of ethics).

NEW MEXICO

A. *Implied Contracts*

1. Handbooks. The New Mexico Supreme Court has recognized an implied contract claim arising from an employer's personnel handbook. *See* Forrester v. Parker, 606 P.2d 191 (N.M. 1980) (employer contractually obligated to follow termination procedures contained in employee manual). The implied contract claim has even been recognized for a probationary employee. *See* Vigil v. Arzola, 687 P.2d 1038 (N.M. 1984). *But see* Ellis v. El Paso Natural Gas Co., 754 F.2d 884 (10th Cir. 1985) (held that employer's handbook was "non-promissory").

2. Implied Covenant of Good Faith and Fair Dealing. A federal district court in New Mexico has refused to recognize a separate cause of action for bad faith breach of the implied covenant. *See* Salazar v. Furr's, Inc., 629 F. Supp. 1403 (D. N.M. 1986).

B. *Public Policy Exceptions*
The New Mexico Supreme Court has not yet recognized any public policy exceptions to the employment-at-will doctrine. A New Mexico appellate court, however, has recognized a public policy exception, holding that the strongest source for such public policy is legislation. *See Vigil, supra;* Zuniga v. Sears, Roebuck & Co., 671 P.2d 662 (N.M. App. 1983); *Salazar, supra* (wrongful discharge cause of action for violation of public policy recognized where employee discharged allegedly to prevent the vesting of her pension benefits thereby contravening ERISA).

NEW YORK *See* chapter VII, *supra,* at 119-138.

NORTH CAROLINA

A. *Implied Contracts*
1. Handbooks. Generally North Carolina courts will not recognize implied contract claims arising from personnel handbooks. *See, e.g.,* Walker v. Westinghouse Electric Corp., 335 S.E.2d 79 (N.C. App. 1985), *rev. denied,* 341 S.E.2d 39 (N.C. 1986) (termination and discipline procedures contained in manual become part of contract only if expressly included); Troutman v. Travenol Laboratories, Inc., 320 S.E.2d 441 (N.C. App. 1984). One North Carolina court, however, has held that an implied contract claim will be recognized if the personnel manual provides for a just cause termination and is expressly incorporated into the employment contract by the employee signing an agreement to abide by the handbook provisions. *See* Trought v. Richardson, 338 S.E.2d 617 (N.C. App. 1986). *But see* Bailey v. Merrill Lynch, Pierce, Fenner & Smith, Inc., No. 85-1066 (4th Cir. Jan. 14, 1986) (even if handbook is incorporated into the employment contract, it is not contractually binding, because the employer reserves the right to unilaterally alter the handbook).
2. Oral Promises. The North Carolina Supreme Court has permitted the use of parol evidence to establish a definite duration of employment and thereby alter an employee's at-will status. *See, e.g.,* Hall v. Hotel L'Europe, Inc., 318 S.E.2d 99 (N.C. 1984); Beal v. K. H. Stephenson Supply Co., 244 S.E.2d 463 (N.C. 1978).
3. Promissory Estoppel. A North Carolina appellate court has held that an employer may be estopped from discharging its at-will employee without just cause where the employee has

given sufficient consideration, such as relocating, or relin-
quishing claims for personal injuries against the employer.
See Burkhimer v. Gealy, 250 S.E.2d 678 (N.C. App.1979), *rev.
denied,* 254 S.E.2d 918 (N.C. 1979); Sides v. Duke Hospital,
328 S.E.2d 818 (N.C. App. 1985), *rev. denied,* 333 S.E.2d 490
(N.C. 1985).

B. *Public Policy Exceptions*
North Carolina has recognized a public policy exception to the
at-will rule where the employee is discharged for testifying
against his employer. *See Sides, supra.* A violation of public policy has also been recognized where an employee was discharged
in retaliation for filing a worker's compensation claim. *See, e.g.,
Trought, supra;* Henderson v. Traditional Log Homes, Inc., 319
S.E.2d 290 (N.C. App.), *rev. denied,* 323 S.E.2d (N.C. 1984).

NORTH DAKOTA

A. *Implied Contracts*
  1. Handbooks. The North Dakota Supreme Court rejected an
  employee's implied contract claim based on a handbook where
  the employer's manual spoke of "lifetime opportunity" and
  "permanent and stable business." *See* Wadeson v. American
  Family Mutual Ins. Co., 343 N.W.2d 267 (N.D. 1984). *See also*
  Gowin v. Hazen Memorial Hospital Assoc., 349 N.W.2d 4
  (N.D. 1984).

B. *Public Policy Exceptions*
At this date North Dakota has not recognized any public policy
exceptions to the at-will rule.

OHIO

A. *Implied Contracts*
  1. Handbooks. The Ohio Supreme Court has held that employee
  handbooks may constitute evidence of an employment contract and contractually obligate the employer. *See, e.g.,* Mers
  v. Dispatch Printing Co., 483 N.E.2d 150 (Ohio 1985). *See
  also* Hedrick v. Center for Comprehensive Alcoholism Treatment, 454 N.E.2d 1343 (Ohio App. 1982); Day v. Good Samar-
  itan Hospital and Health Center, No. 8062 (Ohio App. 1983)
  (recognizing implied contract claims arising from handbooks). Ohio courts appear to be split on the effectiveness of

at-will disclaimers to defeat implied contract claims. *Compare Day, supra* (disclaimer enforced) *with* Kochis v. Sears, Roebuck & Co., No. CA 2175 (Ohio App. Feb. 23, 1984) (at-will disclaimer modified by employer's later oral assurances).

2. Oral Promises. Ohio courts have consistently held that oral assurances made by the employer may modify an otherwise at-will employment relationship. *See, e.g., Mers supra; Kochis, supra.* The use of statute of frauds defense to defeat oral agreements has not been successful. *See, e.g.,* Kidd v. Ral Partha Enterprises, Inc., No. C-840268 (Hamilton App., March 6, 1985); Gathagan v. Firestone Tire & Rubber Co., No. 11803 (Summitt App., Feb. 13, 1985).

3. Promissory Estoppel. The Ohio courts have held that an employer may be estopped from discharging his at-will employee if the employee detrimentally relied on an employer's promise. *See, e.g., Hedrick, supra;* Jones v. East Center for Community Mental Health, Inc., 482 N.E.2d 969 (Ohio App. 1984).

B. *Public Policy Exceptions*

Generally, Ohio has declined to recognize any public policy exceptions to the at-will rule. *See, e.g.,* Phung v. Waste Management, Inc., 491 N.E.2d 1114 (Ohio 1986) (court deferred to legislature to create public policy exception to at-will doctrine); Henkel v. Education Research Council of America, 344 N.E.2d 118 (Ohio 1976); Peterson v. Scott Construction Co., 451 N.E.2d 1236 (Ohio App. 1982). A limited public policy exception has been recognized in one case by a federal court applying Ohio law where the employee was discharged for refusing to commit perjury. *See* Merkel v. Scovill, 570 F. Supp. 133 (S.D. Ohio 1983). *See also* Lovorn v. Dayco Corp., 101 CCH Lab. Cases ¶ 55482 (Montgomery App., Jan. 30, 1984) (public policy exception recognized where employee discharged allegedly for refusing to commit illegal acts).

OKLAHOMA

A. *Implied Contracts*

1. Handbooks. Oklahoma courts have recognized an implied contract claim arising from an employer's personnel handbook. *See* Vinyard v. King, 728 P.2d 428 (10th Cir. 1984); Langdon v. Saga Corp., 569 P.2d 524 (Okla. App. 1976).

2. Implied Covenant of Good Faith and Fair Dealing. The Oklahoma Supreme Court has recognized the implied covenant in an employment contract where the employer discharged his employee in order to deprive him of commissions. *See* Hall v. Farmers Insurance Exchange, 713 P.2d 1027 (Okla. 1985). Where a handbook provides for discharge only for good cause, the covenant of good faith and fair dealing is implied. *See, e.g.,* Grayson v. American Airlines, Inc., 803 F.2d 1097 (10th Cir. 1986); Hinson v. Cameron and Comanche County Hospital Authority, 57 Okla. B. J. 1229 (1986).

B. *Public Policy Exceptions*
   Oklahoma has not yet recognized any public policy exceptions to the at-will rule.

OREGON

A. *Implied Contracts*
   1. Handbooks. The Oregon Supreme Court has recognized that an employer's personnel handbook may become impliedly incorporated into the employment contract and obligate the employer to discharge for cause only. *See, e.g.,* Wyss v. Inskeep, 699 P.2d 1161, *rev. denied,* 707 P.2d 582 (Ore. 1985); Fleming v. Kids & Kin Head Start, 693 P.2d 1363 (Ore. 1985); Sabin v. Willamette-Western Corp., 557 P.2d 1344 (Ore. 1976) (implied contract found to exist based on employer's administrative bulletin).
   2. Implied Covenant of Good Faith and Fair Dealing. In *Wyss, supra,* which involved an employer's use of a written bonus plan to attract employees, the Oregon Supreme Court noted that there is an implied obligation of good faith performance in every contract. *See Wyss, supra.*

B. *Public Policy Exceptions*
   Oregon has recognized an expansive public policy exception to the at-will rule which prohibits an employer from discharging an at-will employee for any "socially undesirable motive." *See* Nee's v. Hocks, 536 P.2d 512 (Ore. 1975) (employee discharged for serving on jury duty when her employer did not want her to). This broad exception has been interpreted to include: discharge for filing a worker's compensation claim [*see* Brown v. Transcon Lines, 588 P.2d 1087 (Ore. 1978)]; discharge for reporting suspected patient abuse [*see* McQuary v. Bel Air Convalescent

Home, Inc., 684 P.2d 21, *rev. denied,* 688 P.2d 845 (Ore. 1984)]; discharge for refusing to sign a false statement concerning fellow employee's discharge [*see* Delaney v. Taco Time International, Inc., 681 P.2d 114 (Ore. 1984)].

PENNSYLVANIA *See* chapter VI, *supra,* at 101-117.

PUERTO RICO

Puerto Rico is unique among American jurisdictions in that it has enacted a Discharge Indemnity Law, Title 29, Section 185 (a), which provides that every employee working under a contract without a fixed duration who is terminated without good cause can recover one month's salary and one week's salary for each year of service.

RHODE ISLAND

A. *Implied Contracts To date*
   Rhode Island has not yet recognized any implied contract exceptions to the at-will rule.

B. *Public Policy Exceptions*
   Rhode Island has not yet recognized any public policy exceptions to the at-will rule. A federal district court applying Rhode Island law rejected a plaintiff's public policy claim where he alleged he was discharged in retaliation for testifying against his employer in a civil action. *See* Brainard v. Imperial Manufacturing Co., 571 F. Supp. 37 (D. R.I. 1983).

SOUTH CAROLINA

A. *Implied Contracts*
   1. Handbooks. A federal district court applying South Carolina law specifically rejected a plaintiff's implied contract claim arising from an employer's handbook. *See* Satterfield v. Lockheed Missiles & Space Co., Inc., 617 F. Supp. 1359 (D. S.C. 1985) (summary judgment granted, held manual designed for "informational and instructional purposes" only); Small v. Springs Industries, Inc., S.C. Sup. Ct. No. 22737 (June 8, 1987) (employer's deviation from termination procedure in handbook constituted a breach of contract).
   2. Implied Covenant of Good Faith and Fair Dealing. In *Satterfield, supra,* the court also specifically rejected an extension of the implied covenant to employment contracts. *Id.*

B. *Public Policy Exceptions*

The South Carolina Supreme Court has recognized a narrow public policy exception to the at-will rule where an employee was discharged for testifying before a state employment security commission. *See* Ludwick v. This Minute of Carolina, Inc., 337 S.E.2d 213 (S.C. 1985). A public policy exception has also been recognized where an employee was discharged for being a union member in violation of the state's right-to-work laws. *See* Layne v. Int'l Brotherhood of Elect. Workers, Local 382, 247 S.E.2d 346 (S.C. 1978). Note, however, that the South Carolina Supreme Court has refused to recognize a public policy exception where an employee was allegedly discharged for pursuing a worker's compensation claim. *See, e.g.,* Hudson v. Zenith Engraving Co., 259 S.E.2d 812 (S.C. 1979); Raley v. Darling Shop of Greenville, Inc., 59 S.E.2d 148 (S.C. 1950).

SOUTH DAKOTA

A. *Implied Contracts*

1. Handbooks. The South Dakota Supreme Court has held in one case that the disciplinary procedures contained in employer's handbook were contractually binding. *See* Osterkamp v. Alkota Manufacturing, Inc., 332 N.W.2d 275 (S.D. 1983).

B. *Public Policy Exceptions*

There are no cases as of this date in which South Dakota has recognized a public policy exception to the at-will rule. *But see* note below.

NOTE: South Dakota has expressly limited the employment-at-will doctrine by law. While termination at will is permitted for employment with no specific duration, the South Dakota statute provides, in part, that: "Servant is presumed to be hired for such length as the parties adopt for the estimation of wages. A hiring at a yearly rate is presumed to be for one year." S.D. Codified Laws Ann. § 60-1-3. *See* Goodwyn v. Sencore, Inc., 389 F. Supp. 824 (D. S.D. 1975) (where employee hired at an annual salary of $15,000, employer has the burden of proving grounds for termination).

TENNESSEE

A. *Implied Contracts*

1. Handbooks. Tennessee courts have generally held that handbooks can constitute an implied contract with respect to certain benefits stated therein. *See, e.g.,* Abbott v. Kellwood Company, 10 T.A.M. 38-30 (W.D. Tenn. Aug. 3, 1985) (employees entitled to accrued vacation pay as provided for in employee handbook on a pro rata basis following sale of company). Under Tennessee law, however, it appears clear that handbooks cannot create implied employment contracts for a definite term. *See, e.g.,* Graves v. Anchor Wire Corp., 692 S.W.2d 420 (Tenn. App. 1985); Whittaker v. Care-More, Inc., 621 S.W.2d 395 (Tenn. App. 1981); Lieber v. Union Carbide Corp., Nuclear Div., 577 F. Supp. 563 (E.D. Tenn. 1983) (handbook merely an expression of internal management policy). Furthermore, it appears that at-will disclaimers are enforceable to defeat an employee's implied contract claims. *See* Blalock v. Hecks Discount Stores, No. 140, slip op. (Tenn. App., April 14, 1986).

2. Oral Promises. Although oral promises used to modify the at-will status are not barred by the statute of frauds under Tennessee law, the employee making the claim must prove that consideration in addition to the services rendered was given. *See* Price v. Mercury Supply Co., Inc., 682 S.W.2d 924 (Tenn. App. 1984), *appeal denied,* 682 S.W.2d 924 (Tenn. 1984).

B. *Public Policy Exceptions*

The Tennessee Supreme Court has recognized a public policy exception to the at-will rule where an employee is discharged for filing a worker's compensation claim. *See* Clanton v. Cain-Sloan Co., 677 S.W.2d 441 (Tenn. 1984). *See also* Williams v. Tennessee In-Home Health Service, Inc., slip op. (Tenn. App., April 26, 1985) (court reversed trial court's dismissal of plaintiff's claim that her discharge for refusing to falsify employer's reports violated public policy); Watson v. Cleveland Chair Co., 122 L.R.R.M. 2076 (Tenn. App. 1985) (public policy claim recognized where employees discharged for refusing to violate state law regarding truck vehicle speed). *But see* Wrather v. Pizza Hut of America, Inc., 10 T.A.M. 17-3 (Tenn. App., March 29, 1985) (public policy exceptions under Tennessee law limited to those specifically recognized by the state supreme court).

TEXAS

A. *Implied Contracts*
   1. Handbooks. Generally, Texas courts have been hesitant to recognize implied contract claims arising from an employer's personnel manual and have held that they constitute only general guidelines and do not limit the procedures by which employees can be discharged. *See, e.g.,* Joachim v. A.T.&T. Information Systems, 793 F.2d 113 (5th Cir. 1986); Berry v. Doctor's Health Facilities, 715 S.W.2d 60 (Tex. App. 1986); Reynolds Manufacturing Co. v. Mendoza, 644 S.W.2d 536 (Tex. App. 1982).
   2. Oral Promises. Texas has held that oral promises made by the employer may alter the at-will status of an employee. *See* Chessher v. Southwestern Bell Telephone Co., 671 S.W.2d 901 (Tex. App. 1983); Kelley v. Apache Products, Inc., 709 S.W.2d 772 (Tex. App. 1986).

B. *Public Policy Exceptions*
   The Texas Supreme Court has recognized a public policy exception to the at-will doctrine in a case where the employee demonstrated that he was discharged for his refusal to perform an illegal act. *See* Sabine Pilot Service, Inc. v. Hauck, 687 S.W.2d 60 (Tex. 1985) (employee refused to pump vessel's bilge at a place prohibited by federal law). *But see* Phillips v. Goodyear Tire & Rubber Co., 651 F.2d 1051 (5th Cir. 1981), *reh'g denied,* 671 F.2d 860 (5th Cir. 1982) (no cause of action where employee discharged allegedly for testifying against employer). Note that under Texas law, there is statutory protection against retaliatory discharge for employees filing worker's compensation claims. *See* Murray Corporation of Maryland v. Brooks, 600 S.W.2d 897 (Tex. Civ. App. 1980).

UTAH

A. *Implied Contracts*
   1. Handbooks. The Utah Supreme Court has held in several cases that a handbook, absent a specific duration term, cannot create a contract of fixed duration. *See, e.g.,* Bullock v. Desert Dodge Truck Center, Inc., 354 P.2d 559 (Utah 1960); Held v. American Linen Supply Co., 307 P.2d 210 (Utah 1957).
   2. Promissory Estoppel. The Utah Supreme Court held that an employee's incurring moving expenses and leaving his former

job in reliance on employer's promise of employment did not constitute sufficient grounds to estop employer from discharging employee at will. *See Bullock, supra.*

B. *Public Policy Exceptions*
Utah has not yet recognized any public policy exceptions to the at-will rule.

VERMONT

A. *Implied Contracts*
  1. Handbooks. The Vermont Supreme Court has held that an employer's handbook and other representations may give rise to an employee's implied contract claim. *See, e.g.,* Benoir v. Ethan-Allen Inc., 514 A.2d 716 (Vt. 1986) (employer's discipline procedure contained in handbook precluded discharge without cause); Sherman v. Rutland Hospital, Inc., 500 A.2d 230 (Vt. 1985). *But see* Larose v. Agway, Inc., 508 A.2d 1364 (Vt. 1986) (unbargained for handbook provisions are not contractually binding on employer).

B. *Public Policy Exceptions*
The Vermont Supreme Court has refused to recognize any public policy exceptions to the at-will rule, holding that such action should be left to the state legislature. *See* Jones v. Keogh, 409 A.2d 581 (Vt. 1979); Brower v. Holmes Transport, Inc., 435 A.2d 952 (Vt. 1981).

VIRGINIA

A. *Implied Contracts*
  1. Handbooks. A federal district court in Virginia recognized the possibility that an employer's personnel handbook may constitute an implied promise to discharge for cause only. *See, e.g.,* Frazier v. Colonial Williamsburg Foundation, 574 F. Supp. 318 (E.D. Va. 1983); Barger v. General Electric Co., 599 F. Supp. 1154 (W.D. Va. 1984); Thompson v. American Motor Inns, Inc., 623 F. Supp. 409 (W. D. Va. 1985).
  2. Oral Promises. Oral assurances made by an employer may be used to modify the at-will status of an employee. *See* Sea-Land Service, Inc. v. O'Neal, 297 S.E.2d 647 (Va. 1982).
  3. Implied Covenant of Good Faith and Fair Dealing. One federal district court has held in *dicta* that Virginia law does not recognize the implied covenant exception to the at-will doc-

trine. *See* Mason v. Richmond Motor Co., 625 F. Supp. 883 (E.D. Va. 1986).

B. *Public Policy Exceptions*

The Virginia Supreme Court has recognized a public policy exception to the at-will rule where an employee is discharged for exercising a statutory right. *See* Bowman v. State Bank of Keysville, 331 S.E.2d 797 (Va. 1985) (employee, a stockholder of bank, effectively denied his right under Virginia law to vote his shares where he was discharged for voting against management's directives). It is uncertain whether Virginia's public policy exception extends to non-statutory claims. *See* Blevins v. General Electric Co., 491 F. Supp. 521 (W.D. Va. 1980).

WASHINGTON

A. *Implied Contracts*

1. Handbooks. The Washington Supreme Court has held that an employer's personnel handbook provides evidence of the parties' intentions to be bound and may support an employee's implied contract claim. *See, e.g.,* Roberts v. Atlantic Richfield Co., 568 P.2d 764 (Wash. 1977); Parker v. United Airlines, 649 P.2d 181, *rev. denied,* 98 Wash. 2d 1011 (1982); Thompson v. St. Regis Paper Co., 685 P.2d 1081 (Wash. S. Ct. 1984). Use of disclaimers in the handbook, however, may be effective in defeating such implied contract claims. *See, Thompson, supra.*

2. Oral Promises. Specific promises made by an employer may be binding if the employee reasonably relied on such assurances. *See, e.g., Thompson, supra;* Sarruf v. Miller, 586 P.2d 466 (Wash. 1978).

3. Implied Covenant of Good Faith and Fair Dealing. The Washington Supreme Court has specifically refused to recognize the implied covenant in an employment contract. *See Thompson, supra.*

B. *Public Policy Exceptions*

Although the Washington Supreme Court has recognized a public policy exception to the at-will rule, it appears that such policy is limited to that which is statutorily defined. *See, e.g., Thompson, supra* (exception would be recognized if employee actually discharged for bringing company's accounting practices in line with federal law); Krystad v. Lau, 400 P.2d 72 (Wash. 1965) (employee discharged for joining a union).

WEST VIRGINIA

A. *Implied Contracts*
   1. Handbooks. The West Virginia Supreme Court has held that it will recognize an implied contract claim arising from an employer's personnel handbook where the handbook contains a definite promise not to discharge the employee except for specific reasons. *See, e.g.,* Cook v. Heck's, Inc., 342 S.E.2d 453 (W. Va. 1986); Berry v. Boone County Ambulance Authority, 341 S.E.2d 418 (W.Va. 1986).

B. *Public Policy Exceptions*
   The West Virginia Supreme Court has recognized public policy exceptions to the at-will rule in the following cases: Harless v. First National Bank in Fairmont, 246 S.E.2d 270 (W. Va. 1978) (employee discharged for attempting to make his employer comply with federal consumer credit laws); Shanholtz v. Monongahela Power Co., 270 S.E.2d 178 (W. Va. 1980) (worker's compensation claim); Cordle v. General Hugh Mercer Corp., 325 S.E.2d 111 (W. Va. 1984) (employee discharged for refusing to take polygraph examination in contravention of state law).

WISCONSIN

A. *Implied Contracts*
   1. Handbooks. The Wisconsin Supreme Court has recognized that an employer's personnel manual may give rise to an implied contract claim. *See* Ferraro v. Koelsch, 368 N.W.2d 666 (Wis. 1985). *See also* Mursch v. Dan Dorn Co., 627 F. Supp. 1310 (W.D. Wis. 1986) (employer's violation of handbook provision supports breach of contract claim); Hale v. Stoughton Hospital Association, Inc., 376 N.W.2d 89 (Wis. App. 1986). *But see* Holloway v. K-Mart Corp., 334 N.W.2d 570 (Wis. 1983) (employer not bound by handbook provisions concerning termination procedure).

B. *Public Policy Exceptions*
   Wisconsin has recognized a public policy exception to the at-will rule where the discharge is contrary to statutory provisions. *See, e.g.,* Brockmeyer v. Dun & Bradstreet, 335 N.W.2d 834

(Wis. 1983) (public policy favoring reinstatement must be based on existing law before exception can be recognized); Wandry v. Bull's Eye Credit Union, 384 N.W.2d 325 (Wis. 1986) (public policy exception recognized where employee discharged for refusing to violate statutory procedures concerning reimbursement for bad checks).

WYOMING

A. *Implied Contracts*
1. Handbooks. The Wyoming Supreme Court has recognized that provisions in an employer's personnel handbook may give rise to implied contract claims. *See, e.g.,* Armstrong v. American Colloid Co., 721 P.2d 1069 (Wyo. 1986); Leithead v. American Colloid Co., 721 P.2d 1059 (Wyo. 1986); Mobil Coal Producing, Inc. v. Parks, 704 P.2d 702 (Wyo. 1985); Alexander v. Phillips Oil Co., No. 85-28 (Wyo. S. Ct. Oct. 23, 1985).
2. Implied Covenant of Good Faith and Fair Dealing. The Wyoming Supreme Court has specifically rejected the implied covenant as a limitation on the employer's ability to discharge at-will employees. *See, e.g., Mobil, supra;* Rompf v. Hammans Hotels, Inc., 685 P.2d 25 (Wyo. 1984); *Alexander, supra.*
3. Promissory Estoppel. The Wyoming Supreme Court has held that an employer was not estopped from discharging his at-will employee, even when the employee quit his former job and accepted a wage cut. *See Rompf, supra.*

B. *Public Policy Exceptions*
The Wyoming Supreme Court rejected an employee's public policy claim based on an alleged violation of his first amendment free speech rights, pension rights, sex discrimination, and marriage status. *See* Allen v. Safeway Stores, Inc., 699 P.2d 277 (Wyo. 1985). *See also* Siebken v. Town of Wheatland, 700 P.2d 1236 (Wyo. 1985).

Appendix B

Full Text Versions of Pennsylvania
and New Jersey
Proposed "Just Cause" Legislation

THE GENERAL ASSEMBLY OF PENNSYLVANIA HOUSE BILL

No. 1020 Session of 1985

INTRODUCED BY MANDERINO, IRVIS, COHEN, KUKOVICH, ITKIN, STABACK, AFFLERBACH, DROMBOWSKI, LASHINGER, SEVENTY, BURNS, CALTAGIRONE, LEV-DANKSY, KOSINSKI, GALLAGHER, PIEVSKY, TELEK, D.W. SNYDER, PETRONE, DALEY, JOSEPHS, LINTON, RYBAK, PERZEL, DeLUCA, PRATT, BELARDI, OLIVER, CARN, PRESTON, TRELLO, WOZNIAK, PISTELLA, PETRARCA, FREEMAN, WAMBACH, BARBER, HARPER, WIGGINS, OLASZ, STEIGHNER, KASUNIC, FEE, FATTAH, EVANS, MICHLOVIC, VAN HORNE AND BATTISTO, APRIL 22, 1985

REFERRED TO COMMITTEE ON LABOR RELATIONS, APRIL 23, 1985

AN ACT

Protecting employees from unjust dismissal; providing for mediation and arbitration proceedings; and providing legal remedies.

TABLE OF CONTENTS

Section 12. Contempt.

Section 13. Construction of act.

Section 14. Posting copy of act.

Section 15. Effective date.

The General Assembly of the Commonwealth of Pennsylvania hereby enacts as follows:

Section 1. Short title.

This act shall be known and may be cited as the Unjust Dismissal Act.

Section 2. Legislative statement of purpose.

In recent years it has become a well established principle in Pennsylvania case law that employers do not have an absolute right to terminate employees when the cause of dismissal arises from issues dealing with public health and safety or matters of public policy. The right of an employee to be protected from unjust dismissal has, therefore, been significantly advanced. The purpose of this law is to further establish these employee rights and to advance them to the point that all employees would have a process to seek redress when they have been dismissed from employment for any reason other than just cause.

Section 3. Definitions.

The following words and phrases when used in this act shall have the meanings given to them in this section unless the context clearly indicates otherwise:

"Bureau." The Bureau of Mediation of the Department of Labor and Industry.

"Dismiss," "dismisses" or "dismissed." Derivatives of "dismissal."

"Dismissal." An involuntary discharge from employment, including a resignation or voluntary quit resulting from an improper or unreasonable action or inaction of the employer. This term and its derivatives shall not be construed to include layoff or any other type of temporary dismissal.

"Employee." A person who performs a service for wages or other remuneration under a contract of hire, written or oral, express or implied. This term does not include those protected by a collective bargaining agreement or those protected by civil service or tenure against unjust dismissal or a person who has a written employment contract of not less than two years and whose contract requires not less than six months' notice of termination.

"Employer." A person who has one or more employees, including an agent of an employer.

"Registered mail." Includes certified mail.

Section 4. Dismissal of employees.

(a) Grounds.—An employer may not dismiss an employee except for just cause.

(b) Notice.—An employer who dismisses an employee shall notify the employee orally at the time of dismissal and in writing by registered mail within 15 calendar days after the dismissal of all reasons for the dismissal. The written notice shall set forth the employee's rights and the procedural time limitations prescribed by this act.

Section 5. Complaints of unjust dismissal.

(a) Form.—The complaint may be in narrative form or in numbered paragraph form. It shall set forth the name and address of the employer and the employee, the date of dismissal and a statement by the employee of the issues. If the employee has been provided with a written dismissal notice, the notice may be attached to the complaint.

(b) Time for filing.—An employee who believes that he or she has been dismissed in violation of section 4(a) may file by registered mail a written complaint with the bureau not later than 30 days after receipt of the employer's written notification of dismissal as provided in section 4(b).

(c) Time when notice requirement not met.—If an employer fails to provide the dismissed employee with written notification of the dismissal and the reason for the action, the dismissed employee may file by registered mail a written complaint, with the bureau not later than 45 calendar days after the date of the oral notification of the dismissal.

Section 6. Mediation.

(a) Appointment of a mediator.—Upon receipt of a complaint from a dismissed employee, the bureau shall appoint a mediator to assist the employer and the dismissed employee in attempting to resolve the dispute.

(b) Explanation of the arbitration option.—If the dispute is not resolved within 30 days after the commencement of the mediation, the mediator shall explain to the employer and employee the process and purpose of final and binding arbitration.

Section 7. Arbitration proceedings.

(a) Request for arbitration.—After the option of arbitration is made available to the dismissed employee, the employee or employer may request a continuance of mediation if he or she believes that a mutual resolution of the dispute is possible. If mutual resolution is not likely, the dismissed employee or the employer may file by registered mail a written request with the bureau for arbitration of the dispute. If continued mediation breaks down and mutual resolution becomes impossible, either party may request arbitration at that time in this same manner.

(b) Hearing.—Within 60 calendar days after the appointment of an arbitrator, or within further additional periods to which the parties may agree, the arbitrator shall call a final hearing and shall give reasonable notice of the time and place of the hearing to the employer and the employee.

Section 8. Decision of the arbitrator.

(a) Time of decision.—Within 30 days after the close of the hearing, or within further additional periods to which the parties may agree, the arbitrator shall render a signed opinion and award based upon the issues presented. The arbitrator shall deliver by registered mail a copy of the award to the employer, the employee and the bureau.

(b) Remedies.—The remedies which the arbitrator may select include, but are not limited to, the following:

(1) Sustaining the dismissal.

(2) Reinstating the employee without back pay or with partial or full back pay.

(3) A severance payment.

(c) Settlement.—If the employer and the employee settle their dispute during the course of the arbitration proceeding, the arbitrator, upon their request, may set forth the terms of the settlement in the award.

Section 9. Effect of award.

An award of the arbitrator shall be final and binding upon the employer and the employee and may be enforced, at the instance of either the employer or the employee, in the court of common pleas for the county in which the dispute arose or in which the employee resides.

Section 10. Cost of mediation and arbitration.

The normal and necessary expenses of mediation and arbitration, including the cost of producing a witness, shall be borne by the complainant, but the expenses may be reimbursed if in the judgment of the arbitrator it would be reasonable and proper to do so.

Section 11. Judicial review.

The court of common pleas for the county in which the dispute arose or in which the employee resides may review an award of the arbitrator but only for the reason that the arbitrator was without, or exceeded the scope of, his jurisdiction, or that the award was procured by fraud, collusion or other similar and unlawful means. The pendency of a proceeding for review shall not stay automatically the award of the arbitrator.

Section 12. Contempt.

An employer or employee who willfully disobeys a lawful order of enforcement issued by the court may be held in contempt. The punishment for each day after the issuance that the contempt order remains in effect shall be a fine not to exceed $250 per day.

Section 13. Construction of act.

This act shall not supersede an employer's grievance procedure that provides for impartial, final and binding arbitration of dismissal-related grievances. Upon the request of an employer or employee, the bureau shall determine whether or not an employer's grievance procedure meets this standard.

Section 14. Posting copy of act.

An employer shall post a copy of this act in a prominent place in the work area.

Section 15. Effective date.

This act shall take effect immediately.

ASSEMBLY, No. 2550

STATE OF NEW JERSEY

INTRODUCED SEPTEMBER 20, 1984
By Assemblyman S. ADUBATO

AN ACT concerning certain personnel actions affecting certain
public employees and supplementing P. L. 1941, c. 100 (C.34:13A-1 et
seq.).

BE IT ENACTED *by the State and General Assembly of the State of
New Jersey:*

1. As used in this act:

a. "Dismissal" means an act of dismissal, suspension, reduction in
rank or compensation, or deprivation of professional or other advantages.

b. "Just cause" means an action based on the performance of an
employee or on valid fiscal problems or programmatic changes of the
employer and excludes any action based on performance which
depends largely on frivolous, arbitrary, capricious or other unreasonable considerations which renders the act unfair or unwarranted. It
shall include criteria, not inconsistent with this definition, that have
been adopted for the purpose of evaluating the performance of
employees.

2. Public employers shall negotiate written policies setting forth
grievance procedures governing just cause dismissals by means of
which their employees or representatives of employees may appeal
an employee's dismissal on grounds that it was not a just cause dismissal. Grievance procedures governing just cause dismissals shall
be included in any agreement entered into between the public
employer and the representative.

3. a. The grievance procedures governing just cause dismissals
shall provide for binding arbitration as a terminal step for resolving
any just cause dismissal dispute. Any grievance procedure governing just cause dismissals shall provide for a hearing before, and decision by, the public employer prior to arbitration.

b. The decision of an arbitrator shall include an opinion and an
award, which shall be final and binding upon the parties, except
where there is submitted to a court, extrinsic evidence upon which
the court may vacate, modify or correct that award pursuant to
N.J.S. 2A:24-7 et seq.

c. If a grievance is submitted to arbitration, the arbitrator may restore the employee to continued employment and may restore any reduction in rank, compensation, benefits or advantages retroactively to which the employee would be entitled under terms and conditions of employment required by law or agreement.

4. The procedures agreed to by the parties may not replace or be inconsistent with any alternate statutory appeal procedures governing dismissals for employees who have obtained civil service or tenure status, or who, because they have served a statutorily mandated probation period, are eligible for civil service or tenure status.

5. Nothing in this act shall limit the right of a public employer and a representative to agree to a probationary period applicable to a class of employees, which, for the purposes of this act, shall not exceed 120 days and shall be satisfied by any employee before the grievance procedures governing just cause dismissals set forth in this act become applicable to him.

6. This act shall take effect immediately.

STATEMENT

This bill supplements the "New Jersey Employer-Employee Relations Act" to provide a negotiated appeal mechanism for organized employees whose job security is not protected by tenure or classified civil service status. Under its provisions, these employees could obtain review of decisions dismissing them from their employment on the basis of the quality of their performance. This bill would not permit negotiation of the criteria for dismissal, but would permit review of the application of such criteria to individual employees. It would require that such dismissals first be reviewed through a hearing before the employer (such as a school board), followed by binding arbitration. The results of the arbitration proceeding could, in turn, be confirmed, modified, or vacated in the Superior Court in the same manner as is currently provided in all arbitration matters.

This bill would parallel, in many respects, the 1982 amendments to the "New Jersey Employer-Employee Relations Act" which permit binding arbitration of disciplinary disputes.

The bill broadly defines the scope of the term "dismissal," recognizing that, in some instances, employers may seek a penalty of lesser severity than actual dismissal. Neither the employer nor arbitrator need choose between actual dismissal and no action.

Finally, it is the opinion of the sponsor of this bill, that its protections for employees not protected from unjust dismissal by reason of tenure or civil service status are necessary, but that there should be some period of time spent on the job before which an employee can become entitled to such protection. Therefore, this bill authorizes and encourages negotiations on the establishment of employee probationary periods (not exceeding 120 days), the completion of which could be required before these just cause dismissal grievance procedures could be invoked.

Index of Cases

Baynard v. Guardian Life Ins. Co.,
399 So.2d 1200 (La. App. 1981), 199

Becker v. Interstate Properties, 569
F.2d 1203 (3d Cir. 1977), *cert. denied,* 436 U.S. 906 (1978), 108

Beeler v. Chicago R.I. & P. Ry., 169
F.2d 557 (10th Cir. 1948), *cert.
denied,* 335 U.S. 903 (1949), 8

Beers v. Southern Pacific Trans. Co.,
703 F.2d 425 (9th Cir. 1983), 45

Beeston v. Collyer, 130 Eng. Rep. 786
(C.P. 1827), 3

Beidler v. W.R. Grace, Inc., 461 F.
Supp. 1013 (E.D. Pa. 1978), *aff'd,*
609 F. 2d 500 (3d Cir, 1979), 22, 111,
112, 113, 115

Bender Ship Repair Inc. v. Stevens,
379 So.2d 594 (Ala. 1980), 186

Benoir v. Ethan-Allen Inc., 514 A.2d
716 (Vt. 1986), 217

Bergamini v. The Manhattan and
Bronx Transit Operating Authority, 62 N.Y.2d 521, 478 N.Y.S.2d
857 (1984), 128

Blake v. Voight, 134 N.Y. 69, 31 N.E.
256 (1892), 130, 131

Blalock v. Hecks Discount Stores, No.
140, slip op. (Tenn. App. April 14,
1986), 215

Blevins v. General Electric Co., 491 F.
Supp. 521 (W.D. Va. 1980), 218

Bohm v. Transworld Airlines, Inc.
No. C-84-5004 JPV (N.D. Cal. May
5, 1986), 59

Bonham v. Dresser Industries, Inc.,
569 F.2d 187 (3d Cir. 1977), *cert.
denied,* 439 U.S. 821 (1978), 32, 105,
110, 115

Boreson v. Rohm & Haas, Inc., 526 F.
Supp. 1230 (E.D. Pa. 1981), 110,
114, 115

Bowman v. State Bank of Keyesville,
331 S.E.2d 797 (Va. 1985), 218

Boyle v. Eyewear, Inc., 700 S.W.2d
859 (Mo. App. 1985), 204

Boynton v. TRW, Inc., No. 83-1773
(E.D. Mich. June 1986), 93

Brainard v. Imperial Manufacturing
Co., 571 F. Supp. 37 (D.R.I. 1983),
213

Braun v. Kelsey-Hayes Co., No. 85-
2377, slip op. (E.D. Pa. March 14,
1986), 109

Breeden v. City of Nome, 628 P.2d 924
(Alas. 1981), 186

Brockmeyer v. Dun & Bradstreet, 335
N.W. 2d 834 (Wis. 1983), 219

Broniman v. Great Atl. & Pac. Tea
Co., 353 F.2d 559 (6th Cir. 1965),
cert. denied, 384 U.S. 907 (1966),
45

Broussard v. CACI, Inc., 780 F.2d 162
(1st Cir. 1986), 200

Brown v. Chris Nelsen & Son, Inc., 10
Mich. App. 95, 158 N.W.2d 818
(1968), 78

Brown v. Physician's Mutual Ins. Co.,
679 S.W.2d 836 (Ky. App. 1984),
199

Brown v. Safeway Stores, Inc., 190 F.
Supp. 295 (E.D.N.Y. 1960), 8

Brown v. Transcon Lines, 588 P.2d
1087 (Ore. 1978), 212

Brudnicki v. General Electric Co., 535
F. Supp. 84 (N.D. Ill. 1982), 195

Bruffett v. Warner Communications,
Inc., 692 F.2d 910 (3d Cir. 1982), 27,
32, 107, 108

Bryant v. Southern Screw Machine
Products Co., Inc., 707 S.W.2d 321
(Ark. 1986), 188

Buckmon v. Wilmington Dry Goods
Store, No. 82-1167 (E.D. Pa. Feb. 6,
1984), 115

Bucyrus-Erie Co. v. Dept. of Industry
and Labor, 599 F.2d 205 (7th Cir.
1979), *cert. denied,* 444 U.S. 1031
(1980), 51

Buian v. J.L. Jacobs & Co., 428 F.2d
531 (7th Cir. 1970), 8

Bullock v. Desert Dodge Truck Center, Inc., 354 P.2d 559 (Utah 1960),
216

Burkhimer v. Gealy, 250 S.E.2d 678
(N.C. App. 1979), *rev. denied,* 254
S.E.2d 918 (N.C. 1979), 210

Buscemi v. McDonnell Douglas Corp.,
736 F.2d 1348 (9th Cir. 1984), 47,
70, 71

Walker v. Univ. of Pittsburgh, 457 F. Supp. 1000 (W.D. Pa. 1978), 115

Walker v. Westinghouse Electric Corp., 335 S.E.2d 79 (N.C. App. 1985), *rev. denied*, 341 S.E.2d 39 (N.C. 1986), 209

Wandry v. Bull's Eye Credit Union, 384 N.W.2d 325 (Wis. 1986), 220

Ward v. Frito-Lay, Inc., 95 Wis. 2d 372, 290 N.W.2d 536 (1980), 28

Warthen v. Tom's River Community memorial Hospital, 118 L.R.R.M. 3179 (N.J. Super. Ct. App. Div. 1985), 30, 208

Washington Welfare Association v. Wheeler, 496 A.2d 613 (D.C. App. 1985), 191

Watassek v. Michigan Department of Mental Health, 143 Mich. App. 556, 372 N.W.2d 617 (1985), 81, 84-85

Watson v. Cleveland Chair Co., 122 L.R.R.M. 2076 (Tenn. App. 1985), 215

Watson v. Gugino, 204 N.Y. 535, 98 N.E. 18 (1912), 120

Wehr v. Burroughs, 438 F. Supp. 1052 (E.D. Pa. 1977), 27, 110, 115

Weiner v. McGraw Hill, Inc., 57 N.Y.2d 458, 443 N.E.2d 441, 457 N.Y.S.2d 198 (1982), 20, 25, 119, 122, 132-37, 167

Weisse v. Engelhard Minerals and Chem. Corp., 571 F.2d 117 (2d Cir. 1978), 120, 130

Wells v. Thomas, 569 F. Supp. 426 (E.D. Pa. 1983), 114

Wenham v. The Right Reverend Paul Moore, Jr., N.Y.L.J. 7 (Sup. Ct. April 15, 1985), 137

Wexler v. Newsweek, Inc., 109 A.D.2d 714, 487 N.Y.S.2d 330 (App. Div. 1985), 132, 136-37

Wheeler v. Caterpillar Tractor Co., 485 N.E.2d 372 (Ill. 1985), 196

White v. I.T. & T., 718 F.2d 994 (11th Cir. 1983), *cert. denied*, 104 S. Ct. 914, *reh'g denied*, 104 S. Ct. 267 (1984), 193

Whitney v. Stearns, 16 Me. 394 (1839), 19

Wickes v. Olympic Airways, 745 F.2d 363 (6th Cir. 1984),

Williams v. Caterpillar Tractor Co., 786 F.2d 928 (9th Cir. 1986), *cert. granted*, No. 86-526 (Nov. 11, 1986), 70

Williams v. Tennessee In-Home Health Service, Inc., slip op. (Tenn. App., April 26, 1985), 215

Wilson v. Red Bluff Daily News, 237 Cal. App. 2d 87, 46 Cal. Rptr. 591 (1965), 8

Wilson v. Vlasic Foods, Inc., 116 L.R.R.M. 2419 (C.D. Cal. 1984), 49, 62, 73

Wilson v. Vulcan Rivet and Bolt Corp., 439 So.2d 65 (Ala. 1983), 185

Wing v. JMB Property Management Corp., 714 P.2d 916 (Colo. App. 1985), 189

Winslow v. Roberts Numbering Mach. Co., 17 Misc. 2d 18, 183 N.Y.S.2d 817 (Sup. Ct. 1959), 8

Winther v. DEC Int'l, Inc., 625 F. Supp. 100 (D. Colo. 1985), 189

Witowski v. St. Anne's Hospital, 113 Ill. App. 3d 745, 447 N.E.2d 1016 (1983), 50

Wolber v. Service Corp. Int'l, 612 F. Supp. 235 (D. Nev. 1985), 206

Wolk v. Saks Fifth Avenue, Inc., 115 L.R.R.M. 3064 (3d Cir. 1984), 728 F.2d 221 (3d Cir. 1984), 27, 32, 51, 107, 108-09

Wood v. Burlington Indusries, 536 F. Supp. 56 (E.D. Pa. 1981), 115

Wood v. Lucy, Lady Duff-Gordon, 222 N.Y. 88, 118 N.E. 214 (1917), 91

Woolley v. Hoffman-LaRoche, Inc., 119 L.R.R.M. 2370, 99 N.J. 284, 491 A.2d 1257 (1985), 20, 23, 164, 207

Wrather v. Pizza Hut of America, Inc., 10 T.A.M. 17-3 (Tenn. App. March 29, 1985), 215

Wynn v. Boeing Military Airplane Co., 595 F. Supp. 727 (D. Kan. 1984), 198